The Functions of the COMMERCIAL BANKING SYSTEM

The Functions of the COMMERCIAL BANKING SYSTEM

By JOHN BROOKE WILLIS

SUBMITTED IN PARTIAL FULFILLMENT OF THE REQUIREMENTS FOR THE DEGREE OF DOCTOR OF PHILOSOPHY UNDER THE JOINT COMMITTEE ON GRADUATE INSTRUCTION, COLUMBIA UNIVERSITY

KING'S CROWN PRESS
MORNINGSIDE HEIGHTS · NEW YORK
1943

Printed in the United States of America

King's Crown Press is a division of Columbia University Press organized for the purpose of making certain scholarly material available at minimum cost. Toward that end, the publishers have adopted every reasonable economy except such as would interfere with a legible format. The work is presented substantially as submitted by the author, without the usual editorial attention of Columbia University Press.

To

H. PARKER WILLIS

PREFACE

THIS WORK examines the nature of the commercial banking process from the standpoint of function. It is not concerned with the technical operating practices of individual banks, but with the functioning of the banking system as a whole. By "commercial" banking is meant the system in which banks issue demand liabilities transferable by check. No consideration is given to other types of financial institutions except incidentally. The study is confined roughly to the period between the First and the Second World War, the era in which modern banking reached a zenith, and is based almost exclusively upon American banking practice. However, an introductory chapter is included in order to give perspective to the purely financial nature of modern banking and distinguish it from its antecedent institutions.

The principal aims of the project are, first, to differentiate commercial banking in regard to function from other types of financial institutions; second, to analyze the essential and peculiar features of the process; and third, to develop the relation between banking and the financing of debts In this procedure stress is laid upon the importance of the distinction between the individual bank and the banking system, a distinction prerequisite to reaching agreement on banking theory. This is covered in the first five chapters. A sixth chapter examines critically the inadequacies of both monetary and credit theory, and the divergent paths which they have followed. The final portion of the book is concerned, first, with the reasons for the changing relation of banking to the economy and its implications; and second, with an expansion of the theory of bank capital and its importance to the type of banking policy which is pursued. A final chapter summarizes the findings and indicates certain basic problems which face the administrators of banking policy.

I wish to record my gratitude to those persons whose criticism and advice have aided me in the preparation of this book. I am indebted especially to Professor Benjamin Haggott Beckhart for his guidance and encouragement, to Professor John M. Chapman for his patient advice, and to Professor Archibald H. Stockder for his generous comment and helpful criticisms regarding the first chapter. The National Bureau of Economic Research kindly permitted the use of data from certain preliminary and confidential manuscripts not yet published in final form. The responsibility for the use made of all suggestions, criticism and factual information is solely mine.

J. BROOKE WILLIS

New York, New York. May 29, 1942

CONTENTS

TABLES

CHARTS

Chapter I

THE ANTECEDENTS OF CONTEMPORARY BANKING FUNCTIONS

SINCE THIS WORK endeavors to examine the functional nature of what is now known as the "commercial" or "deposit" banking system, it seems desirable first to sketch briefly the evolution of the principal banking functions. These functions are not to be regarded as abstract and immutable. Their importance, therefore, must be considered in the light of the role played by banks as ancillary institutions in an ever changing system of political economy.

It is well to observe at the outset that the modern commercial banking system is an institution which performs a combination of related functions. Commercial banks have often been described as institutions which use the machinery of deposit, discount, and issue; but this kind of definition fails to illuminate the temporal sequence which these operations observe. Contemporary banking is predominantly concerned with the active issuance of bank credit in the form of deposits against various forms of debt, as well as against money; this phenomenon is not immediately conditional upon the anterior receipt or collection of deposits. For the system as a whole, the sequence runs from the making of loans, or buying of investments, to the issuance of deposits, not the reverse. Moreover, even this combination of elements has only existed in the same institution during comparatively modern times, roughly since the end, or perhaps the middle, of the eighteenth century.

The early evolution of banking is necessarily confined to tracing the separate development of specific functions still performed by modern banks, while the study of modern banking proper resolves itself into a study of the coalescence of functions which, in earlier times, had been independently performed by institutions called banks, but which, in some respects, bear only a generic resemblance to their modern counterparts.

Contemporary banking finds its historical roots, not in any one function, but rather in all of them. Various authors maintain that the function of serving as a storage place for the deposit of coins and specie was among the first, historically speaking, if it was not antecedent to the functions of serving as a payments mechanism, or as a source of loans.[1] Other writers, however, contend that banking sprang from the business of usurers, or persons who lent their own money at interest.[2] Still others regard banking as the end product of a progressive evolution from barter, to the use of money, and finally to the use of credit, in other words, as a phase of development in monetary science. However, as Willis said:

> The only really important matter in this whole historical discussion regarding the successive steps by which money (and banking) were brought to its present status . . . is that methods or processes of exchange differ from period to period, there being no single or universally most advantageous way of exchanging goods.[3]

Historically, the sixteenth century was a period in which the use of money was widespread, while the nineteenth century and the beginning of the twentieth century was essentially a credit period in which banking assumed a development theretofore unknown.[4] For ages, banks had performed various functions, but at no time prior to the nineteenth century were all these functions combined with one another and performed simultaneously by a system of fairly uniform, highly specialized institutions of a purely financial nature, as they are today. Rist has observed that "The development of credit institutions and particularly large banks is one of the most important facts in Nineteenth Century economic history." [5] This development assumed significant proportions around the middle of the century in England, somewhat later in the United States, and, after the war of 1870–71, in France and Germany.

BANKING IN ANCIENT TIMES

It has long been suspected that the functions of banking were much more highly developed by the Assyro-Babylonian civilization of Mesopotamia, even as early as the third millennium B. C., than among any other people of antiquity. As translations of the business records written by these peoples in the cuneiform script have become available in greater number, this assumption has been confirmed. Indeed, it may now definitely be said that the

[1] A. De Viti De Marco, *Die Funktion der Bank,* tr. from the Italian by H. Fried (Vienna, 1935), p. 2.

[2] Henry Dunning Macleod, *The Theory and Practice of Banking with the Elementary Principles of Currency, Prices, Credit, and Exchanges* (London, 1885), I, 341. See also, by the same author, *The Theory of Credit* (London, 1890), II, 349 f.

[3] H. Parker Willis and George W. Edwards, *Banking and Business* (rev. ed.; New York, 1925), p. 6.

[4] *Ibid.,* p. 9.

[5] Charles Rist, *History of Monetary and Credit Theory from John Law to the Present Day,* tr. by Jane Degras (New York, 1940), p. 261.

great temples of Marduk and Samas, at a period even prior to 2000 B. C., were actively engaged in banking operations of all sorts.

Even at this early date, the shekel of silver had already become the chief measure of value and medium of exchange. The shekel was a weight unit and not a coin. Its exchange value relative to other commodities, such as grain, oil, copper, wool, etc., which also were used extensively to make payment, was set by decree. Such a monetary system obviously was based upon rigidly maintained standards of capacity and weight. Each of the great temples, by setting its own standards of capacity and weight, therefore became a regulator of the media of payment. The records disclose, further, that loans at interest were made in great numbers by these temples. They served also, though less extensively, as depositaries holding in trust the grain of their tenants to be disposed of in accordance with written instructions. A comparison of such contracts as these with their modern forms discloses an amazing correspondence. But the granting of credit, as well as the service of custodian of deposit, was also extensively performed by the individual capitalist who nearly always caused the contract to be executed in the presence of witnesses before a scribe who served as notary public.[6]

Westermann has described the contemporaneous existence in ancient economic life of exchange *in natura* and exchange in money.[7] In Egypt and Babylonia in the eighth century B. C. the storage of goods and exchange in kind (warehouse banking) predominated, but in the Neo-Babylonian period (sixth century B. C.) there arose private organizations, such as the Egibi Sons in Babylonia, which developed a considerable business based upon money and kind.[8] Among other things, they made loans on a substantial scale to monarchs as well as to private merchants; accepted orders to pay from one account to another; acted as commission men; received loans and paid interest thereon; opened warehouses for deposits in kind and took a fee for safekeeping; advanced loans on the security of mortgages; and entered partnerships with traders.

In the seventh century, in Lydia in Asia Minor, state monopoly of coinage was adopted, a system which guaranteed a definite weight and quality of precious metal used in each coin of a particular type. This was copied soon afterward by the Greeks when, in the late fifth century B. C., money-changers

[6] For these observations regarding the system of money and banking in Assyro-Babylonian times I am indebted to Professor Archibald H. Stockder, School of Business, Columbia University. See Walter Schwenzer, *Zum Altbabylonischen Wirtschaftsleben* (Leipzig, 1915), and C. H. W. Johns, *Assyrian Deeds and Documents* (Cambridge, England, 1898–1923).

[7] W. L. Westermann, "Warehousing and Trapezite Banking in Antiquity," *Journal of Economic and Business History*, III, No. 1 (November, 1930), 31.

[8] *Ibid.*, p. 30.

in Athens perceived the opportunities in opening banks which could compete with the temples as depositaries of surpluses of coin.[9] This "trapezite" banking spread throughout the Greek city-states. In Westermann's words,

> these private banks exchanged money in behalf of merchants who had been dealing in coins of other states, and converted them either one way or the other. In such cases the coins would be contained in bags which were sealed; and no use could be made of the money by the banks. A part of their business was essentially pawn-broking.[10]

By the fourth century B. C. Greek private bankers loaned money to city-states as well as to individuals.

In Egypt, banking advanced more slowly than in Greece, but "all the elements of the financial accounting system, developed in the private banking business of the Greeks in the Fourth Century, recur in Ptolemaic Egypt." [11] However, the warehousing system in kind persisted strongly, and the granary system,

> actually shows a higher development than the banking system; for the state granaries permitted transfers from the grain account of one client to another on order of the first client, under the system called *giro* in European financial parlance, in which no actual transfer of grain occurred.[12]

Also,

> a real payment in grain could be made on order of a depositor of grain in the state *theosauros* to another person who carried no grain account at the granary. This is an actual application of the check system to payment in kind; but no transaction of the money banks similar to this has as yet been found.[13]

Rome copied the Greek financial models and the *argentarius* soon developed, along with money changing, other banking functions already familiar to the Greeks.[14] Despite the predominance of the money economy in the first two centuries of the Roman Empire, government agencies existed which perpetuated the old system of exchange in kind. Under the regime of Augustus Caesar, the Ptolemaic system of state monopoly of banking was abolished in Egypt, and this led to the growth and development of private banks [15] which employed the practices common to the banks of the Greek city-states, including the receiving of deposits for safekeeping, payments of debts by the bank for depositors, money-lending at interest, and the service of acting as receivers of money taxes on behalf of the State. New departures included the practice of permitting transfers from the deposit account of one client to that of a second in the same bank and the provision that pay-

[9] *Ibid.*, p. 38. [10] *Ibid.*, p. 39. [11] *Ibid.*, p. 49. [12] *Ibid.*
[13] *Ibid.* [14] *Ibid.*, p. 50. [15] *Ibid.*, p. 52.

ments could be made, on direct order of a depositor, from his account to a second person even though that second person had no account with the bank. Westermann explained that "this development brings a certain analogy to the modern check system," but "the practice of check endorsement and payment 'to order or bearer' does not occur." [16] It is worth noting that the monetary and credit practices of the ancient states did not contemplate the issuance of paper money. Furthermore, "the custom of bookkeeping transfer and direct payments on order of a depositor were actually more highly developed on the warehouse side of this double economy system than on the banking side." [17] Nevertheless, Macleod was sufficiently impressed with the practices of the Roman private bankers in keeping customers' accounts and facilitating payments by use of checks that he attributed to them "the first step in the great engine for the promotion of commerce, which conduced so much to the prosperity of modern times, viz., the transferability of the debt apart from the coined money." [18] However, he observed that they were never able to advance beyond that first step.

The Rise of Other Types of Lenders

In the late Roman Empire, the landowners of a given district were organized into a *curia*. The State then assessed taxes upon this *curia* as a body rather than upon the individual members. For this reason some local organization was necessary to make the collections and pay the tax. Local capitalists organized with others what were called *vectigalia*, whose function it was to pay the Government in return for the right to collect from the members of the *curia* individually. This practice was to some extent later adopted by the Church. Ecclesiastical tax collectors were replaced by agents of the Italian commercial houses and the establishment, by the middle of the thirteenth century, of regular deposit relations between the *camera apostolica* and these commercial houses. Deposits sometimes were not withdrawn for long periods and constituted a considerable part of the working capital necessary for the organization of an international system of branch houses. Other resources were obtained through a widespread net of depositaries open to all strata of the population, and through the establishment of credit relations with business associates.[19]

In the medieval cities the Jews and, later, the Lombards occupied an important place as lenders for consumption purposes to the urban aristocracy and for handicraft production. One of the principal sources of funds

[16] *Ibid.*, p. 53.
[17] *Ibid.*
[18] Macleod, *The Theory and Practice of Banking*, I, 350.
[19] See F. Cyril James, *The Economics of Money, Credit, and Banking* (3d. ed. rev. New York, 1940), pp. 111–12.

for such loans appears to have been the receipt of interest-bearing deposits. Monasteries, because of their security, served as important depositaries of wealth and even as lenders in times of emergency. Likewise, the militant religious orders, particularly the Knights Templars and the knights hospitaler, by the thirteenth century had become important financial institutions. Their functions included serving as depositaries of idle funds, as lenders to impoverished monarchs, and as fiscal agents for the royal Treasury of France. According to James, the funds received in the form of deposits were mingled with the general assets of the Order so that depositors became also general rather than specific creditors.[20] By receiving deposits at one office of the Order and undertaking to make payments to designated beneficiaries at distant points the Templars were able to develop an efficient transfer mechanism which linked together all the commercial centers of Western Europe. Local merchants were enabled to deposit funds and have them credited to others who likewise kept running accounts at the Temple.

By the time of the Renaissance several distinct groups of lenders had arisen among the private financial houses: the Italians, whose business relations were with the *curia,* vassals of the Church, and the kings of France, England, and Naples; the South German financiers, who were the chief creditors of the Hapsburgs of Austria and Spain and of the German princes; and the Hansards, who were creditors of the English and Scandinavian rulers.[21] These houses perished by the end of the sixteenth century, owing to a variety of causes. During the Spanish conquest of the Netherlands the troops twice sacked the city of Antwerp. In Germany the upheavals accompanying the Reformation, e. g., the great peasant revolts, brought ruin. In Italy the incursion of the Turks into Eastern Europe cut the old commercial ties and caused a general decline. State bankruptcies were widespread.

In the seventeenth century the tax farmers in France and Italy were able to lend to private persons and discount bills of exchange, depending for funds upon the receipt of interest-bearing deposits. The Jews regained a position of financial prominence which was associated with their mercantile pursuits, and were able to obtain additional capital from coreligionists which was lent to various governments. Private banking developed out of wholesale trade, shipping, and the commission business. The specialized pursuit of dealing in bills of exchange became associated with security brokerage, the flotation of government loans, and with the management of private fortunes. By the second half of the eighteenth century these various types had evolved into international banking houses, like that of Rothschild,

[20] *Ibid.*, p. 109.

[21] Julius Landmann, "Banking, Commercial, History to the Close of the Eighteenth Century," in *The Encyclopaedia of the Social Sciences* (New York, 1933), II, 426.

which were to be found in various international commercial ports, and which confined themselves largely to wholesale finance or security speculation.

The acceptance of deposits and the lending of money were also developed in connection with the specialized pursuit of money changing. The money-changers generally held minting concessions and performed certain fiscal duties, but their chief function was that of exchanging old coins for new, and domestic for foreign.[22] Merchants acquired the habit of depositing surplus funds with them and paid fees for safekeeping. These deposits became the basis of a book transfer or clearing system of local payments and were also used for the extension of credit.[23] By the close of the twelfth century the exchange of actual coin was replaced by the written promises of the money-changers to pay in foreign places in coin of those places the equivalent of sums received in domestic coin.

Special bills of exchange were developed which were payable at the great international fairs, and from these grew the custom of clearing mercantile indebtedness and of grants of credit from one fair to the next. Out of these practices there arose the great money fairs of the fifteenth and sixteenth centuries, such as those at Lyons, Genoa, Medina del Campo, Seville, etc.

Transfer Banks

As long as coinage disorder persisted, that is, until about the eighteenth century and, in some places, until the nineteenth, money-changers and a system of book transfer for payments were essential.[24] It is noteworthy that as soon as money-changers began the practice of lending out the sums deposited, their effectiveness in serving their original function became impaired. Regulatory measures designed to prevent money-changers from operating deposit accounts for clearing purposes proved ineffective. The municipal authorities, therefore, established public transfer banks in which deposited coins were to remain untouched in the vaults of the bank so as to serve as a safe foundation for a book-transfer system of payments. The main function of such banks was not the making of loans, but the receiving of deposits against which 100 percent bullion reserves were kept. Pure transfer banks were monetary institutions, the function of their deposits being to serve as a collateral basis for transfer accounts. These banks established a separate standard unit of account, which represented a fixed quantity of specified metal and in which bills of exchange were to be drawn. Customers of the bank formed a closed community within which payments were made

22 James, *op. cit.*, p. 113.

23 Landmann, *op. cit.*, pp. 424–25.

24 J. G. Van Dillen, *History of the Principal Public Banks, Accompanied by Extensive Bibliographies of the History of Banking and Credit in Eleven European Countries* (The Hague, 1934), pp. 80–84.

by transferred entries in the books. Although prohibited from granting credit, transfer banks could not on occasion resist pressure to make secret loans. No interest was paid on deposits; on the contrary, a charge was levied to cover cost of administration.

At various times the banks of Barcelona, Genoa, Venice, Milan, Amsterdam, and Hamburg satisfied the description given above, but it would be false to assume that the functions of such institutions remained the same throughout the centuries of their existence. Some, like the Bank of Genoa, did not really become a bank in the sense of a *giro* bank until about 1500. Prior to 1500 a number of the banks mentioned were more in the nature of modern investment trusts than banks.[25]

The Bank of Amsterdam, which was established as a municipal bank of exchange in 1609, according to its ordinance, was to be concerned exclusively with receiving of money on deposit, transfer and clearing business, exchanging money, and purchasing both precious metal and *billioen* (uncurrent coins) to have them minted into good commercial coins by the mints.[26] In order to compel merchants to open a bank account it was regulated that all bills of exchange of 100 pounds Flemish and upward were to be made payable at the bank. However, from the beginning, bills were also paid outside the bank in current money. To draw in excess of the amount to the credit of the drawer (overdrafts) was strictly prohibited, so that granting of credit by this method was out of the question.[27] Granting of credits had not been expressly prohibited in the ordinance of 1609, but "properly speaking it is excluded by the whole plan and organization of the bank." [28] However, Van Dillen observed that the granting of credits to the East India Company commenced as early as 1615 and proved very profitable.[29]

The paying in specie to holders of accounts current fell into desuetude by the beginning of the eighteenth century, and the bank thereafter supplied an inconvertible currency. After 1863 the bank broadened its activities and began making advances to merchants who deposited with it gold and silver, but with the right to withdraw such deposits whenever desired.[30] Such receipts were readily sold on the exchange, being worth the difference between the current price of specie and the amount advanced on the same. In the eighteenth century, the bank refrained from taking part in operations such as the dealing in exchange, acceptances, and the issuance of loans, as was the common practice of private bankers, nor did it normally trade in precious metals.[31] It contented itself for the most part with making advances on specie deposited with it, providing a clearing service, and ex-

[25] *Ibid., passim.* [26] *Ibid.*, p. 84. [27] *Ibid.*, p. 24. [28] *Ibid.*, p. 94.
[29] *Ibid.* [30] *Ibid.*, p. 102. [31] *Ibid.*, p. 107.

tending credit to the East India Company. After 1780 and the advent of the fourth war between the Republic and England, an unusually large credit was extended to the Municipal Loan Chamber and the town treasury. An offer to pay holders in silver bars at a depreciated rate was rejected, and the bank's money fell to a discount and gradual disuse, although in 1802, by means of a forced loan to the municipality, aided by the Government of the new Batavian Republic, the specie cover for the credit balances was restored.[32]

Although Rist lays emphasis upon the statement that at Amsterdam and Venice a merchant could not withdraw in coin sums deposited by him, once he had been credited upon the bank's books with a sum corresponding to the silver or gold content of the deposited coin, the above description, based on Van Dillen, indicates that this was not always so.[33] A study of the accounts of the Bank of Amsterdam shows rapid variation from year to year in the deposit of bullion on hand, indicating at times heavy withdrawals. In the case of the Bank of Venice there apparently were few withdrawals, because the State had expropriated the bullion and the bank notes became fiat money when they were made legal tender by the Government.

In describing the foundation of the Chamber of Loans in Venice in 1173 for the purpose of managing the public debt, Macleod explained that this institution could scarcely be called a bank since it merely represented the citizens who had been forced to contribute a loan to the State.[34] However, several centuries later the chamber became the Bank of Venice (1587) and assumed certain banking functions. In order to obviate the difficulties connected with the use of bills of exchange in the face of clipped and worn foreign coins, the plan was devised of having the chamber receive deposits from private persons who, in turn, received a corresponding number of the bank's notes payable to bearer in the full amount in bullion on demand. All bills of exchange were made payable in the notes of the bank. It is to be observed that the State made the bank's notes legal tender and required that bills of exchange be paid in it. The result was that bills of exchange were usually drawn on the Genoese fairs, in which case they were payable in gold *scud di marche*. This was a money of account specifying gold of a given weight and fineness, but not a coin in circulation. The rules of this fair did not accept notes of the Bank of Genoa or of any other bank as valid payment. However, the Bank of Venice, according to Macleod, does not appear ever to have discounted bills upon its own account, and its paper only represented the sum of bullion actually in its coffers; it made no increase in the quantity of money in circulation.[35]

[32] *Ibid.*, p. 115.
[33] Rist, *op. cit.*, p. 45.
[34] Macleod, *The Theory and Practice of Banking*, I, 355.
[35] *Ibid.*, p. 356.

Like the Bank of Venice, the Bank of St. George at Genoa (1408) originated from the necessities of the State and was established as the Chamber of St. George to permit the consolidation and management of the public debt of the Republic of Genoa. To it were assigned for collection several branches of the public revenue. Like the Bank of Venice it was primarily a bank of deposit and issue, and all bills of exchange were payable in bank money.

The Bank of Barcelona (1401) had been established a few years earlier by the magistrates for the receiving of deposits of customers, and discounting of bills for merchants. The public property of the city was pledged as security for the deposits. It does not appear that the bank issued notes, or that its customers paid by means of checks, but since it used the deposits of its customers in discounting bills, it was perhaps of greater service to commerce than the Bank of Venice, which kept its specie idle most of the time in its vaults.

THE BANKING ORGANIZATION AT THE END OF THE SEVENTEENTH CENTURY

By the end of the seventeenth century there were in several parts of Europe twenty-five different institutions named banks, which Macleod divided into three main classes:

1. Those for the benefit of income only: such as the Italian *monti* which were nothing but creditors of the State, who advanced money to them upon the security of terminable or perpetual annuities which were transferable (the management of the revenues and their distribution among the proprietors, as well as the transference of the annuities, being handled by commissioners).

2. For safekeeping of cash, for the insuring of a uniform standard of value, and for the convenience of transferring debts from one account to another: such as those in Amsterdam, Rotterdam, Hamburg, and Stockholm, and that of Venice which engrafted this business on its original constitution. Banks of this description had no shareholders and were not intended to make any profits beyond what was necessary for paying their expenses.

3. Those instituted for the express purpose of trading and profit, in which the proprietors by receiving money from the public on deposit, and lending it at interest, realized a profit, which they shared among themselves. This type was illustrated by the banks of Barcelona and Scotland.

It is to be emphasized that none of the Continental public banks issued paper notes on their own credit, or upon any other basis than gold or silver actually deposited with them, so that they did not in any way add to the quantity of the currency.[36] These banks were not credit banks, they were "purely monetary institutions." [37] During the period from 1500 to 1700 the public banks had little or nothing to do with the quantity of the circulating medium. This was the function of the private bankers. The chief circulating medium of the period (i. e., money) was the bill of exchange. The Tudor kings of England tried to make a state monopoly of the right of exchange and then sought to farm it out. For that reason it did not develop so extensively there as elsewhere, and when the Bank of England was established the way had already been paved to permit that bank to discount or even to draw such bills.

Thus it would appear that the transfer banks were chiefly of value as institutions which provided a uniform and sound paper currency, as a substitute for specie issued against the deposit of 100 percent specie reserves, and were not of service as lenders, although there were exceptions to this. It was long suspected that the Bank of Amsterdam took advantage of its credit and lent out money at interest. John Law so accused it, and the fact seems to have been verified in 1796 when the French took possession of Amsterdam and found that the bank had lent upward of ten million guilders to the Government of Holland.[38] Pure transfer banks, although prohibited from granting credit, could not on occasion resist inducements to make secret loans.

It is of historical interest that a number of these transfer banks had originally been organized in connection with the requirements of public credit, composed as they were of creditors of the Italian city-states who had participated in public loans. Although Macleod fails to see how these chambers performed banking functions, other writers have observed that they did.[39] The corporations were charged with the collection of revenues pledged as security and with the distribution of interest. Since income was more uniformly spread over time than were interest payments, periodic accumulations of funds could be utilized for occasional loans to the State and were loaned, on rare occasions, to private persons. The flotation of public loans led eventually to the creation of organized bourses, or securities exchanges, such as those at Antwerp and Lyons. The Continental bourse was for a long time a commodity exchange before it became also the seat of trading in securities and foreign exchange. Even today these Continental institutions combine these three functions.

[36] *Ibid.*, p. 367.

[37] Rist, *op. cit.*, p. 45.

[38] Macleod, *The Theory and Practice of Banking*, I, 365.

[39] *Ibid.*, p. 3; Landmann, *op. cit.*, pp. 427–28.

Banks of Issue

Private banking houses, such as that of Fugger and Company of Augsburg, began the issue and circulation of interest-bearing promissory notes as early as about 1525. Bills of exchange also served as money and were issued by private bankers long before the public banks assumed that function. The private bankers of Italy, as well as banks operating under public grant or permit during the sixteenth century, issued freely transferable certificates of deposit or certificates of credit, as the case might be. These were called *di deposito* or *di credito,* respectively.

In Antwerp, as also in Holland during the sixteenth century, it became the custom of merchants to deposit funds with "cashiers" and to pay their bills by issuing written memoranda and orders upon the cashier—in other words, checks. These cashiers also often employed the cash deposited with them to their own advantage. They profited, not only by making loans, but also by sorting coins and paying out in worn pieces that barely passed current requirements.

Heckscher has observed that the part played by public banks, up to the middle of the nineteenth century, was small in its bearing upon the credit system when compared with the activities of private bankers, goldsmiths, scriveners, money-lenders and usurers.[40] Public banks of issue first appeared at the end of the seventeenth century and the beginning of the eighteenth century in response to the need for capital by the centralized State and expanding commerce and industry. Early forms of note issue were found in certain transfer banks already described. The Casa di San Giorgio in Genoa began in 1675 to issue deposit vouchers, payable to individual persons and transferable by endorsement. Other banks followed the same practice. The Bank of Sweden, which was founded by Palmstruch in 1656, had already issued certificates, at first as receipts for deposits of copper coin, but later in amounts exceeding the deposits. According to Heckscher, Palmstruch was influenced by what he believed to be the practice of the Bank of Amsterdam, the granting of credits of a banking character. He had in mind the extension of credit by the Bank of Amsterdam through an independent institution, the Huys van Leening. This was adapted to the Bank of Sweden by giving it two departments, the Bank of Exchange and the Lending Bank. The small amounts deposited with the Bank of Exchange were given out in credits "so that the bank became a credit institution, insofar as it was anything at all." [41] The significant departure was the issuance of bank notes

[40] Eli F. Heckscher, "The Bank of Sweden in Its Connection with the Bank of Amsterdam," in Van Dillen, *op. cit.*, p. 161.

[41] *Ibid.*, p. 169.

which differed in important respects from the certificates which had earlier been issued by the Italian banks, namely, they were not issued against deposits with the bank and their amounts were in round numbers upon printed forms. Promissory notes later issued by the Scottish and English banks were of the same character. These paper notes at first proved popular owing to their superior convenience over the heavy standard copper coins, but by 1663, when copper flowed out of the country, the notes were presented to the bank in amounts exceeding its power to redeem them, so that in 1664 the Government prohibited their issue.

The Bank of Sweden thus became, during its first half century of operations, a bank of credit, but without the complementary device of note issue. Deposits were essential to the working of the bank, for it had small capital.[42] However, the bank experienced difficulties in finding loan outlets since it was restricted principally to loans on real estate, and was unimportant with regard to commercial credit. Later the bank's note issue came into greater use, playing an important part in causing inflation.

In England the beginnings of note issue are attributed to the goldsmiths who, about the year 1640, after Charles I destroyed confidence in the safety of the Royal Mint by seizing the deposits of the London merchants, became depositaries for merchants and landed nobility, though later, in 1672, they were bankrupted owing to suspension of specie payments by the Government. This is not to say that the goldsmiths were the first bankers, for it is evident that the scrivener was the first financial intermediary to make a practice of keeping money deposits for the purpose of lending such deposits at interest.[43]

Goldsmiths first served as trustees or bailees who accepted money deposits in trust and were not allowed to use the sums deposited. Later, as deposit keepers, they were allowed to use these monies provided an equivalent sum was returnable to the depositor on demand. Thus the goldsmith became the debtor of the depositor. The first notes issued by the goldsmiths were, therefore, bailee notes, or nonassignable warehouse receipts, later supplemented by promissory notes, representing the holding of cash withdrawable on demand. Finally, notes were issued which possessed no specific metallic banking, based merely on the banker's judgment of the probable demand for specie.[44]

In contrast to the principles of the Continental transfer banks, the goldsmiths did not assume the obligation of keeping the deposits untouched, but only to repay them on demand or short notice.[45] They did not disguise the

[42] *Ibid.*, p. 172.
[43] R. D. Richards, *The Early History of Banking in England* (London, 1929), p. 15.
[44] *Ibid.*, p. 225.
[45] See Landmann, *op. cit.*, p. 428.

fact that they were making loans. Various practices existed, including the transfer of deposits by order, by draft, similar to modern checks, and by issuance of deposit vouchers or goldsmiths' notes for circulation. The goldsmiths illustrate one of the first real developments of the principle of using the note-issue technique as a means of granting loans. The fact that the amount of notes which were presented for payment was less than the amount of deposits outstanding allowed the note issue customarily to exceed the deposited cash balance on hand.

The failure of the goldsmiths left unsatisfied the need for a convenient means of payment. William Patterson's plan of combining a bank of issue with the granting of a loan to the Government was adopted in 1694 with the chartering of the Governors and Company of the Bank of England. This institution was empowered to raise working capital, not only by accepting deposits, but also by issuing notes against negotiable securities to the amount of its capital. It was copied elsewhere, although the principles of limiting note issue to negotiable securities were not always observed. However, a sharp distinction is to be made according to the basis upon which banks issue their own obligations. Rist has made this quite clear in pointing out that "bank money" may take two forms: [46]

1. A simple receipt certificate, transferable by a mutual clearing agreement, as was the custom at the *giro* specie banks. For each receipt there was in the repositories of the bank an exactly equivalent amount of metal.

2. The bank note in the more modern sense (and the bank deposit in the contemporary meaning), that is, a circulating credit; in this case, the bank undertakes to exchange it on sight for coin (or whatever is the legal standard of value), but it does not undertake to keep always on hand an equivalent amount of metal; this was true of the Bank of England and the Scottish banks.

Macleod contends that the Scottish banks were among the first institutions which deliberately operated upon the use of their own credit.[47] The Bank of Scotland was the first instance, he says, of a private joint stock bank, formed by private persons for the express purpose of making a trade of banking, wholly unconnected with the State, and depending upon its own private capital.[48] In view of these features of its organization, it became

[46] Rist, *op. cit.*, p. 33.

[47] It is to be observed that during the seventeenth century it became quite customary for merchants as well as bankers to draw bills of exchange upon correspondents with whom they had accounts, leaving it up to the person or bank drawn upon either to accept or reject. This resulted in credit accommodations, which was quite common, especially in Catholic countries. Therefore, Macleod's emphasis upon the importance of Scotch banks as users of their own credit should not be allowed to overshadow the importance of earlier devices used in the granting of credit.

[48] Macleod, *The Theory and Practice of Banking*, I, 339.

necessary to derive a profit from its business sufficient to pay the usual interest upon the stock and indemnify the proprietors for the risk they ran. It was not restricted to the amount of its issues and might issue as many notes as the public was willing to receive. The significant feature of these notes was that they were issued upon the basis of the bank's own credit. The bank apparently did not at first receive deposits from the public but contented itself with issuing its own notes based ultimately upon the security of the stock subscriptions of its proprietors. Macleod attributed the stopping of payment in 1704 to overissue of paper and this, he explained, induced the bank in 1707 to receive public deposits upon which it gave interest.

Macleod believed that it was the lack of limitation upon note issue which facilitated the development of the cash credit or accommodation credit system in Scotland, administered through a branch network which proved so beneficial in the development of the economy of Scotland. The significant fact is that banks up to that time had merely issued notes as receipts for the coin, or bullion, deposited with them, and, as in the case of the Bank of England, were strictly forbidden under penalties from issuing notes or bills to a greater amount than their subscribed capital which had been advanced to the Government. Scottish banks, on the other hand, were able to issue as many notes as the public was willing to receive and can be viewed as early examples of banks of credit.

It would seem that Macleod's description of the Scottish banks could apply with some modification to the private banking houses of the sixteenth century. The chief difference was that the latter were organized as universal partnerships, to which were attached subpartnerships entered into with factors operating as branches of the main firm, while the former was in the nature of a general partnership, or what would now be called a joint stock company with or without a charter. The old private banking houses made loans against pledges of taxes, mining properties, exclusive markets for spices, etc., under which they were required to reimburse themselves by operating these concessions. The Scottish banks were more inclined to avoid such operating duties, and therefore observed more closely what is considered today to be the proper banking function.

On the Continent the founding of banks of issue was delayed until some years later. In France, John Law's bank (1716) was authorized to issue circulating notes without limitation which, like the notes of the Bank of Amsterdam, were stated in terms of an ideal unit representing a fixed weight of bullion in which its notes were redeemable on demand. The bank was not expected to hold reserves of coin and bullion in excess of amounts necessary to meet demands for them. Lending operations of various kinds were authorized; deposits were accepted and interest paid thereon. The bank was so successful in the beginning that it was taken over and operated as a government institution, the Royal Bank, in 1718. However, its *modus operandi* underwent significant changes. The bank notes were declared legal tender and were made redeemable, not in the original ideal unit representing a fixed weight of bullion, but in current coin of the realm. The implication of these changes was realized too late after the overexpansion of the bank's issue and the subsequent loss of confidence in the bank's credit.[49]

Despite the collapse of Law's financial system through the abuse of the power inherent in an institution of this kind, his system marks a signal experiment with the technique of modern banking since it involved the combination and complementary use of various functions, particularly lending and note issue, in one institution—the bank. It is this feature which distinguishes commercial banking of the present day and which makes its successful operation depend upon principles peculiar to this method of finance.

THE RISE OF MODERN BANKING

Various writers agree that prior to the seventeenth century the basic techniques of deposit, discount, and note issue had all been practiced by various institutions, but that these operations had not been combined in the same institution. Thus the money-changers and transfer banks had forged the mechanism of deposit and clearance, while private financiers and merchants had developed the market for loans and the discount of commercial paper, and the banks of issue supplied the other essential element.[50] These elements were developed in various places, at different times, and under different circumstances, and did not coexist within the framework of the same institution until the end of the eighteenth century. During the following century, the basic functions of modern banking, the providing of credit, and the issuance and clearance of circulating media were still further integrated and specialized by banks, as purely financial institutions no longer as closely identified with other pursuits. Likewise, the establishment of closer relations among individual banks and their fusion into a system occurred in the course of the nineteenth century. In the twentieth century, the practice of note issue was limited and finally, for all practical purposes, reserved to the central bank or to the government, while the commercial banking system through the perfection of the deposit technique emancipated itself from its former reliance on limited note issue and was integrated into a system of deposit issue bound together through interbank accounts and

[49] A convenient summary of Law's financial system is to be found in James, *op. cit.*, pp. 125–34.

[50] Landmann, *op. cit.*, p. 431.

devoted to the function of facilitating payments. It thereby has become an autonomous business granting credit on its own account, no longer dependent within limits on the disposition of specie deposits. But at the same time it was the combination of the function of lending and investing with the function of undertaking to make demand payments that introduced the basic and inherent contradiction in banking. This contradiction became stronger the more the practice spread of using the banking machinery to make payments and to provide borrowers with money capital and led necessarily to distinctions in theory between credit and capital.

Chapter II

THE BASIC FUNCTIONS OF MODERN BANKS

THE MODERN deposit banking system performs two basic functions. In the first place, it provides and maintains the machinery by which the bulk of all payments are made. Secondly, it comprises a principal source of loanable funds. On the one hand, commercial banks are the most important money-issuing institutions; on the other, they are a source of credit and, in the opinion of many writers, a source of capital as well. In this chapter it is intended to examine in turn the nature of each of these basic functions, and then the manner in which they are interrelated.

THE MONETARY FUNCTION OF BANKS

It has been widely recognized that in countries like the United States, where the use of credit is highly developed, the banking system to an increasing extent has assumed functions which, according to older theory, were attributable to money. Both British and American writers for many years have treated the subject of money from a functional standpoint, assigning to it three basic functions: (1) a measure of value, or means of comparing values; (2) a means of payment; and (3) a store of value. Unless the system of exchange is to be conducted on a barter basis in which price comparisons are limited to two commodities at a time, there is need for a common denominator of value so as to permit simultaneous price comparisons of several or all commodities. In the second place, without a common and generally acceptable medium of exchange or means of payment, it would be impossible to effectuate the division of labor and specialization which renders possible the present-day methods of indirect production and exchange. Finally, the uncertainty of the future and the fact that, to the individual person, the exchange process involves the element of time, require that individual persons and firms in the system possess something which will serve as a store of value, that is, a means of postponing decisions and guarding against contingencies.

Broadly speaking, the term "money" has come to be applied to any instrument which satisfies any or all of the functions enumerated above, and in modern usage money is said to consist of the various categories of media of exchange, including not only the older forms of money like gold and silver, but also the nonphysical forms comprising transferable bank deposits and even bills of exchange. Unfortunately, it is not clear what particular function of money is regarded as being served by those instruments upon which the name "money" is conferred. Other functions often have been wrongly imputed to particular instruments simply because money in the broad sense comprehends a variety of functions. Therefore, it is important to consider in what sense bank deposits function as money and whether they are capable of performing all the functions just described and, if so, under what conditions.

Evidently, bank deposits transferable by check have assimilated the means-of-payments function which in earlier times was performed by bank notes, and still earlier by government notes and standard coins, but it is not clear to what extent this depends upon their own suitability as a store of value, or requires that some other object serve as a store of value. A number of writers today, particularly those who seem to believe in the unlimited elasticity of bank deposits, deliberately or unconsciously neglect the interconnection in society between the store-of-value function and the means-of-payment function, implying that because these functions are performed by separate institutions or instruments, they are independent of one another.

The antimetallists, like Knapp, who regard money merely as a means of payment have completely denied its function as a store of value, while the metallists, who have always considered the store-of-value function essential, have refused to admit that paper money is money because of its inability to perform the store-of-value function. Between these two extremes are found writers like Wicksell, Hawtrey, and Robertson, who have mainly stressed the means-of-payment function and denied the importance of, ignored, or neglected to consider, the store-of-value function.

Wicksell has pointed out that for a long time one class of commodities, the precious metals, have been used as a medium of exchange, while other commodities such as grain have been used contemporaneously as a measure of value, especially in fixing wages and paying taxes.[1] He argued that only the medium-of-payment function "is in a true sense characteristic of money," that "as a measure of value any commodity whatever might serve," and that "the function of acting as a store of value is not an essential characteristic of money." Thus, he viewed these functions as independent of one another, but a close reading of his work reveals that he perceived significant interconnections between them. While he said that, for society as a whole, money never has the function of a store of value, and that, from the individual point of view, the object of the individual in hoarding money is to conserve some-

[1] Knut Wicksell, *Lectures on Political Economy* (New York, 1935), II, 7–8.

thing else for a future time, his statement that "it is money as a future medium of exchange which is hoarded," reveals that he could not avoid the interconnection between money as a store of value and money as a medium of exchange.

On the other hand, Rist has argued that the store-of-value function is the origin of the other functions.[2] Money as a store of value is a means of settling balances without waiting until such balances are offset by further operations. The function of serving as a means of exchange presupposes the function of serving as a store of value since there is always a certain interval between the receipt of money and expenditures. Thus the function of money, according to Rist, cannot be understood in a society of static equilibrium but only in a dynamic society where money functions to guard against uncertainties of the future.

The important question is not whether the term "money" should be applied to bank deposits; there is no reason why it should not, provided it is understood that bank deposits are given the appellation "money" because of their service as a means of payment, and provided it is clearly understood that bank deposits will only function as a satisfactory means of payment to the extent that they also serve as a store of value, or to the extent that some other material into which they are convertible serves that function. Rist's criticism of Hawtrey, Robertson, Keynes, and others for neglect of the relation between the means of payment and the store of value seems valid, because in this neglect they have been tempted to assume unlimited creation of bank deposits and at times thus implied the belief that the only function of money is to serve as a means of payment, while at other times they have been compelled to admit that the successful use of bank deposits as a means of payment is conditioned by the necessity of these deposits continuing to serve as a store of value, or of there being available reserves to satisfy this function.

Thus Rist said:

> What matters to the economist is not so much a good definition of money, as a knowledge and an understanding of "monetary phenomena"; that is to say, of the way in which the very varied and numerous instruments that are in fact in existence and that we call money behave in different circumstances.[3]

Similarly, he believed that the antimetallists have been wrong in denying that one of the functions of money is to act as a store of value, while the

[2] Charles Rist, *History of Monetary and Credit Theory from John Law to the Present Day,* tr. by Jane Degras (New York, 1940), pp. 324–37.

[3] *Ibid.*, p. 335.

metallists have been wrong in believing that paper money and other fiduciary forms (bank deposits) cannot fulfill this function.[4]

A significant monetary development of the nineteenth and twentieth centuries was the apparent separation in practice of the performance of the means-of-payment function from the performance of the store-of-value function. It was found possible to dispense with the use of standard money, especially those forms like gold which possess intrinsic value, as a means of payment, though gold continued to serve as a store of value. The banking system gradually took over the means-of-payment function, and accounts came to be settled more and more by clearing arrangements. Thus Willis in his writings regarded the banking and credit mechanism as a means of avoiding the use of money, meaning by "money," the legal tender or standard forms.[5] However, the fact which many students have neglected is that, in using the term "money" to refer to bank credit (deposits), they have assumed the absence of any interconnection between the successful functioning of these deposits as a means of payment and the need for some other instrument to perform the store-of-value function.

The perfection of clearance in the banking system depends in no small measure upon the kinds of bank assets against which the system generates its deposit liabilities, and in a real world, even under conditions where bank assets permit satisfactory clearance, there always remain net balances which have to be settled at some time since they cannot be carried forward indefinitely. The situation in domestic trade is analogous to that in international trade where there exist various means of balancing accounts which cannot be carried forward indefinitely and in the end must be paid in real wealth. Under the gold standard, settlement normally took place in gold, and this is still true in the case of the international transactions of the United States despite the departure from the strict orthodoxy of the pre-1933 gold standard. Where satisfactory arrangements for ultimate or final settlement in real wealth cannot be arranged, the adjustment may be consummated through fluctuating prices of currencies, theories of which fall outside the scope of this discussion.

In domestic affairs when clearance is not perfect, settlements have to be made and were normally made, even before suspension of the redemption in gold, either in legal tender currency or in debits and credits to reserve accounts at the central bank. But here again, unless it can be assumed that

[4] *Ibid.*, p. 337.

[5] H. Parker Willis and George W. Edwards, *Banking and Business* (rev. ed.; New York, 1925), p. 8; also H. Parker Willis, John M. Chapman, and Ralph W. Robey, *Contemporary Banking* (New York, 1933), Chap. 1.

these reserve accounts can be acquired free and are of unlimited elasticity, the only way an individual bank which is deficient in reserves can effect settlement of net balances owing to other banks is by liquidation of its assets. This may or may not involve changes in valuation of its assets (as will be discussed at a later point).

Thus it is that reserve accounts with the central bank, which, like notes, are liabilities of the central bank and only technically different, are a kind of money which serves both as a store of value and as a means of payment. Reserves are in actual practice the principal means which banks use to effect payment among one another.

In connection with the use of commercial bank as well as central bank deposits as a means of payment, it is important to observe that the function of acting as a means of payment presupposes that the function of serving as a store of value can also be satisfactorily served. From the standpoint of the individual bank the need for a reserve is the need for a store of value, and this need is the result of the necessity of guarding against the uncertainties of the future, specifically the risk that settlements will have to be made so long as foresight and judgment are not certain.

The uninterrupted use of bank deposits and of central bank deposits as a means of payment presupposes their successful employment as a store of value. The question whether they can or will perform this function satisfactorily depends, in the final analysis, upon the conditions upon which they are issued and, once issued, the disposition of them by their holders.

Whereas bank deposits and similar instruments, under a given unit-of-account money system, may serve as ideal instruments for performing the mechanical service of a means of payments, it does not follow that they will do so under all conditions. One essential condition is that they remain generally acceptable to those who desire money to hold, which is another way of saying that they must serve as a satisfactory store of value. One great advantage of gold and other precious metals, and the reason why they were chosen as legal standards, was their admirable quality as a store of value which, in turn, was derived from their intrinsic value. The real question is whether bank credit can be controlled in such a way as satisfactorily to replace or dispense with other materials which formerly were used for this purpose. This question can only be answered by rather careful analysis of the nature of bank credit (deposits) and the way in which it differs from other forms of money, including legal tender and standard money. But the essential point is that the soundness of bank credit as a means of payment is measured by the degree to which the clearance of deposits is perfect, that is, the degree to which the use of money as a means of final net settlement is avoided. Bank deposits will function satisfactorily as a means of payment, or medium of exchange, and obviate the need for money as a store of value so long as they can be cleared.

It is worth while to mention the essential differences between bank deposits, bank notes, and gold. Any or all of these may be selected and used by the public as a means of payment without the prior necessity of being endowed with legal characteristics. However, there can hardly be any question that a society, built upon intricate series of complex legal relations between debtor and creditor, requires that some one form, or forms, be vested with the attribute of acceptability in the eyes of custom or law, hence the practice of legislating what particular kinds of money shall be legal tender in the settlement of debts. In the United States this quality has been granted only to certain hand-to-hand forms of currency, namely, the issues of the Government and the central bank. Today, bank deposits are claims to payment in legal tender money and therefore, *de jure* at least, to be distinguished from it. It is of interest to observe in passing that interbank deposits, that is, checks on banks other than the remitting bank, under the Negotiable Instruments Law, are a satisfactory means of payment, while under the regulations of the Board of Governors of the Federal Reserve System, a Federal Reserve bank may accept cash, bank drafts, transfer of funds or banks credits, or other forms of payment or remittance acceptable to the collecting Federal Reserve bank, in payment for checks.

But aside from these legal features, it is obvious that the economic and financial characteristics of various types of money are determined by an entirely different set of considerations. Basically, the bank note and bank deposit differ from all other forms of money in that their issue is conditional upon the acquisition of assets by the commercial banks while cancellation depends on disposal of these assets. The same is true of the note and deposit issues of central banks. Indeed, this is the essence of their mechanical elasticity. In the case of government note issues, there is no corresponding acquisition or sale of assets, except in the case of representative forms of money which are secured 100 percent and, hence, are synonymous with precious metals or some other valuable object of wealth. On the other hand, the precious metals are subject to their own peculiar conditions of production and use, and therefore their elasticity is conditional upon an entirely different set of factors.

In principle, both notes and deposits of banks are alternative forms of bank credit, both being liabilities assumed by the issuers. Technically and practically speaking, there are significant differences between these two types of liability, but these differences are institutional in nature. The differences, so far as the banking process is concerned, depends upon the type of collateral or of legal reserve required to be held behind each, for this imposes an upper limit upon the power of the issuing bank to expand or multiply its liabilities. In the United States the limits which operate in the case of deposits, which are merely a general creditor's claim in liquidation on the assets of the issuing bank, under a fractional reserve system greatly exceed the limits under a fully covered note issue system, like that of the national banks, where specific assets were also pledged to secure the notes. But under the same set of hypothetical reserve and collateral requirements, these differences would disappear. From the standpoint of the note or deposit holder, there are, of course, practical differences of convenience as well as legal protection which may under certain circumstances tend to destroy the theoretical identity of notes and deposits as alternative forms of circulating bank liability.

The volume of unsecured fiat government issues obviously are subject to arbitrary control dependent upon the wisdom of the issuing authority, but ordinarily in the past not subject in practice to any fixed limitation except that imposed by the requirements of budgetary deficits.

Consequently, additions to and contractions of the money supply are determined by entirely different factors in each case. Furthermore, additions to, or contractions of the available supply have quite different repercussions upon other aspects of economic life. For example, the creation of paper money issues by the Government represents an absolute addition to the money supply which continues in existence indefinitely until canceled or paid off, as for example, through taxation, or refunded into an interest-bearing obligation by the issuer. The precious metals represent a more permanent addition to the money supply, but differ principally in that they are valuable in themselves and need never be paid off or retired. Bank credit, however, is subject to reduction and expansion, but only in consequence of changes in the volume of bank assets which, in turn, are governed in part by the policy of the bankers, in part by the decisions of borrowers and the willingness of the non-bank public to buy or sell securities, and limited by the demands of the public for legal tender money, that is, their distrust of bank deposits as a store of value, in other words, by the condition of bank reserves. In some respects, and within limits, the supply of money is subject indirectly to deliberate alteration by the central bank or the Treasury. In any case, the principles which control the volume of bank credit are entirely different from those which operate in the case of either gold or fiat forms of government issue.

The important everyday fact is that deposits which are transferable by check afford the chief means of payment and that the banking system, through its power to issue both notes and deposits, supplies the means by which the bulk of all transactions are paid for in the monetary sense. Money in the form of hand-to-hand currency (legal tender) is now used only in making small change, in retail trade, sometimes in meeting pay rolls, while central bank deposits are used in bringing about the net settlement of transactions between banks which cannot be cleared, in the ordinary course of events, without the use of legal tender. In the case of interbank clearance, the technique has been refined to the point where clearing is accomplished through debits and credits to reserve accounts with the Federal Reserve bank. In turn, these central banks effect net settlements with each other in gold certificates, that is, standard money.

In the United States bank deposits represent about 85 percent of the aggregate money supply (demand deposits plus various types of note circulation outside the Treasury) and are employed in financing over 85 percent of all money payments.[6] Since 1935 the national banks have been prevented from issuing their own notes, so that today notes are issued only by the Government and the Federal Reserve banks, principally in the form of silver certificates and Federal Reserve notes, both of which are legal tender, although they can no longer be redeemed in the standard money gold which, in turn, from a domestic standpoint, now serves mainly as a reserve limitation upon the issuance by the central banks of notes and deposits and in no sense circulates or performs the medium-of-exchange function. Hand-to-hand currency forms (i. e., note issues), therefore, have become either fiduciary or fiat, even though the fiction of their representative character continues nominally to be preserved. Bank deposits which comprise the bulk of the means of payment are not subject to quite the same kind of limitations upon issue, nor do they yet possess the legal tender property. In normal times their acceptability is derived from their convenience as well as their redeemability in legal tender currency which, in turn, for domestic purposes is no longer redeemable under present laws in the standard gold but only redeemable in itself.[7] Therefore it would appear that the means of payment for domestic purposes consists today entirely of fiduciary or fiat elements, since even silver certificates issued by the Treasury possess intrinsic value which is only a fraction of their face value. But even the bank deposits have been given the effectiveness of legal tender character by means of Federal insurance of deposits while, from the economic standpoint, they are to an

[6] See Frederick A. Bradford, *Money and Banking* (rev. ed.; New York, 1941), pp. 259–60. See also Willis, Chapman, and Robey, *op. cit.*, pp. 39–42.

[7] It should be noted that, in so far as the external relation between the unit of account, the dollar, and gold is fixed by the $35 per ounce buying price, and theoretically by a comparable selling price, as long as the Treasury buys or sells gold for or from its monetary stocks, the reserves of the deposit banks will be affected, as will the deposits issued against these reserves, so that in a quantitative sense, the supply of the means of payment is related to the standard money gold and is redeemable in it even if only indirectly, and even if subject to the discretion of the Treasury or central bank.

increasing extent being issued upon the basis of Government credit subject to variable limits imposed by legal reserve requirements as to balances required at central banks.

As Gregory observed:

> We are compelled at the outset to disregard those older theories which asserted the view that the value of money is derived from its intrinsic content and not from its function as a medium of exchange, as well as those of the Nineteenth Century which regarded money as a valuable commodity which for various reasons came to exercise the functions of a medium of exchange, and to adhere to the general view taken by more recent 'unit of account' theories which consider money as the objective representative of debts and the legally authorized means of settling them, which derives its value from the quantitative [and qualitative] relations between itself and these debts.[8]

It becomes necessary to examine the extent to which money is an autonomous creation of the exchange economy, and to decide to what extent it has become merely an instrument devised by the State and imposed from without, and to what extent the State can or cannot escape the consequences of its own action. If the bulk of the means of payment consists of fiduciary and fiat elements, it is obviously necessary to study the methods of fixing and controlling these elements, and the extent to which new methods can be substituted for the older tests of redemption or convertibility into standard money when that standard money itself served as a store of value and also as a means of payment.

The most important basic difference between banks and other financial institutions is the fact that only banks of deposit perform the means-of-payment function. This difference is not merely a difference in technique of operation based upon the device of securing funds for loan or investment. There is a fundamental difference in economic function which lies beneath the mere mechanical function of transferring legal titles. The function is to operate the entire system of payments so that the goods and services which flow in the process of exchange are cleared successfully. This requires that banks conduct their affairs and manage their relations to that process in such a way as to accomplish this result. The real test of their success, in the final analysis, lies in their ability to manage or limit the supply of circulating media so that they satisfy at the same time their own requirements of liquidity and solvency and the requirements of society as a whole for financial assistance in promoting the uninterrupted flow of goods and services.

[8] T. E. Gregory, "Money," in *The Encyclopaedia of the Social Sciences* (New York, 1933), p. 604.

Chapter III

THE LENDING FUNCTIONS OF BANKS

THE COMPOUND NATURE OF BANKING FUNCTIONS

THE VIEWS of various authors regarding the functional aspects of banking can be traced to their personal conception of the banking system. Some look at banking from the narrow standpoint of the individual bank, others from the standpoint of the entire system, while still others identify the system with one great large single bank.[1] Any theory, whatever the framework within which it is confined, must concern itself with the interrelation of bank assets and liabilities, and this means with the interrelation of the two basic functions of banking. Neither is a simple independent function, though frequently for the purposes of analysis it is necessary to separate them.

It is a common but serious fault which runs through much of the literature on money and banking that no distinction is clearly drawn between the system and the individual bank, or if such a distinction is made, it is soon disregarded or modified by the author when he comes to deal with the subject of the expansion and contraction of bank credit. The older concepts of banking regard deposits as being accumulated out of the thrift and industry of the community. This is a notion which can be traced to those writers who denied that banks had the power to create deposits, and has always been implied in the *cliché* that, after all, the banker only lends "other people's money," a belief which is quite fallacious in so far as the banking system as a whole is concerned.[2] This notion, however, has been presented in different form by some of the modern writers. Reasoning on the assumption of the big single bank, they have discovered that deposits can never be paid out of the system by their holders, and, on this premise, have committed themselves to the paralogism that deposits are the equivalent of "savings."[3]

[1] The assumption of the large single bank in a closed system is usually implied but seldom stated by contemporary writers on the subject of monetary theory. D. H. Robertson, for example, makes such an assumption. See his *Banking Policy and the Price Level* (rev. ed.; London, 1932), pp. 52–3.

[2] Many bankers entertain this view of their operations.

[3] See *infra*, Chap. VI.

The power of banks to supply credit or money capital to borrowers by making loans or buying investments is derived in an entirely different way from the comparable power of other lenders. Furthermore, banks do not serve merely as simple "transporters of capital," that is, intermediaries in the transfer of monetary savings to investment. The function of making loans or buying investments in practice and theory is inextricably tied up with their power to issue deposit liabilities, that is to say, with the issuance of bank money.

In this connection, Harrod said:

> The banking system performs two functions which are perfectly distinct in principle but closely related in practice. On the one hand, it provides the effective circulating medium. On the other hand, it is a channel by which the savings which people do not wish to lock up in long term investments are made available for industry and trade. Since every time the banking system makes a loan it necessarily adds an equivalent amount to the circulating medium, the interconnexion of the two functions is evident.[4]

Hawtrey took a somewhat different view when he said:

> There is no necessary connection between the two sides of a banker's business—the demand liabilities which provide the means of payment and the temporary advances to traders. The union of these two functions in one agency is a great advantage from the point of view of convenience, and important consequences flow from their being so united. But in some respects it is desirable to study each in isolation from the other.[5]

Keynes gave a clear description of the inherent conflict in the duality of banking functions. Speaking on this subject he said:

> In so far as his (the banker's) deposits are Savings-Deposits, he is acting merely as an intermediary for the transfer of loan capital. In so far as they are Cash-Deposits, he is acting both as a provider of money for his depositors, and also as a provider of resources for his borrowing customers. Thus the modern banker performs two distinct sets of services. He supplies a substitute for State Money by acting as a clearing-house and transferring current payments backwards and forwards between his different customers by means of book entries on the credit and debit sides. But he is also acting as a middleman in respect to a particular type of lending, receiving deposits from the public which he employs in purchasing securities, or in making loans to industry and trade mainly to meet demands for working capital. This duality of function is the clue

[4] *What Everybody Wants to Know about Money*, ed. G. D. H. Cole (London, 1933). See Chap. III, by R. F. Harrod, p. 135.

[5] R. G. Hawtrey, *Currency and Credit* (2d ed.; London, 1923), p. 193.

to many difficulties in the modern theory of Money and Credit and the source of some serious confusions of thought. . . . The dilemma of modern banking is satisfactorily to combine these two functions.[6]

THE DIFFERENCES BETWEEN BANKS AND OTHER FINANCIAL INSTITUTIONS

In the United States there are nearly fifty different types of financial institutions, which may be classified into three general groups depending upon their method of operation: those which employ the deposit technique, i. e., banks; those which operate through some form of mediation, like the investment trust which issues its own obligations through sale to individual savers and invests the proceeds thus raised; and those whose activities are virtually limited to suretyship, for example, the Federal Housing Administration, which guarantees, or insures, loans made by lending institutions but which does not itself make loans.[7]

A general list of the various sources and means by which funds are raised would include: sale of stock, accumulation of surplus, short- and long-term borrowing, and issue of deposit credits. With regard to these, commercial banks are peculiar in several respects. The banking system, unlike all other financial institutions and business concerns, with the possible exception of the Government, acquires its assets almost entirely by virtue of its power to issue liabilities which function as money.[8] The resources of the individual bank in a system are derived in two peculiar ways: first, the receipt of cash items in the form of legal tender or checks drawn on other banks in return for which deposit credit is issued; and second, the origination of demand deposits transferable by check. The deposit technique is not employed; in fact, it cannot legally be employed by other institutions. The term "bank" is ordinarily only applied in reference to "deposit" institutions, although several exceptions are to be found in the law and in current usage, for example, the Morris Plan banks and the so-called investment banker, or underwriter, as he is more properly designated. The savings bank is a special exception since it holds "deposits," but it does not originate them, nor are they transferable by check. On the other hand, the other financial institutions find the principal source of their funds either in the sale of stock; the issuance of their own time obligations, i. e., time deposits, notes, or bonds;

[6] John Maynard Keynes, *A Treatise on Money* (New York, 1930), II, 213, 215.

[7] Cf. W. H. Steiner, *Money and Banking* (New York, 1933), pp. 153–58.

[8] The United States Treasury, contrary to popular assumption, does not incur budgetary expense when it buys gold and silver. It pays for these assets by issuing against them gold certificates or silver certificates or standard coins. This represents the monetization of particular assets, the metals, which are carried as such in the accounts.

or, in some cases, through a form of special contribution or tax, as is the case with insurance companies.

Banks are not unlike many other lending and investing institutions in so far as resources are obtained from the sale of capital stock or the accumulation of surplus. In this respect, they serve merely as channels through which a portion of the monetary savings of the community are routed. The function of the bank may be nothing more than that of reinvesting the sums so obtained. In so far as funds are obtained by the individual bank through the receipt of cash items in return for demand or time deposit credits, the individual bank functions in much the same way as the savings bank. However, as will be shown, the banking system is the originating source of all deposit credits, and loans of the system are not conditional upon the antecedent receipt of cash items, as is the case with the individual bank. Furthermore, as already mentioned, the deposit credits which banks issue are subject to transfer by check, while the deposit credits in savings banks are not subject to the same right of action by their owners.

THE SOURCES OF BANK LENDING POWER

The sources from which an individual bank derives its power to lend or invest are set forth on the liability side of its balance sheet. Except for minor miscellaneous liabilities, which may be safely neglected, these consist of deposits and capital account. In the United States, deposits typically are about ten times the size of the capital account, in recent years somewhat less. These items simply show the kind of claim which the bank issued at some time in the past against the acquisition of various kinds of assets. So far as the present is concerned, there is no justification for relating particular liabilities to particular assets.

The capital account indicates the amounts of cash which were obtained in the past by sale of common and preferred stock, and the sums accumulated out of past earnings and designated as surplus, undivided profits, or reserves for contingencies.

Deposits are classified in various ways but, for the moment, may be treated as all of one class. They represent in the case of the individual bank, amounts which at some time in the past were lodged with the bank and which the bank was at liberty to lend or invest. In addition, however, the individual bank, acting on its own initiative, may have made loans or purchased investments, and paid for them merely by writing up deposit liabilities, that is, by assuming a liability to pay money.

Economists early recognized that the power of the individual bank to continue making loans by writing up deposits is subject to real limitations, since the borrowers from a bank may promptly write checks against the newly acquired deposits, which are paid to persons who deposit them in other banks, which, in turn, present them to the drawee bank for payment. This means that the drawee bank, in order to honor the checks presented to it, must remit cash, suffer a reduction in its deposit balances with correspondent banks, or in its balance with the Federal Reserve bank; in other words, lose reserves, unless it happens that the checks presented to it can be offset or cleared against reciprocal items which the given bank is simultaneously trying to collect from the other banks. The only conditions under which the given bank would not lose reserves would be: (1) when the lending bank is the only bank in the community; or (2) when the other banks in the community are also simultaneously and at the same rate expanding their loans by assuming deposit liabilities.

As Hawtrey expressed it, there is a tendency for banks "to keep pace in granting credits" [9] as, otherwise, if a bank is too free with its loans, its customers will, on balance, pay away greater sums to customers of other banks than they will receive. Hence, if a bank is to keep a cash reserve in due proportion to its liabilities, it must restrict its advances, or perhaps transform its other assets into cash, but whatever it does, the result is that it no longer outstrips its competitors in granting credit. On the other hand, if it is unduly cautious, its cash reserves will grow at the expense of other assets, and its profits will suffer because its earning assets are too small.

The mechanics of this expansion are perhaps most easily understood by recognizing that an individual bank, finding itself in possession of additional reserve (legal tender, gold, or central bank credit), "lends" or "invests" this reserve by first granting deposit credit, i. e., issuing "rights of action" against the bank, to borrowers in return for promissory notes or bonds, and in this way makes itself vulnerable to loss of reserves in the event that the deposit holders transfer their rights against the bank by checks to persons who "deposit" them in other banks. The reserves are loaned, i. e., converted into another asset, say promissory notes, only in the sense that their availability for withdrawal permitted the loan to be made. But the acquisition by the bank of this asset was not *per se* dependent upon the reserves; it was acquired by mere creation of "rights of action" against the bank (deposits). Other banks in the system, upon receipt of the checks, collect them, thereby acquiring the reserves and gaining a position which permits them, in their turn, to make loans or investments. The result is that a given quantity of reserves is repeatedly used over and over again by a succession of banks, the aggregate quantity of such reserves for the banking system remaining constant all the while. The multiple expansion of credit

[9] Hawtrey, *op. cit.*, p. 201.

upon the basis of this reserve is made possible by the successive loans of individual banks with the result that, if none of these loans are repaid to the banks, a volume of deposits several times the reserves may be issued by the banking system. The device of deposit issue is the mechanical means by which a given volume of reserves is made to serve repeatedly for an indefinite series of credit transactions, the amount of reserves remaining unchanged but becoming subdistributed among many banks. Some writers, therefore, speak of this phenomenon as one in which bank credit (notes or deposit issues) makes money (reserves) circulate.[10] In this sense the erection of a volume of deposits requires the repeated circulation of a given volume of reserves. In actual practice, however, it is to be observed that expansion of bank deposits may take place simultaneously in many banks, so there may result no actual net shift in the ownership of reserves.

The individual banker habitually regards deposits as having resulted from funds entrusted to the bank by the depositors to be loaned or invested. For this attitude he has been roundly condemned by a number of writers on the subject, and yet in terms of his own narrow point of view his attitude normally would seem to be a reasonable one in that his freedom to make loans and buy investments is conditioned by his reserves. As Keynes put it, the rate at which a bank actively creates deposits is conditioned by the rate at which it passively acquires them. However, under certain conditions, namely, if other banks are simultaneously following the same lending policy, the individual bank may write up and actively incur deposit liabilities without there having been any previous receipt of cash reserves. This is merely another way of saying that, so long as the receipt of claims by one bank against other banks (reserves to the individual bank) offsets their claims on it, there will be clearance and no need for the settlement of net balances.

On the other hand, a number of theorists are inclined to neglect the vital assumption that expansion by all banks must be simultaneous and the internal payments among banks in the system must clear perfectly if the need for reserves is to be obviated, and an infinite series of credit transactions rendered possible. To the extent that clearance is perfect, bank credit obviates the use of money as such, i. e., reserves. But this assumes in theory the complete absence of a desire to hold money; that is to say, it assumes away the need for a store of value.

Reserves, then, are to the individual bankers a kind of money, while to the system of banks they are in the aggregate a set of clearing accounts through which net settlements among banks are effected by redivision of their ownership in the common fund. The need for reserves in the case of

[10] Charles Rist, *History of Monetary and Credit Theory from John Law to the Present Day*, tr. by Jane Degras (New York, 1940), pp. 38–43.

an individual bank *vis à vis* other banks disappears when clearance is perfect and, under such circumstances, credit stands forth as the means of avoiding the use of reserves as money. For the system of banks *vis à vis* the public, the need for reserves disappears only when the public does not demand to redeem the deposits which it owns in legal tender, or in gold in the case of international transactions.

The individual banker is activated, on the one hand, by the desire to make profits and, on the other, by the risks involved in relation to his ability to absorb loss, but his reserve position is the proximate factor of influence. For the system, however, the volume of loans is not conditioned by the volume of reserves. Loans are not made out of reserves. This is obvious, since any given aggregate of reserves will be the same before as after the expansion of bank deposits. All that the reserves do in this case is to serve as a means of payment among the banks by which the transfer of deposits within the system is accomplished. Reserves may be enlarged by: (1) gold imports; (2) return of hand-to-hand currency by the public; (3) their creation by the central bank, through open-market operations or rediscounts; and (4) their creation by the Treasury, through issuance of fiat currency, expenditure of gold revaluation profits, or direct borrowing from the central banks and subsequent expenditure of the deposit credits thus acquired on the books of the central bank.

An increase in reserves by any of these means may induce individual bankers to be more willing to lend, but the loans would not be made out of the reserves, but merely because of their presence and their increased volume relative to deposit liabilities. Conversely, for the system, contraction of loans and investments does not require a destruction of reserves. A contraction of reserves owing to a reversal of any one of the above factors would not in itself cancel loans or reduce bank assets, although it would undoubtedly induce such action by the banks if they were already fully loaned.

An examination of the consolidated balance sheet of the banking system will quickly show that the bulk of the offsets to assets consists, not of stock outstanding, but of deposit liabilities. Manifestly, deposits are liabilities which have been assumed by the banks severally. As of June 29, 1940, the insured commercial banks showed total deposits of $58,400,000,000.[11] These certainly did not represent sums of money which were contributed to the banks from outside the banking system, since cash plus reserves with Federal Reserve banks amounted to only $14,700,000,000.

From the standpoint of the system, deposits are the creation of the banks in the sense that they represent the assumption of liabilities and are the

[11] Federal Deposit Insurance Corporation, *Assets and Liabilities of Operating Insured Banks*, Report No. 13.

result of the purchase of assets by the banks, whether these assets be loans, investments, central bank credit, or gold. Only a small portion of the total assets resulted from sale of stock. Deposits, on the other hand, are created by the expansion of assets and destroyed by the contraction of assets. In other words, the volume of deposits of the system is functionally dependent on the assets of the system, and not the reverse.

At some point in the banking process individual banks, or the banks severally, wrote up by way of credits to borrowers the very deposits which the individual banker says were brought to him in the form of cash by his depositors. But once generated, their identity with the transaction by which they were created is soon lost somewhere along the devious routes and by-passes of the flow of funds, with the result that to the individual banker who later acquires these funds, because his customers transfer them to him in the form of reserves from banks by which they were originally issued, they appear as funds entrusted to him which he can safely lend or invest. For the system, deposits once created remain outstanding as a liability of some bank somewhere in the system until the then owners decide to employ them to repay loans or investments or to redeem them in legal gender currency or gold. Thus, for the system, the assets beget the liabilities, while for the individual bank the liability begets the asset. For the system, there is no real passive acquisition of funds except through gold and silver imports or the issuance of fiat money by the Treasury.[12]

The individual bank in the system may passively incur deposit obligations because depositors of other banks elect to transfer their claims to the given bank; but such changes are internal to the system and in every case are found to be either the mere transference of claims against the banking system from one individual to another, or substitutions of one kind of claim for another, as when an individual converts a note claim into a deposit claim. These changes are of the greatest importance to the conduct of the affairs of an individual bank because they impose a change in its relations *vis à vis* all other banks in the system. Thus, if the given bank is expanding loans and thereby deposits, and if the owners of these deposit credits draw them down and pay them into other banks, the given bank will suffer an adverse drain of legal tender money in its possession or will suffer a reduction in its own claims against other banks, or against the central bank, all of which merely means its working reserves will be reduced, a reduction which it cannot suffer indefinitely. This interrelationship of banks is the result of their

[12] This statement is meant to apply to the entire banking system, including the central bank. The member banking system, outside the central bank, of course, may passively acquire reserves if the central bank takes the initiative to create them, for example, by open-market operations.

joint performance of the function of providing the means of payment; and, therefore, this function must be conceived as a function of the system and is not to be regarded as a separate independent function of any single bank unless that bank is the only bank.

To the extent that the banking system approximates the idea of a large single bank, the means-of-payment function becomes attributable to the single bank; but in the United States, where there are nearly fifteen thousand banks, the function has no reality except in relation to the system of banks. This means that the joint performance by the banks of the function of providing the means of payments, or circulating media of the community, imposes upon the banks the necessity of acting in consonance with one another. In other words, in order to perform their joint function successfully, the degree of individual freedom in the matter of expanding loans and buying investments is automatically restricted, and so banks are to an important extent molded into a common behavioristic pattern with a definite trammel of action.

THE LIMITS TO EXPANSION AND CONTRACTION

The question of how far the banks can go in expanding their liabilities in the way indicated has been discussed by various writers who have shown that, under the following assumptions, there is no limit to expansion power: (1) that everyone uses checks in making payments; that is, there is no demand for money proper; (2) that the economy is closed; that is, there is no importation or exportation of gold and commensurate change in bank reserves; (3) that all banks follow a uniform lending and investing policy; specifically, that they expand loans or suffer repayments at the same rate; (4) that the system is composed of homogeneous banking units; and (5) that there are no legal reserve requirements.

These assumptions are not realized in practice, and accordingly, the system of banks faces real limits upon its power to expand even where a strong and consistent demand for bank credit is being expressed continually by the borrowing public at the interest cost which banks must charge to cover possible losses and overhead. The maximum potential limit to expansion is popularly said to be established by the fractional legal reserve requirement, but this imposes an outside legal limit which, as a matter of fact, cannot be realized unless all other assumptions hold good. In reality, there will be expressed a demand for hand-to-hand legal tender money, which normally is likely to grow with any expansion of deposits but may move otherwise. There is also the influence of the country's international balance of payments with its attendant international shift of bank deposits and analogous shift of gold, silver, or whatever may be the means of payment by which net balances are settled. There is also the fact that banks do not necessarily follow uniform policies as regards interest charges on loans or yields at which investments are purchased. Nor do the individual banks always keep the same proportion of reserves to deposits. Nor are banks uniform in respect to size; and, therefore, some units are more vulnerable than others to fluctuations in reserves, because newly created deposits are more likely to be paid away to other banks.

These factors give rise to frictions in the processes of clearance among banks and result in imperfections in that process, and hence, in limitations upon the realization by the system of any such maximum expansion as is frequently but erroneously predicated upon the sole consideration of the legal reserve requirement. For the short run, the individual policies of banks in regard to types of loans and investments govern their reserve policy as much as it is governed by it and this fact renders invalid the assumption of a common average reserve limitation. Furthermore, the types and kinds of loans which are made in one region of the country may affect the balance of payments between it and other areas and give rise to internal disequilibrium which will be reflected in the clearing mechanism.

Many writers have been inclined to overlook the fact that even in the presence of legal reserve requirements, the realization of such an expansion as that indicated can take place only on the following assumptions: (1) there is no need for reserves among individual banks; and (2) there is no demand for legal tender by the public; that is, the public is quite willing to hold bank deposits as a store of value, as well as a means of payment. These conditions, in turn, subsume: (*a*) a continuous demand for loans by borrowers at the rates imposed by lending banks; (*b*) that the standards of credit observed by the lending banks can be relaxed so as to enable the bank to compete with loans being offered by voluntary savers; (*c*) in the case of securities investments, an active policy on the part of the purchasing banks based on a desire for earnings and a belief in the maintenance of the existing level of money rates; (*d*) perfection of clearance, since that determines the reserve position of the individual banker.

Few writers have concerned themselves with the multiple contraction of bank deposits, but this seems to be of importance equal to that of the analysis of the conditions upon which expansion can occur. The contraction of bank deposits may be brought about by: (1) a need for reserves by individual banks, which must be obtained from other banks in the system, in the absence of the creation of new ones, since the contraction of one bank will force contraction of others; (2) a demand for legal tender by the public. Under either of these conditions, there must necessarily result one or all of the following: (*a*) the repayment of loans by borrowers, at least a faster rate of repayments as compared with the rate at which new loans are made, which will depend upon the ability of borrowers to repay; (*b*) a tightening of credit standards by the lending bank, which will mean denial of credit to borrowers who formerly depended upon it, and who must therefore appeal to the supply of funds available from voluntary savings; (*c*) in the case of securities investments, the banks may be forced to sell, and this will necessitate selling at reduced valuations unless the nonbank public has the willingness and capacity to absorb the securities disgorged by banks—otherwise the selling banks must absorb losses.

With full recognition of the factors which may interfere with the free and easy realization by the banking system of an expansion or contraction of deposit liabilities, it cannot be denied that the system possesses great powers of expansion merely by the making of loans and acquiring of investments even in the absence of variation in reserves. Of course, in periods when gold imports are heavy, as in the last ten years, the resulting increases in reserves under fixed legal ratio requirements in effect suspend or render ineffective those legal limitations. Within variable limits, therefore, bank deposits vary rather widely throughout the season and the business cycle and always basically as the result of changes in assets.

On the other hand, it seems to be true, logically and pragmatically, that the banking system has only limited powers of contraction without becoming involved in serious losses, or without imposing hardship upon an economic system which has become adjusted to the preceding expansion. If the system does not possess assets, gold or legal tender, loans, or investments, which the community is able and willing to receive or pay off in cancellation of deposits at existing values, the banks must absorb the losses, since they cannot revalue their liabilities. Under past banking practice these losses were absorbed by writing down the stated capital account of the banks, that is, by the stockholders; but, where that was not sufficient, the deposit creditors themselves suffered the losses. Deposit insurance, as will be shown in Chapter VIII, provides a means of redistributing these losses. It is to be emphasized that the voluntary repayment of loans is based in normal times upon a calculated decision by borrowers in relation to the marginal efficiency of capital, whereas the sale of securities by banks does not wait upon this factor as much as it does upon liquidity preference. Thus for the system, liquidity and solvency dissolve into much the same thing. The system can give the individual bank liquidity, but it cannot give it to itself except by being solvent.

Chapter IV

THE POSITION OF BANKS AS INTERMEDIARIES

ECONOMIES EFFECTED BY BANKS AS SIMPLE INTERMEDIARIES

IN FUNCTIONING as an intermediary, or transporter of "capital," commercial banks, like other lenders, such as the savings bank, life insurance company, etc., effectuate certain economies. Lavington has given an excellent description of these.[1] First, by collecting and pooling small amounts of capital, individually unimportant, they make a large stock of capital permanently available for business and other users. Secondly, as expert lenders they supply this capital to borrowers at average rates lower than would otherwise be the case. Regarded as a supply of capital, deposits (what Lavington calls "lodgements") constitute one large aggregate which has been formed out of many small quantities which, individually considered, would have been useless, owing to their size or to the lack of correspondence between the time for which borrowers wished to borrow and lenders were willing to lend. The banks succeed in offsetting the ebb and flow of one account by the flow and ebb of another, while at the same time, the "short lengths of capital" are added together, or averaged, the net result being that a continuous portion of the "capital," that is, the funds lodged with commercial banks as deposits, becomes available for continuous employment in trade and industry.

The extent of the economy thus effected by the banking system in turn is related to the structure of the system and the degree to which it succeeds in economizing reserves through the development of central and branch banking. As explained elsewhere, the shifting of deposits within the banking system is accomplished by an analogous shifting of reserves among the banking units in the system. The necessity for reserves arises from the need of individual banks for a means of payment and from the need of the country for a means of settling its international balance of payments. Other things being equal, the greater the degree to which these reserves are centralized and rendered elastic through being held by central banks, and the greater

[1] F. Lavington, *The English Capital Market* (London, 1921), Chap. XX, especially p. 134.

the degree to which they are rendered unnecessary through the consolidation of banks or the development of branch banking, the greater is the economy effected, and the more completely the banking system can succeed in applying the funds received from depositors to productive use by borrowers. To the extent that these economies are not effected, the individual banking units are restrained by the need for liquidity, and necessarily must confine a larger fraction of their resources to loans for short periods, or at least to loans which can be easily and quickly recovered without loss. This means that borrowers must bear the risk arising from the fact that the lending banks can recall their loans at short notice, and it also means that banks will be inclined to confine their investments to the less venturesome types of financing in order that they be assured of being able, if necessary, to dispose of such assets to other buyers without sacrifice in value.

THE IMPORTANCE OF BANKS AS INTERMEDIARIES

To portray the importance of the banking system as an intermediary in the process of savings and investment, it is necessary first to describe the framework within which that process is carried out in the United States.[2] This description is concerned with that part of the capital formation process which is essentially institutional and financial in nature, and therefore it does not attempt to explain, except in a general way, the sources of monetary savings or the distribution and application of funds under the control and discretion of the institutions in question.

The general process of capital formation has been conveniently epitomized in the following way:

First Stage: Savings.—When savings are made in any country (i. e.,

[2] Descriptions of this framework are to be found in the following publications:

H. Parker Willis and Jules I. Bogen, *Investment Banking* (rev. ed.; New York, 1936), p. 19.

League of Nations, *Statistics Relating to Capital Formation,* Studies and Reports on Statistical Methods, No. 4 (Geneva, 1938).

H. G. Moulton, *The Financial Organization and the Economic System* (New York, 1938), Chaps. III and X, especially pp. 132–36.

F. Cyril James, *The Economics of Money, Credit, and Banking* (3d ed., rev.; New York, 1940), p. 558.

Temporary National Economic Committee, 76th Cong., 1st Sess., Hearings, *Investigation of Concentration of Economic Power* (Washington, D.C., 1940), Part IX, "Savings and Investment," testimony of Dr. Donald H. Davenport, pp. 3726 ff.

Temporary National Economic Committee, *Savings, Investment, and National Income,* Monograph No. 37 (Washington, D.C., 1941), especially Part III.

National Resources Committee, *The Structure of the American Economy* (Washington, D.C., 1939), Part I, Chap. VI.

Murray Shields, *Interest Rates: an Analysis of Supply and Demand Factors* (lithographed ms, copyrighted 1941), Chap. IV.

when individual households or business enterprises or public authorities set aside part of their incomes), these may (*a*) be used for other purposes than investment within the country—e. g., either exported or hoarded or transferred to other persons for purposes of consumption by them; (*b*) be used directly for the acquisition of capital goods; (*c*) become available for investment by business enterprises, public authorities or private households.

Second Stage: Funds available for investment.—Out of the three streams of money savings enumerated above, the last two become available for investment. Stream (*b*) goes directly to investment without passing out of the control of the saver (e. g., investment in the enterprise of the saver himself, purchase of consumers' capital goods). Stream (*c*) finds its way to investment through the capital market either directly or through the intermediary of banks and similar institutions.

The streams coming from savings do not, however, represent all funds available for investment. Thus the money streams leading to the banks need not be equal to savings put at the latter's disposal, as the funds supplied by banks may in particular have been increased as a result of an increase of the credit-base or a reduction in reserve ratios, and by funds accumulated for maintenance or replacement of existing capital goods.

Third Stage: The value of newly created capital goods (money outlay for the acquisition of such goods).—The last stage of the process described consists in the actual acquisition of capital goods. Here again the money outlay for the acquisition of these goods need not correspond to the funds available for investment as described above. The difference is partly due to the time lag between the accumulation of funds and the acquisition of capital goods, as funds may remain idle over a period. Furthermore, parts of these funds may be used for other purposes than the acquisition of capital goods—e. g., by business enterprises for covering losses or by Governments for paying unemployment benefits, etc.[3]

The commercial bank occupies a position in the second stage alongside a large number of other intermediary financial institutions through which the large proportion of total money savings are channeled en route to the various users of funds who finally, in the third stage, employ them in the acquisition of physical capital goods.

Professor Donald H. Davenport has estimated the relative size of the various reservoirs of money savings under the control of the principal intermediary institutions already mentioned as well as for certain others, such as the social security, United States Government life insurance, and all governmental pension funds, the postal savings system, and the sale of

[3] League of Nations, *op. cit.*

United States Savings Bonds.[4] His estimates for the year 1938 are given in Table 1.

TABLE 1

SIZE OF RESERVOIRS OF MONEY SAVINGS, 1938

(In Billions of Dollars)

Life insurance assets (including fraternal associations)	28,775
Commercial bank time deposits	14,359
Mutual savings bank assets	11,572
Building and loan association assets	5,712
Governmental pension and trust funds	6,169
Postal savings	1,252
Baby bonds	1,238
Total	$69,077

These data afford some idea of the relative size of several formal institutions in whose care the savings of individuals are customarily entrusted, but they do not show the importance of sums invested by individuals directly in bonds and mortgages, stocks, and real estate, or those entrusted to individual or corporate trustees. While the exact size of the latter sums are not known, their general order of magnitude is considerable.

The importance of commercial banks in this scheme of things cannot be appraised from a mere examination of the framework, or even from estimates of quantitative size as determined by any of the usual criteria. These institutions differ radically from all other financial institutions, not only in their technical method of operation, but in the relation of these operations to other financial institutions, and in the fact that they touch virtually every phase of economic life. Thus they not only obtain funds from individuals and business firms, but they also have the power to create them, while in turn they make funds available to all types of businesses, individual consumers, and governments. Their peculiar importance in the general process of capital formation arises from their basic functions as providers of credit and money capital, and as creators of the means of payments. Generally speaking, the other financial institutions, whether they are investing institutions or institutional investors, are engaged primarily in collecting the funds of a large number of individual savers and in investing them in various directions. Techniques of collection differ, as do the particular directions in which the funds so collected are applied; but the common characteristic of all these institutions is that they serve as channels through which savings

[4] T.N.E.C., Hearings, *Investigation of Concentration of Economic Power*, Part IX, Appendix, Exhibit No. 601, p. 4052.
T.N.E.C., Monograph No. 37, pp. 31–32.

flow and are directed. This characteristic is also common to the commercial banks. They also collect savings of individuals and others and direct them to various uses by either lending or investing them. In this respect they function in much the same way as savings banks, although the law does not require segregation of that portion of their liabilities and assets which represents the performance of this function. Their difference from other financial institutions lies in the fact that they also serve as issuers of the means of payments, and this function is inseparably bound with their function as providers of credit. Therefore, in addition to the sources of savings which are commonly listed, there must be added the commercial banks themselves.

The principal sources from which savings are derived are said to include:

1. The monetary savings of individual persons, i. e., that part of current monetary incomes which is not consumed; sometimes described as "consumers' thrift."

2. Business savings, i. e., that part of the monetary receipts of business concerns which is withheld from distribution to meet current cash outlays. This, perhaps, is more accurately described as "corporate reinvestment," since funds withheld are often directly reinvested within the corporation in maintenance or replacement, although these funds may flow into the money market for varying periods depending upon the policy of depreciation in relation to actual maintenance and replacement.

3. Taxation; under conditions where a government receives revenue which is larger than needed for current operating expenditure, the surplus may be used to retire outstanding debt. This was the case during the late twenties in the United States, and it was also true in 1936–37 when the net cash outlay of the Government became negative despite a budgetary deficit.

4. Bank credit comprises a peculiar source of savings in that newly created bank credit may be employed directly, or indirectly, for the purpose of financing the purchase or construction of fixed assets; or, the banking system indirectly may "force" savings upon the community through the pricing process and the consequently altered distribution or amount of real income; or, by lowering interest rates, it may induce investment and expand incomes from which savings are made; and expansion of bank credit may give rise to deposits in savings institutions.[5]

There is no question that bank assets fluctuate widely, not only during the business cycle, but also seasonally. This means that at times the banks may be injecting into the streams of money payments amounts which bear no relation to the current volume of money savings as such; conversely, they

[5] Cf. James, *op. cit.*, pp. 557–62. See also T.N.E.C. Monograph No. 37, Part II; B. M. Anderson, "Bank Money and the Capital Supply," *Chase Economic Bulletin*, November 8, 1926.

may be withdrawing from circulation sums irrespective of the normal flow of savings into investment.

While it is quite true that other types of financial institutions, such as the savings bank, or the building and loan association, may interrupt this flow of savings into investment by holding more or less of their assets in the form of cash, the commercial banks have powers to interrupt the flow of funds in ways not available to these other institutions simply because the banks have the power to assume liabilities instantaneously, i. e., create money, although they cannot contract them always quite as easily. The decision of various financial institutions, business corporations, and individual consumers to hold, or not to hold, cash in the form of deposits with banks does not imply variation in their total cash holdings, but merely in the distribution of the total deposit liabilities owing to changes in ownership. In the case of the savings bank or, say, the life insurance company, the decision to accumulate cash is virtually a decision not to expend funds received on loans or securities, and conversely. These limits are narrow, since neither the savings bank nor the life insurance company can buy securities, or make loans, to any extent greater than the rate at which funds are accumulated.

They can accumulate cash, but only at the expense of a reduction in the cash holdings of others. On the other hand, the banks, which have the power to issue demand deposits, can enlarge their loans and investments considerably, assuming attractive outlets, and contract them depending upon the ability of borrowers to repay and/or the ability and willingness of the public to buy securities at attractive prices. The expansion or contraction of bank assets, however, has its analogue in the creation or destruction of the aggregate supply of deposit money.

Since banks are peculiar in the respect that they are the institutions which create the bulk of the money supply which is extant at any time in the system, their action may be such as to neutralize action of the other groups, or it may not, but it is obvious that the banks through their power as a system to expand and contract their assets, and hence the supply of deposit money, initially, at least, may control the direction of money flows in such a way as either to finance current consumption, the formation of fixed or working capital, or the activities of government. The decision may be passed along or it may be exercised by the banks. The decisions of other economic classes, in turn, may have a reflex action upon the banks owing to the central position which banks occupy as the institutions against which these other groups hold claims.

The axiom that the quantity of deposit money is determined by the quantity of bank assets, as it stands, does not imply the extent to which the nonbank holders of deposits have power to negate the action of the banks. The effective supply of money has two components, its quantity and its velocity, or rate of turnover. The non-bank holders, it is true, cannot in the aggregate reduce the size of their balances by spending them without the banks' either deciding to reduce the size of bank assets, or being compelled to do so, as when borrowers repay loans, assuming no change in credit standards.[6] But non-bank holders can, in spending such balances, cause a given quantity of them to circulate at a faster rate, and this in effect constitutes a change in the nature of the demand for money from a demand for money to hold, to a demand for balances as a means of payment. Thus the functioning of the money system may be affected by the manipulation of money balances in the possession of the various non-bank holders, regardless of the deliberate action of the banks.

The amount of balances in the hands of the various non-bank groups, in recent years, is indicated in tables 2 and 3.

TABLE 2

DISTRIBUTION OF DEMAND DEPOSITS BY CLASSES OF DEPOSITORS, 1933–37 [a]

Estimated Figures for End-of-Year Dates

In Billions of Dollars

	1933	*1935*	*1936*	*1937*
Business	6.1	7.6	8.5	7.7
Finance	2.4	5.0	5.4	5.1
Public bodies	2.7	4.1	4.1	3.6
Unclassified (consumers)	3.9	5.1	6.8	6.9
Total demand deposits adjusted for items in transit	15.1	21.9	24.8	23.4
In Percentages of Total				
Business	40.6	34.9	34.2	33.1
Finance	15.8	22.7	21.7	21.9
Public bodies	17.9	18.9	16.8	15.6
Unclassified	25.7	23.5	27.3	29.4
Total demand deposits adjusted for items in transit	100.0	100.0	100.0	100.0

[a] Source: *Federal Reserve Bulletin,* October, 1939, pp. 871–74; May, 1940, pp. 401–3.

Roughly, business enterprises held about one third of the deposit balances in all checking accounts; financial groups, including foreign depositors and banks' trust departments, one fifth; and public bodies, one sixth. The un-

[6] This is a matter which Keynes (*The General Theory of Employment, Interest and Money* [New York, 1935], p. 174) seems inclined to neglect, but which Durbin (*The Problem of Credit Policy* [London, 1935], pp. 57, 78–79), among others, emphasizes.

TABLE 3

DISTRIBUTION OF TIME DEPOSITS BY CLASSES OF DEPOSITORS, 1933–37 [a]

Estimated Figures for End-of-Year Dates

	1933	1935	1936	1937
In Billions of Dollars				
Business	1.1	0.6	0.7	0.6
Finance	0.4	0.5	0.4	0.4
Public bodies	0.4	0.4	0.4	0.6
Unclassified	20.0	22.7	23.9	24.7
Total time deposits	21.8	24.2	25.4	26.3
In Percentages of Total				
Business	5.0	2.5	2.7	2.3
Finance	1.8	1.9	1.7	1.6
Public bodies	1.6	1.7	1.4	2.2
Unclassified	91.6	93.9	94.2	93.9
Total time deposits	100.0	100.0	100.0	100.0

[a] Source: *Federal Reserve Bulletin,* October, 1939, pp. 871–74; May, 1940, pp. 401-3.

classified remainder comprises mainly consumer balances, the large balances of individuals, and balances of nonprofit organizations and some unincorporated groups for which estimates were lacking.[7] In the case of time deposits, more than 90 percent of the total were held by depositors of the unclassified group. This is because deposits of other groups are held mostly as demand deposits, since time deposits are not subject to check.

The data give a rough indication of the relative distribution of money balances, although they are not available with sufficient frequency to afford measurement of their short-term fluctuation. However, in Chapter VII, some attention will be given to the causes of the decline and expansion of total deposits and the attendant redistribution of the total among various groups.

For the moment it is sufficient to observe that the bulk of deposit money outstanding is held by those business enterprises, financial institutions, and individuals who are primarily concerned with the investment of funds and likely to use their money balances only to a minor extent to purchase goods for consumption.[8] The bulk of consumers apparently live on a more or less hand-to-mouth basis, since their balances are estimated as only sufficient to finance approximately a month of expenditure at the 1935–36 rate.[9] It has been concluded, therefore, that great increases in expenditure of the

[7] *Federal Reserve Bulletin,* October, 1939, p. 871.
[8] National Resources Committee, *op. cit.*, pp. 88–89.
[9] *Ibid.*, p. 89.

bulk of consumers could not arise directly out of the use of money balances already held by consumers. They could arise only if consumers received increased incomes or if they either borrowed or trenched on previous investments.[10]

On the other hand, there is some indication that in the period covered by the 1933–37 data the largest absolute increase in deposits occurred in the deposits of the "unclassified" or consumer group. On a relative basis, the increased holdings of the financial groups, especially bank trust departments, life insurance companies, and foreign banks, reflect the difficulties in finding attractive outlets for funds of savers entrusted to them, and the failure of expenditures to correspond with changes in deposit holdings.[11]

[10] *Ibid.*

[11] Martin Krost, "The Significance of American Deposit Movements since 1929," unpublished address before the American Economic Association, Philadelphia, December 28, 1939.

Chapter V

THE DEPENDENCE OF THE MONETARY FUNCTIONS OF BANKS UPON THEIR CREDIT FUNCTIONS

IN ORDER to place the relation between the monetary function of banking and its credit function in clearer perspective, the analysis of the banking process will be further refined. Several phases of this process may be differentiated, as follows: (1) appraisal of the credit worthiness of borrowers; (2) substitution of bank credit for non-bank credit; (3) monetization of debt; and (4) transference of titles to bank credit.[1]

In the first place, the making of loans, or buying of investments, enfolds a process of "recognizing rights to credit." The question as to who is entitled to credit might be answered in terms of political, sociological, or economic considerations; but in the economy of the United States, the main consideration in credit analysis has been of an economic nature—certainly this has been true of individual bank loans and investments. The recognition of credit is based upon an analysis and appraisal of the credit standing of the individual borrower as measured in the light of the transactions in which he is engaged or proposes to engage, and the use to which he proposes to apply the proceeds of loans. In the case of securities purchases, analysis is concerned with the differentiation of credit risks of various debtors, as well as the money risks attached to all titles to future income. With regard to these matters the credit function of banks does not differ fundamentally from that of other lenders.

Having recognized and measured the credit standing of borrowers, the bank then makes the loan. It is at this point that the function of banks differs in a peculiar fashion from the corresponding functions of other lenders. The act of making a loan becomes an action in which the bank substitutes its own credit for that of the borrower, by placing at his command a so-called deposit credit (bank credit) in exchange for the acquisition of an obligation of the borrower (personal, corporate, or governmental credit). The granting of loans, therefore, is a process which involves the substitution

[1] This analysis of lending functions follows in outline the approach in Willis and Edwards, *Banking and Business* (New York, 1925), pp. 20–21.

of bank for individual credit. It involves the substitution of one form of credit which has wide acceptability for another which has only limited acceptability.

Some writers describe this operation as a "creation" of bank credit, neglecting the fact that it also involves the substitution of one kind of credit for another, bank credit for individual credit. The answer to the question whether it involves creation as well as substitution would seem to depend upon whether the banking system is making new loans at a faster rate than old ones are being repaid, or making net additions to its holding of securities.[2] Whatever the case may be, substitution of bank credit is involved in the individual transactions which make up the total of bank loans.[3]

The individual borrower, in the absence of bank intervention, might have been able to acquire deposits already outstanding from other holders merely on the basis of his individual credit. However, the intervention of the bank assures him of this. Furthermore, if the banking system is rendering available a net increase in a volume of loanable funds, which compete for employment with those already being offered from voluntary savings, it may enable borrowers to obtain command of bank deposits on terms more advantageous than would otherwise have been the case.

Whether the process is viewed from the individual transaction or from the standpoint of the system, the extension of bank credit is essentially a process in which individual or corporate debts are monetized, in the sense that against these debts, deposits are being issued which function as a current means of payment.

The obligation of the bank in the form of a deposit credit remains outstanding as a liability of the banking system regardless of the eventual goodness of the borrower's debt. The bank, therefore, has assumed the risk of goodness of the individual debt. In this respect, the bank performs an underwriting function, since it undertakes to absorb any loss which may result from mistakes in judgment of the original basis of credit. These losses must be absorbed out of current earnings derived from charging interest or from reduction in the bank's capital account, that is, the equity of the owners. Banking, therefore, is an institution which averages risks, the losses being absorbed by the owners of the banks, while at the same time profits are taken as a reward for bearing risks and the expense of maintaining the overhead connected with the maintenance of the banking facilities.

[2] The ramifications of this matter are discussed *infra*.

[3] Contemporary "monetary theory" embraces an entirely different conception from this. Many theorists abstract from the banking framework and assume that the supply of money is a given independent variable. Their view, obviously, disregards the dependence of the "creation" of bank money (deposits subject to check) upon the acquisition by banks of debts of borrowers; i. e., it disregards the fact of substitution.

It has already been stated that the process of substitution of bank for individual credit amounts to the monetization of debt. The borrower, having gained possession of a widely acceptable credit instrument, the bank deposit, is placed in a position to exercise command over goods and services. In spending these deposits, he is in reality transferring them to others, to the sellers of goods and services; and, in a going society, deposits, once established by the loan process, thus circulate, the aggregate deposit liabilities of the system being increased unless an equivalent amount of deposits is canceled through repayment by the same or some other borrower.

The bank, having substituted its credit for that of the borrower, undertakes to transfer the ownership of the deposits thus established, at the direction and on the order of their owners. Its function in this respect is concerned with maintaining the machinery by which payments are effected. The acceptability of the bank credit, in turn, is partially derived from the fact that the deposit credits thus established are legally payable at any time to their holders in legal tender money; and therefore banks must be prepared to redeem such liabilities in legal tender. This does not mean that the deposits are legal tender money—they are credits which are payable or redeemable in legal tender and are functionally and legally to be distinguished from it.[4] If banks are to maintain the acceptability of the credit thus established, they must at all times be able to demonstrate an ability to pay in legal tender.

The ability of the individual bank to redeem the deposits it issues will depend, not merely upon the volume of its legal tender holdings, but upon its power to require the borrowing public to repay its debts, in other words, to surrender deposit credits against the cancellation of indebtedness. At this point, numerous misconceptions about the banking process have arisen.

The individual bank, it is true, in the first instance, meets a demand for legal tender by its depositors, or an adverse clearing balance resulting from the transfer of deposits to another bank, in either legal tender or central bank credit. The banking system, likewise, must be prepared to satisfy the demands of depositors for legal tender if there is a demand for hand-to-hand currency, but its ability to do so is limited by the total amount of holdings of legal tender or of reserve credit with the central bank. Once legal tender holdings are exhausted, or reserves at the central bank reduced to their legal minimum, the system must collect or sell its other assets, loans and investments. Therefore, in the final analysis, the ability of the system

[4] The distinction between bank credit (deposits) and money, insisted upon by Willis and Edwards, *op. cit.*, and earlier authorities like Macleod (*The Theory of Credit* [London, 1890]), is fundamental to credit and hence to banking theory.

to meet any general demand by depositors for payment depends upon the ability of borrowers to repay their debts to the banking system or to purchase securities from the banks. In the aggregate, assuming a given quantity of legal tender money or reserves and no new creations of these, there can be no cancellation of deposits without equivalent cancellation of the indebtedness of the non-bank public to the banks.

Bank credit rests upon individual credit, while individual credit, in turn, consists of personal, corporate, or government credit. Before entering upon an analysis of the nature of individual credit and the suitability of various kinds of credit as a basis for bank credit, it seems preferable to explore, first, the relation between the issuance of debt by borrowers, its absorption by various holders, and the consequent effect upon the supply of bank deposits.

THE CREATION OF DEBT AND ITS OWNERSHIP

One of the innate features of the credit system is, on the one hand, the issuance of indebtedness by borrowers (promissory notes, bonds, stocks, etc.) and, on the other, the repayment or cancellation of indebtedness. Debt, for the purposes of the discussion which follows, is therefore merely another name for credit instruments.[5]

These instruments may be issued by: consumers for the purchase of goods; business firms for the purchase of goods or the hiring of labor; and governments for meeting cash deficits, that is, for the purchase of goods, the hiring of labor, or payment of subsidies. If a distinction is made between public, or non-bank, and bank buyers of debt, the following possibilities exist with regard to the absorption of new or outstanding forms of debt:

The public may absorb them by: (1) refusing to spend current income on goods and services; or (2) by refusing to hold money balances. As sometimes expressed, the public may purchase securities out of "savings" or by "dishoarding." On the other hand the banking system may absorb securities only with a consequent issue of deposit liabilities. Bank absorption involves, therefore, the creation of bank "money," while conversely, a reduction in bank holdings involves the obliteration of "money." It has already been explained that banks do not and cannot in the aggregate absorb securities by spending reserves.

THE ABSORPTION OF SECURITIES BY THE PUBLIC

It is sometimes said that the public's income is devoted either to consumption, savings, or hoarding, but these terms are ambiguous, and it seems

5 To simplify the discussion, various forms of debt will be referred to in what follows as "securities."

preferable in this context to speak of: (1) the spending of money incomes either on goods, labor, or securities; and (2) the holding of money (deposit balances).

A desire to hold larger quantities of deposit balances means an interruption in the circular flow of money, assuming other things remain unchanged. If the quantity of outstanding bank deposits remains unchanged, its velocity of circulation, or turnover, will be decreased by an increased desire for it as a store of value. In other words, in a closed banking system, it is impossible for hoarding, i. e., holding of deposits, to be accompanied by a withdrawal from the banking system unless withdrawals can take place in legal tender currency, and only in that event would deposits be decreased to the accompaniment of an increase in some other form of money in circulation, such as note issues. If this were to take place, on any scale, banks would be forced to meet deposit withdrawals by surrender of other assets, once the reserves of actual money were exhausted. Under the conditions of this analysis, incomes which are not spent on either goods or securities are retained in the form of bank deposits and the phenomenon of "hoarding" takes the form of decreased velocity of the unchanged total of bank deposits. Velocity, in this sense, is merely the converse of a desire to hold money. If withdrawals did take place in legal tender money, it would mean that deposits no longer functioned as a satisfactory store of value and that the public sought some other medium for that purpose.

The holding of bank deposits under certain conditions is not necessarily a reflection of a desire to "hoard," but may be caused by a desire to benefit from interest paid on such deposits, and hence be stimulated like other acts of saving. However, this is no longer legally possible in the United States since payment of interest on demand deposits is prohibited. An exceptional case exists where deposits are used to acquire securities from other holders, banks, or issuers, each of which possibilities will be discussed below. Another possibility exists where depositors in commercial banks elect to transfer their deposits to mutual savings banks. Here commercial bank liabilities would remain unchanged unless the savings bank were, in turn, to purchase securities from commercial banks, which is a case comprehended in the discussion which follows.

The non-bank public in deciding to spend deposit balances on securities may acquire securities from any one of three distinct sources; (1) from other non-bank holders; (2) from issuers; and (3) from bank holders.

SECURITIES ACQUIRED FROM OTHER NON-BANK HOLDERS

If the supply of securities is assumed unchanged, and one section of the public acquires securities from another section, the case represents merely a redistribution of the ownership of outstanding bank deposits. The aggregate volume of deposits would remain at an unchanged amount although the distribution of bank liabilities might undergo significant alteration with respect to the distribution of reserves in the banking system. The decision regarding the functional use of deposits by the buyers of securities would have been passed along to other persons, the sellers of securities. Although the objective of the individual saver to apply a part of income to investment in securities would have been accomplished, the same objective from the standpoint of society might not have been, depending upon the action of the seller of securities to whom the title to bank deposits had been transferred. The same possibility would remain open where savings banks, life insurance companies, or other investing institutions bought already outstanding securities from individual holders, except that here the decision of these institutions regarding the disposition of the deposits so acquired would depend upon different considerations than those affecting the other possible kinds of sellers of securities, such as consumers or business firms.

However, as a general proposition, one part of the public would increase its securities purchases at the same time that another part of the public decreased its holdings, and the effects would be compensating. In the aggregate, the public, under the assumption of no change in the total of outstanding securities, and no change in bank holdings, could not increase the volume of securities purchased.

SECURITIES ACQUIRED FROM ISSUERS

If the non-bank public acquires securities from issuers, it being presupposed that the amount of outstanding securities is enlarged, but that the amount of bank holdings remains constant as above, the additional securities would have to be absorbed by individuals or institutions, that is, outside the commercial banking system. This could only be accomplished if the individual buyers of securities were to apply a portion of their deposits to the purchase of securities directly from borrowers, and this would mean transference of ownership of deposits to borrowers. This would not alter the statistical picture of the banks, but would mean that consumption or investment in goods and labor was being financed by individual savers who had decided or consented to surrender their claims against banks for claims to future payments from borrowers. Essentially, consumption or investment would be financed out of savings, but at the expense of a rise in total debt of the community which would now be held by those persons who had performed individual acts of savings. The banks would have functioned simply as intermediaries, or facilitating agents, bringing about the transfer of the ownership of deposits to those who intended to use them as a means of payment from those who were willing to forego their use. This process, in which borrowers continued to issue more and more indebtedness, under the assumption that banks held constant their own assets, could continue only as long as there were borrowers who found it profitable to borrow and individuals who were willing to refrain from immediate expenditures on goods, or from the holding of money, in order to invest in securities, and there would come a time when the sacrifices to savers outweighed the rewards. A point which requires emphasis is that this process involves a rise of the total debt which, in the long run, under the assumptions of the case, can only be tolerated if the investment, or consumption, undertaken at the expense of savings, proves to be income producing. This implies more value output for given input of raw materials and labor.

The classical theory of capital formation and its allied theory of interest evidently were predicated on some such set of conditions as those just outlined. Here, the banking system would function as a passive intermediary agency, and there would be no change in the supply of bank money. Consumption or investment, in effect, would be financed either out of the individual savings of one section of the public, i. e., nonconsumption, or by virtue of increased velocity of the given stocks of money. Enlarged investment would be accompanied by a rising debt whose amount would be conditioned by the terms upon which the power over the disposal of incomes is rendered transferable, and whose increase would represent the application of incomes to investment in durable goods. Very little attention seems to have been paid in the literature to the mechanics of the expansion of debt. It would seem that the principles which govern the expansion of bank deposits, given certain reserves, would be generally applicable with slight modification to the multiple expansion of debt, given certain volume of money balances. In any event, it is not inherently conditional upon bank financing.

SECURITIES ACQUIRED FROM BANKS

If the non-bank public acquires securities from banks, two assumptions need to be taken into account: (1) the case where the volume of outstanding securities is unchanged; and (2) the case where it is not. The non-bank public might acquire outstanding securities not yet matured from banks, or the non-bank public might repay loans or other indebtedness to banks. In the one case, there is no change in the supply of securities; in the other, there is a contraction in the supply of securities. In both cases the volume of bank deposits would be reduced; in other words, that part of income which was not used for expenditure on goods, or for transference of the ownership of securities among the public, or for the holding of money, would be applied to cancellation of those deposits which were not serving strictly as a means of payment. The result would be that the total assets of the banking system would be reduced and so would the total of bank deposits. If the supply of securities, however, were unchanged, they would have to be absorbed by non-bank holders. This is the reverse of the cases where the banks acquire securities from the public and/or from new issuers, which will be discussed below. It seems desirable now to consider this entire subject from the standpoint of the banks.

THE ABSORPTION OF SECURITIES BY BANKS

It is to be noted at the outset that the decisions of banks in lending or investing are governed by somewhat different considerations than those which govern the non-bank public. Furthermore, banks do not purchase goods or hire labor for use in production or consumption, alternative to holding of money. Banks deal only in debts. In preceding pages, the point has been labored that, whereas the individual bank by virtue of its reserves is enabled to acquire assets, the banking system does not acquire its assets out of its reserves—its assets are acquired by the issuance of deposit obligations. Thus, banks in enlarging their holdings of loans or securities are not motivated by the same considerations which motivate the non-bank public, particularly the business firm or the individual or institutional saver.

The sources from which banks acquire securities are threefold: (1) from other banks; (2) from the non-bank holders; and (3) from new issuers. These cases will be considered in turn.

FROM OTHER BANKS

This case would not alter the position of the banking system, if it is assumed that the distribution of reserves is uniform. The transactions are internal to the banking system and for that reason may be neglected.

FROM NON-BANK HOLDERS

Assuming the supply of securities unchanged, purchase by banks would immediately enlarge deposits, in particular, those in the hands of the sellers of securities.

Under the assumptions of the case, purchase by banks would tend to raise the prices of securities, since the total supply of securities is constant, and therefore encourage sellers to sell. These sellers would then be in a position to spend the additional deposits on goods, or to hold them, but in any case this decision would be made by the sellers of securities and over it the banks would hold no control whatever.

In the converse case, if banks sold securities, the outstanding volume of securities remaining unchanged, the price of securities would fall unless, in the meanwhile, the disposition of the non-bank public with regard to their money balances had changed. In effect, the public would have to be induced to surrender deposits for securities, and it might be unwillling to do this. However, within limits the public might be induced to give up idle deposit balances, but at lower valuations for securities. If the action were actively prosecuted by banks, it would result in a contraction in the supply of deposits. This is what ordinarily occurs in a severe depression in economic activity.

FROM BORROWERS WHO ISSUE NEW SECURITIES

In this case both the total amount of securities outstanding and the total deposits change. Bank holdings of securities rise, while holdings by the public remain unchanged. Here, since the absorption of securities by banks is accompanied by an equivalent rise in deposits, the case is decidedly different from the absorption of new securities by the public by transfer and/or simultaneous increase in the velocity of money (less hoarding). In that case, the prices of securities rise in order to induce the public to give them up in exchange for larger money balances.

In the instant case, where business firms, consumers, or government issue new securities which are bought by banks, no price rise need occur since the increase in securities would be matched by "created" deposits. No price rise would be necessary unless businessmen, for example, were unwilling to borrow. The unwillingness of borrowers to borrow would be conditioned by factors unlike those which condition the unwillingness of non-bank holders of securities to sell.

In the converse case, where borrowers attempt to repay (in a sense, buy back) indebtedness, the motives of borrowers again would be based upon considerations different from the case where the public had to be induced to absorb securities from banks at the expense of a reduction in deposits. The motives of borrowers in repaying indebtedness and their ability to do so rests upon the ability to set aside earnings out of current income. On the other hand, the motives of the public in absorbing securities by buying them from banks rests upon considerations of "liquidity preference" and the "propensity to consume," to use the Keynesian dichotomy.

The Significance of Bank Intervention

A large share of the complexities which arise in the credit system are attributable basically to the fact that when goods are purchased by business, or labor is hired, or when goods are purchased by consumers, indebtedness is increased in some form. The issuance of indebtedness must be absorbed by either the non-bank public or the banks. The ability of the non-bank public to absorb securities, in absence of bank action, is dependent upon the possibility that the public, or some section of it, can or will refrain from spending on goods, can increase the velocity of its money holdings, or that the economy becomes capable of producing the same or a larger quantity of goods more efficiently—that means at lower money prices relative to the previously existing state of affairs. The ability of the banks to absorb securities, in the absence of a different disposition of income by the public, depends upon the ability and willingness of banks to assume deposit liabilities, and this for the system, in turn, depends upon the desire of the banks for earnings, the position of their capital account, and the ability of borrowers to service their indebtedness, i. e., obviate losses to the banks, but within these general limits, upon the perfection of clearance, that is, the need of individual banks for reserves. The ability of borrowers to service indebtedness depends upon the realization of increased output at lower costs.

Since banks by their very nature are institutions which deal only in forms of indebtedness, their influence upon the economy is made effective through their power to induce action on the part of the borrowing or nonborrowing public, or to compensate the behavior of the public by alteration in the terms (price, quantity, and quality) upon which they are ready to grant deposit credits. As already stated, banks do not buy goods, nor undertake entrepreneurial functions by combining the factors of production with a view to the production and sale of goods. Hence, their influence is, to say the least, indirect, and they are never able to engage in action which in any real sense is completely reparative or compensating, that is, never an exact and equivalent substitute for opposite action of the borrowing or nonborrowing public. The power of the banks is basically a power to alter the money value of securities (debts), and this power is the other aspect of their power to "create" and issue money in the form of deposit liabilities.

If banks are buying securities in the face of hoarding by the public (a reduction in the velocity of existing deposits), the compensation takes the form of an increased volume of bank deposits as the analogue to increased bank assets. These increased deposits do not necessarily fall into the hands of the original hoarders, but into the hands of the sellers of securities. For complete compensation, the anticipations of the public would have to be altered.

If banks are purchasing securities in order to stimulate expenditures on goods, they may be successful in inducing consumption or investment by borrowers, but they can only do so at the expense of a rise in their own assets whose validation in terms of price rests in the long run upon the induction of an increase in incomes through more complete employment of the factors of production, or more efficient use of the employed factors, i. e., lower real costs.

The action taken by banks is only reversible in the long run if there occurs a reversal of the factors which were deemed to be the justification for the intervention of banks as a stimulating influence. The fundamental fact which cannot be escaped is that bank intervention requires enlargement of bank assets and enlargement of bank deposit liabilities. These deposit liabilities can never be reduced except by repayment of indebtedness by borrowers or sale of securities to the non-bank public. For this reason, intervention by the banking system involves risk of loss in value of assets. Contraction in asset value can only be absorbed by contraction in capital and surplus accounts, since the whole essence of the banking process is that liabilities to creditors are issued in the form of demand claims to legal tender money and are noncontractible in money value. The amount of deposits is inherently not subject to contraction in money valuation, while the volume of deposits can only be changed by a shift in bank assets to the public. On the other hand, the money valuation of bank loans and investments is subject to change in money value as well as volume, depending upon the competitive or compensatory action of non-bank holders. Bank action is only one factor affecting the valuation of securities, but it is upon the power of banks to affect the valuation of securities that the influence of bank action depends. All theories which explain interest rates solely in terms of the supply of money created by banks overlook this fact.

The Keynesian theory of interest, for example, is based upon the quantity of money and liquidity preference, and money is assumed to be an independent variable.[6] It has been shown above that the volume of money balances is a function of changes in bank assets, that is, bank holdings of securities. Keynes's theory seemingly holds, that where securities are issued by borrowers to banks, and public holdings remain unchanged, if liquidity preference is constant, there would be no change in interest rates. In effect, the purchase of securities by banks provides its own supply of money balances (deposits). On the other hand, the theory holds that, if no issuance of new securities occurs, but if banks purchase outstanding securities from the non-bank public, the prices of securities will rise; i. e., interest rates will fall.

What Keynes has not considered is the case where expansion of output is financed, not by sale of indebtedness to the banks, but to the public. Under

[6] John Maynard Keynes, *The General Theory of Employment, Interest and Money* (New York, 1935), Chap. XIII, "The General Theory of Interest."

these conditions, the money supply would remain the same; the public would absorb the additional securities, but it could do so only at lower valuations, i. e., a rise in interest rates, unless a part of the public decided to hold less money balances or consume less goods. The conclusion is, therefore, that where bank assets, and hence deposits, remain unchanged, that is to say, where the banking system is passive, the interest rate becomes a function of the public's desire to consume or its desire to buy securities. In other words, the interest rate is not solely a function of liquidity preference.

The implication of this reasoning is that Keynes's theory of interest is a special case which holds good only in the short run. Interest is a function of the quantity of money only where banks absorb all new securities issues or sales by the public of its securities holdings. To assume that banks will absorb all new securities issues by borrowers or sales of outstanding securities by the public is to assume unlimited elasticity of the supply of bank money.

THE DIFFERENCE BETWEEN CUSTOMER LOANS AND OPEN-MARKET LOANS FROM THE STANDPOINT OF CREDIT ELASTICITY

As used heretofore, the term "securities" has comprehended generally all kinds of indebtedness issued by borrowers, including promissory notes, bonds, and theoretically stocks. From the banking standpoint a clear distinction exists between what are called loans and what are called investments. The term "loan" refers to indebtedness which has been issued to banks directly by borrowers in the form of a promissory note, running commonly for a specific term of months or even years. These notes arise from transactions between banks and their regular borrowing customers, and hence are called "customer loans." The various kinds of such loans in respect to purpose, maturity, and collateral is of no particular concern at this juncture. The other type of assets, the investment or "open-market loan," in the United States, comprises bonds, that is, long-term promissory notes running for a term of years and for which there is usually a market in which such securities are regularly traded. In the case of national banks, the regulations governing eligible investments require that there be such a ready market. The distinction thus drawn is one between customer-indebtedness, for which there is no real market outside the lending bank, and open-market loans, for which there is such a market.

Customer loans are held by banks until maturity simply because there is no market for them, and are originally made with that intention in mind (even if they may be rediscountable at the central bank). Investments are bought usually to be held and, according to older banking practice, should only be bought on this condition, although in recent years banks have come to rely more and more upon alterations in holdings of high-grade investments for the adjustment of their reserve position.

A significant difference between customer loans and open-market loans lies in the initiative which gives rise to their acquisition by banks. The bank customer loan is made in response to the demands of the borrowing public and is only made when and if demanded, although, of course, banks by alteration of their credit standards could envelop a larger portion of the "unsatisfied fringe" of potential borrowers, or could withdraw credit from the regular class of borrowers by refusing to renew loans. On the other hand, investments, or open-market loans, are purchased at the initiative of the banks and the resulting expansion of deposit credits is, therefore, in response to a somewhat different stimulus than is true of an expansion in customer loans. It seems evident that an expansion of deposit credit in the course of a business cycle which is based upon purchases of investments by banks holds different implications than one based upon regular customer loans.

Most bank assets, in varying degree, are a renewable aggregate, but the renewable character of customer loans and investments obviously differs. In the case of customer loans, the individual bank holds a type of asset which ideally is turned over repeatedly through repayments and renewals. The total loan portfolio remains constant as long as the rate at which new loans are made is equal to the rate at which old loans are repaid. In the lending process, bank deposits are being written up against promissory notes of customers and, as a result, funds are being paid away from the bank; that is, reserves are lost because borrowers draw against these deposit credits and pay them to persons who most probably bank with other banks. But if the loans are short-term and self-liquidating, the process will involve a return flow of reserves by reason of the fact that borrowers pay off their indebtedness to the bank out of receipts realized from the sale of goods to the public. Payments by the public are received most probably in the form of claims against banks other than the creditor bank. This means that the bank can exercise some control over its reserve position through its ability to adjust the rate at which it makes new loans to the rate at which old ones are being paid off. In any event, the flow of repayments carries an assurance of a continuous recovery of reserves. The shorter the term of its loans and the more rapid the turnover, the more accurately can the bank's position be adjusted.

In the case of open-market securities, the situation is quite different. Here the purchasing bank may buy the debt either directly from the borrower or from some previous holder. In either event, the resulting deposit credit is paid away entirely and at once, and the bank loses an equivalent amount of reserves. It is also true that the portfolio of securities involves no dependable source of current repayments. In other words, it does not automatically provide a continuous return flow of funds as is the case with customer loans. Here, the only means of recovering reserves available to the individual bank is through sale of the securities to some other buyer, ordinarily not the original seller. Thus the effects upon the reserve position of individual banks of an expansion of loans, for example, may be to induce an equivalent loss in reserves, but it also will involve in the future a dependent return of reserves when repayment occurs. In the case of investments, the matter can not be contractually controlled. Purchase of investments results in an immediate loss of reserves recoverable only through resale of the securities.

To the extent that proceeds of loans are spent locally, there may not be an actual loss of reserves, particularly if the bank has a monopoly of the local business. This would only be true of investments if they were purchased locally, but usually they are purchased in money market centers, often removed at some distance from the lending bank.

In so far as the banking system as a whole is concerned, there is an essential similarity between the holding of loans and the holding of investments which lies in the fact that expansion of either type of asset for the system is not dependent upon reserves, since for the system the aggregate of reserves may be the same amount after an enlargement of its assets as it was beforehand. However, where the banking system holds a renewable quantity of loans, the users of the bank credits which are granted are also the collecting agencies of repayment. The asset holdings of the banks undergo repeated testing of the ability of debtors to repay, and the behavior of depositors is to a certain extent controlled in the sense that, even though the individual borrower spends the deposits, he must acquire others in order to make repayment. The banking system, by contract, can enforce the nonbank public to take up its debts through repayment. The banks exercise no such power in the case of investments. They cannot directly force obligors to take up securities issues which have not matured. What they can do, is induce the nonborrowing public to purchase the securities, but this may be feasible only at lower valuations unless the public is less inclined to hold money balances or consume goods. Furthermore, in the case of the investments of the banking system, the body of debts is not repeatedly tested and the valuation of the entire debt structure therefore rests upon the disposition and preferences of deposit holders in general as to expenditure, savings, or surrender of deposit through repayment.

Customer loans and investments are also different in their relation to the speed with which the banking system can expand. If loans are all made locally and if the proceeds are not dispersed to other areas, expansion could proceed unhindered. This is never true of investments unless the whole system of banks expands simultaneously. However, the individual bank can adjust its reserve position much more quickly by buying and selling investments than it can by making or demanding repayment of loans. While the purchase and sale of investments appears to be a much more flexible instrument to the individual banker, it is a much less flexible instrument to the banking system as a whole, except where the banking system is prepared and able to absorb fluctuations in securities values. This means that a banking system whose assets consist entirely of long-term nonmaturing investments must be prepared to absorb all losses arising from changes in valuations due to the decisions of the non-bank public, especially the nonborrowing public, and, on the other hand, it may derive profits from increased values of its investments. A banking system whose assets are limited to short-term, regularly maturing debts is in a different position, since it is not forced to suffer the same fluctuations in debt values. The investment type of banking system can only facilitate the clearance of payments by changes in the capitalized values of the assets which it holds, and therefore may be forced to absorb losses due to alterations in the rate at which such capitalization is currently being made. On the other hand, the self-liquidating short-term type of banking system may not be forced to take such losses, but only those which result from misjudgments of individual credit risks. Losses due to "money" risks would be sustained by the borrowing public through alterations in the commodity price structure and through alterations in the volume of goods produced and sold. The cost of uneconomic employment of the proceeds of loans, through overexpansion, would be borne by entrepreneurs.

THE FUNCTIONAL NATURE OF INDIVIDUAL CREDIT AND ITS SUITABILITY AS A BASIS FOR THE EXPANSION OF BANK CREDIT

It is now proposed to consider the nature of individual credit in order to be able to discriminate among various types of debt which may be monetized by the banking system as explained in the first part of this chapter. The question to which banking theory has not satisfactorily addressed itself is: Which of the various types of individual credit are most suitable as a basis for the monetization of debt? Here lies a vast area of disagreement and opinion which will be considered in the next chapter. Meanwhile, it is proposed to note some essential differences between an expansion of bank credit based upon its employment in working capital, fixed capital, consumption, and in government deficits. But first, it is necessary to examine the nature of individual credit.

The Nature of Individual Credit

A credit transaction arises whenever there is an indirect exchange of goods. Unlike a barter system in which goods are exchanged directly against goods without the intervention of a means of payment, a credit system is one in which exchanges of goods take place indirectly through the intervention in the exchange transactions of money or credit. Credit, therefore, involves almost always a postponement of final payment; in other words, it involves the element of time.[7]

The relation between the parties to such transactions is defined by law or custom and is embodied in a formal or legal instrument, such as a promissory note or bill of exchange. In addition, the amount of credit involved in such transactions is measured in terms of a money of account, such as the dollar, and hence, is expressed in money. This merely means that such instruments are payable in money, not that credit is the same thing as money.

Finally, credit presumably rests upon some basis. That basis ultimately resides in the underlying economic transaction rather than in "character," "collateral," or "capital." Naturally, any credit contract presupposes mutual sincerity regarding fulfillment of the terms of the contract, or character of the parties, and may also be supplemented or reinforced by requirements of various sorts as to collateral pledged by the debtor, or capital (equity) available for the absorption of loss before impairment of the creditor's claim.

If a classification of credit is to prove fruitful, it ought to be based upon factors which surround the underlying transaction, that is, upon the use or purpose to which the borrower intends to apply the credit, as well as the way in which he is expected to acquire the means of repayment. The factor of time, or postponement of payment, is not independent of, but is determined by, the use made of the credit. The other terms of the credit contract,

[7] Some writers have questioned the significance of time as an essential element in credit. Their view, however, regards the total volume of credit as constant and assumes that it consists of a renewable aggregate. In the case of bank credit, it is argued that the aggregate volume does not represent an "advance" to society but is merely a way of matching or clearing goods. See, in this connection, Willis and Edwards, *op. cit.*, p. 18; and also W. H. Steiner and E. Shapiro, *Money and Banking* (New York, 1941), p. 97. However, this view does not consider conditions in a society which is not stationary, and in which the aggregate volume of credit is changing. In any event, in so far as individual transactions are concerned, there is no disagreement that time is an essential and ever present element.

such as collateral, endorsement, etc., and the particular type of instrument in which credit is embodied, are technical matters which will be appropriately decided in each case.

The customary classification of credit embraces the tripartite divisions of commercial, investment, and consumption credit. Commercial credit usually is defined as short-term credit but, as already explained, the time factor is not the determining factor, and so there has been a tendency to define such credit to mean broadly any credit which is used to finance the movement of goods in commerce, that is to say, their distributive movement after production through commerce or trade. In recent years the term has been broadened and used to mean credit which finances the movement of goods through production stages. This expansion of meaning overlaps to some extent the field of investment credit, which is usually understood as that credit which finances the acquisition of fixed capital equipment and various other instruments of production which are to be applied to some income-producing purpose. Consumption credit has come to be recognized more and more as a quite distinct category which relates to the financing of acts of consumption of the final users of finished goods, that is, the final utilization or destruction of wealth in the satisfaction of personal wants. It is a type of credit which is applied to personal satisfaction rather than to the satisfaction of the wants of others. From this standpoint, it is nonproductive. Both commercial and investment credit are income-producing in the sense that they are expected to result in the creation of values by giving to goods form or place utility, or even in creating and adding to the value of goods through manufacture.

Credit to Finance Working and Fixed Capital

It will be found helpful if the above classifications are revised somewhat in order to make them more specific and to relate them to the functional nature of the underlying transactions which the respective kinds of credit are intended to finance. A distinction therefore is drawn between credit to finance "working capital" and credit to finance "fixed capital." The distinction between circulating, or working, capital and fixed capital is basic to our present-day conception of manufacturing and accounting. Furthermore, it is a distinction which rests upon technical grounds. For the purpose of this chapter, the term "working capital" will be used to denote the current or circulating assets of a business, that is, the sum of cash, accounts receivable, and inventories of all kinds. These are all things which are continuously being turned over and replaced in the course of a cycle of operations which repeats itself, the general sequence being from cash to raw materials to finished goods, to accounts receivable, to cash, as goods are manufactured and sold. These items comprise the stock in trade and other current assets into which it is immediately convertible or exchangeable.

"Fixed capital," on the other hand, is a term which denotes those assets which do not circulate but which are fixed, are not intended to be sold *in toto,* but are intended to be used as part of the permanent equipment of the business concern and, therefore, are only used up by being worn out through depreciation or by becoming obsolete. Such assets, it must be emphasized, are acquired to be held.

The dividing line between the circulating or current assets of a business and the fixed assets is fairly clear and sharp, though it might be argued that the entire list of assets merely shades off gradually from those which are cash to those which are by degrees convertible into cash. Thus, in any business, accounts receivable mature, in the course of time, into cash, and, if spaced according to maturity, will bring about a fairly continuous inflow of cash. Inventory will also mature into cash through sale. However, in the case of fixed assets, like machinery, the process is more complicated. Here the equipment of a going concern is in the process of being consumed in the manufacture of finished inventory. Therefore, accounting practice, in making a charge for use depreciation, intends that it be recovered over the life of the asset in the sales price of the finished goods. In this sense fixed assets, like current assets, are being turned over and replaced. The significant difference between their behavior and the behavior of the so-called circulating assets is that the cycle of turnover, from the standpoint of the individual concern, is of much longer duration, lasting perhaps many years.

But this similarity of all business assets is by no means as close when the question of their replacement is examined. In the case of circulating assets, the inflow of cash for replacement is derived from gross sales, whereas in the case of fixed assets, ability to replace them depends, in the absence of borrowing outside the firm, upon net income from sales after the current operating expenses of the business have been met. When the process is viewed from the long-run standpoint, the ability to replace fixed assets depends upon the ability of the concern to produce and sell finished goods at a profit above prime costs. Thus the similarity of all the assets, from the standpoint of turnover, is only apparent, since the repetitive nature of the cycle differs significantly between those assets which are replaced from gross sales and those which can only be replaced from net profits after other expenses have been met.

Any matured debt, no matter what its original basis, naturally is paid from the cash holdings of the concern. As already explained, this cash fund is continuously being spent and replenished by the individual business unit.

Its immediate source of replenishment is the sale of inventories for cash, or the collection of receivables if goods are sold on credit. The short-term bank loan has been criticized by a number of writers on the ground that such loans are not self-liquidating in the aggregate.[8] However, these critics have overlooked the fact that the capacity to pay current debts may depend, not only on turnover of current assets, that is, receivables and inventory, but on liquidation of fixed assets through depreciation charges and failure to replace fixed equipment.[9] Thus, the business system does possess a reserve power to liquidate its current debts which is not reflected in the static balance between current liabilities and current assets. This would be a factor of great importance in a system where the volume of repayments which business is called upon to make exceeds its current capacity as measured by potential liquidation of current assets. Hence, current debt may look for repayment, not only to the immediate liquidation of inventories, but also, over a period of time, as in 1929–33, to the consumption of fixed capital.

From a contractual standpoint, long-term loans to finance fixed assets are repaid out of net income, as has already been pointed out. Here too, however, if selling prices can be maintained, and if the equipment is not replaced, depreciation charges may currently render available funds to service the debt. This is possible as long as selling prices exceed prime costs, but once that break-even point is violated, the liquidation of fixed assets is rendered unproductive as a source of cash if the concern is to continue as a going concern.[10]

SELF-LIQUIDATING CREDIT

A self-liquidating debt is one which is predicated upon a transaction, or transactions, which will directly give rise to proceeds which can be applied to the retirement of the debt, upon completion of the underlying transaction. Thus, for example, bills of exchange and promissory notes which arose out of specific transactions which financed the movements of goods have long been regarded as self-liquidating, whereas debts which financed the acquisition of fixed assets of borrowers used in the further production of goods were held to fall outside the definition of a self-liquidating transaction. In

[8] For example: H. G. Moulton; L. Currie; F. Machlup; C. O. Hardy. See *infra*, Chap. VI.

[9] Arthur Winakor, *Capacity to Pay Current Debts*, University of Illinois, Bureau of Business Research, Bulletin No. 53, October 6, 1936; and *Maintenance of Working Capital of Industrial Corporations*, Bulletin No. 49, January 23, 1934.

[10] Cf. O. J. Curry, *Utilization of Corporate Profits in Prosperity and Depression*, University of Michigan, Bureau of Business Research, "Michigan Business Studies," IX, No. 4 (1941), 20.

the contemporary meaning of the term, loans to finance working capital requirements are included in the category of "self-liquidating" provided no more credit is employed than can be liquidated in the course of a normal production period.[11] Loans for working capital are self-liquidating "if the period of time is long enough to enable the borrowed capital to make the cycle—from money to working capital, to salable goods, and back to money again." [12] This definition would leave outside the concept of "self-liquidating" all credit extended for speculative installment buying purposes and, of course, all credit used for fixed capital purposes. A loan is not self-liquidating if it fails to give rise to a chain of events "which will naturally and normally return funds to the borrower within the life of the loan." [13]

Some writers have stretched the idea of self-liquidating to include loans for fixed capital purposes "if the loan were to run for a period of time sufficient for the capital goods to earn back the interest and principal of the loan." [14] However, the objection to this treatment of the concept is that loans for fixed assets purposes depend for repayment upon profits resulting from the use to which the funds are put. It seems best to limit the term to transactions in which there is a direct and simple relation between the use of credit by the borrower and the source of its liquidation. Thus seasonal working capital loans are repaid from gross receipts which arise directly from the turnover of goods, or the collection of current receivables, whereas fixed asset loans or permanent working capital loans may depend for repayment upon net receipts which are the joint result of other operations requiring an indefinite succession of future production periods for their realization.

The self-liquidating concept is functional in nature and, accordingly, bears a close relation to the concept of working capital. As explained, individual loans to finance working capital are liquidated from the movement through production or into consumption of inventories and by the collection of accounts receivable. Individual loans to finance fixed assets, on the contrary, are serviced or liquidated, not from gross receipts derived from sale, but from net income resulting from total operations after current expenditures have been met.

THE VARIOUS BASES OF BANK CREDIT FURTHER CONSIDERED

When the banking system expands credit to finance enlarged working capital requirements, it is in effect monetizing the prospective gross income

[11] Br. Suviranta, "The Shiftability Theory of Bank Liquidity" in *Economic Essays in Honour of Gustav Cassel* (London, 1933), pp. 623–25.

[12] Rollin G. Thomas, *Modern Banking* (New York, 1937), p. 163.

[13] *Ibid.*, p. 164.

[14] *Ibid.*, p. 163.

from the sale of goods. On the other hand, an expansion of bank credit to finance an enlargement of the fixed instruments of production represents the monetization of the capitalized value of future earnings. It represents, at the time of extension, the substitution of bank credit for future savings which are expected to be realized over time by the application of income later received to the servicing or even retirement of the debt. Similarly, an expansion of bank credit to finance consumption involves the monetization of an equivalent volume of future savings which must be withheld from future incomes if the debt is to be serviced or paid off. When bank credit is expanded to finance governmental deficits, it is anticipated that future tax revenues will be applied to servicing or retiring the debt. Accordingly, expansion of credit for this purpose looks to the later imposition of forced savings.

One type of banking theory has held in essence that the only sound basis for the monetization of debt is the self-liquidating commercial loan. It is argued that banks should undertake to finance by creation of credit only those transactions which involve either the production or marketing of goods destined for immediate consumption, since individual debts of this character are contracted upon the basis of present or anticipated prices, and hence their values tested promptly by the consumption and final satisfaction of wants. Under these conditions, it is believed, the volume of bank credit would correspond to the volume of goods currently being produced and sold. Bank credit, therefore, is viewed as a mechanism concerned primarily with financing the working capital requirements of the community.[15]

Other writers have taken the position that banks need not be constrained by such a narrow basis of credit, that banking can and should be employed successfully to finance the expansion of the permanently installed productive instruments of borrowers, and that, as long as the borrowers are able to pay, such credit would be validated.[16] Thus, the basis upon which credit should be advanced is anticipated income. But here it is to be noted that the validation of credit rests upon the later realization of the anticipated income; in other words, the undertakings must actually prove to be income-producing, that is, give rise to a flow of goods and services over time which will satisfy the wants of consumers at estimated prices and enable the borrower to derive earnings from his total operations which will permit the gradual extinction of his indebtedness.

Still others have regarded government debt as a satisfactory basis for the

[15] See, e. g., William E. Dunkman, *Qualitative Credit Control* (New York, 1933).

[16] See, e.g., Joseph A. Schumpeter, *The Theory of Economic Development*, tr. Redvers Opie (English ed.; Cambridge, Mass., 1936), Chaps. II and III; H. G. Moulton, *The Formation of Capital* (Washington, 1935), Chaps. VII and VIII.

extension of credit.[17] Here it is to be noted that until the popularization of Keynes's *General Theory* most advocates of an expansion of bank credit based upon government debt conceded the desirability of eventual cancellation of bank credit in the course of the business cycle. Some have argued that such credit would be self-liquidating since the expenditures of the Government are income-producing. It is only in recent years that the fashion of advocating unlimited credit creation for the purpose of the secular perpetuation of investment has received much imitation. This matter is the subject of later reference in the text. Suffice it to say, at this point, that bank credit when based upon government credit loses the essential character of self-liquidation because the underlying application of the credit bears no direct relation to the sources from which it is to be repaid, while, obviously, the decision and justification as to its use is shifted to the State. Indefinite monetization of government debt by the banking system eventually will require forced saving through taxation, price inflation, or write-off of losses, and, therefore, involve ultimately the necessity of State intervention through the use of nonmonetary powers. Monetization of government debt represents an extreme case of the separation of the use and repayment aspects of credit transactions.

In any case, it must be agreed that bank credit is based upon a corresponding volume of individual, corporate, or government debt, and that the long-run validity of such credit depends upon the ability of the borrowing community to service or erase that debt. The question of the proper basis for bank credit is one aspect of the larger question: Does the borrowing and subsequent use of credit have for its purpose the creation of additional capital wealth in the form of income-producing assets, and will it therefore prove productive, or does it merely anticipate income and later prove unproductive? [18] The borrowing of business firms, from the individual standpoint, appears to belong in the productive category, while that of the consumer falls in the unproductive category. Borrowing by government may be of either kind, although usually it is of the unproductive kind as judged from the narrow standpoint of the purpose to which it is immediately applied, since no new assets are created thereby.[19]

The productivity of bank credit, from the social standpoint, depends upon the productivity of the money capital which it renders available to borrowers in the form of bank deposits. This becomes a question of the use by

[17] See, e.g., Keynes, *op. cit.;* J. W. Angell, *Investment and Business Cycles* (New York, 1941); and Alvin Hansen, *Fiscal Policy and Business Cycles* (New York, 1941).

[18] Cf. E. L. Hargreaves, "Debt" in *What Everybody Wants to Know about Money,* ed. G. D. H. Cole (London, 1933), p. 438.

[19] Cf. Institute of International Finance of New York University, *Some Aspects of the Mounting Public Debt,* Bulletin No. 119, February, 1942, p. 10.

society of the credit so created. From the banking standpoint, the eventual value of the debts monetized in this way will depend upon the income productivity of the additional money capital rendered available to borrowers. There will be no possibility of the banking system's withdrawing the value equivalent of the money capital earlier advanced, or of shifting the burden of ownership of these titles to income to non-bank holders, unless the rate at which the underlying processes produce income is sufficient to support their capitalized values. Thus the productivity of bank credit would seem to rest upon the following factors: (1) the profitability of the ventures in question; (2) the efficacy of expanded credit in inducing the employment of unused labor and capital; and, (3) the response of voluntary savings to enlarged incomes.

Chapter VI

THE DIVERGENCE OF MONETARY AND CREDIT THEORY

THE COMBINATION of its money-issuing function with its lending function differentiates commercial banking from all other types of financial institutions. Banking theory may be said, therefore, to embrace two related fields: first, the study of money, which approaches the subject from the standpoint of the supply of money and hence is concerned with the total amount of money in existence and its relation to prices, interest rates, and capital formation; and second, the study of credit, which is concerned with the lending and investing activities of banks, and hence with the use and repayment of credit. Viewed from the standpoint of the bank balance sheet, the first type of theory may be said to deal with the liability side of bank operations, whereas the second type of theory has regard to the assets.

Owing to the dual character of banking functions these two branches of theory are not mutually exclusive, yet their development has followed separate paths. It might be expected that central banking would furnish a synthesis, but it has become largely a study of the technique of varying the supply of money. Monetary theory, despite its attention to the savings-investment process, has almost completely neglected the qualitative relation of commercial banking to capital formation. This has been due to a persistent neglect of the conditions upon which banks issue credit. Credit theory receives only brief paragraphic treatment in many American textbooks in sections dealing with the classification of credit, although some attention is given to the principles governing individual bank portfolio policy. Texts dealing with the subject of credit itself are usually confined entirely to the study of the differential selection of risks. However, a school of writers known as the Qualitative School, following the tradition of the Banking School, has endeavored in a few published works to postulate criteria of banking policy which are intended to harmonize the dual functions of the bank.[1]

[1] A differentiation of monetary theory and qualitative credit theory is presented in B. H. Beckhart, "Monetary Policy and Commercial Bank Portfolios," *American Economic Review,* Supplement, Vol. XXX, No. 1 (March, 1940); and by the same author, *Qualitative Credit Control,* prepared for the Commission on Banking Law and Practice, Association of Reserve City Bankers, Bulletin No. 10 (June, 1936).

The divergence between monetary theory and qualitative credit theory can be dated for convenience from the controversy between the Currency School and the Banking School after the suspension of specie payments by the Bank of England in 1797. The same basic differences which characterized that controversy underlie more recent disputes over the relative advantages of the quantitative as opposed to the qualitative approach to the study of banking. A related issue concerns the desirability of self-liquidation as opposed to shiftability of bank assets.[2]

THE CHARACTERISTICS OF MONETARY THEORY

The proclivities of contemporary monetary theory include the following: (1) the identification of credit with money and the allied proposition that bank credit is a satisfactory substitute for savings; (2) reliance upon the quantity theory formulation in which the factor money is assumed to be an independent variable; (3) the hypothesis that causation operates from changes in the supply of money to prices, interest rates, or incomes; (4) the assumption that the supply of money is subject to fairly complete control; and (5) the corollary that the function of the banking system is to supply money in quantities deemed appropriate to the attainment of predetermined objectives such as price stability, equality of investment and savings, etc.

THE IDENTIFICATION OF CREDIT AND MONEY

Divergencies between monetary theory and credit theory have arisen over the basic question: Are the issues of banks in the form of notes and deposits the same thing as money? A long and continuous line of writers has taken this position.[3] Thus today the monetary theorists regard bank deposits as a homogeneous mass of money, just as the older quantity theorists, like Fisher, for example, added them together in the same equation and assumed their effects were of similar weight.

Rist has skillfully exposed the origin and development of the confusion between money and credit, and has traced its influence down to contemporary writers.[4] According to Rist, writers of the eighteenth century, with the

[2] It is to be noted that among monetary theorists there are many shades of opinion; not all writers in this general category deny the necessity of qualitative criteria in banking policy. Of late there is increasing evidence that central bankers have discovered the necessity of qualitative controls, not only over credit used to finance operations in the securities markets, but also over consumer credit during wartimes. However, in this connection the term "selective" control seems more appropriate than "qualitative" control. See, *Annual Report of the Federal Reserve Bank of New York* (1941), pp. 25–26.

[3] Ralph W. Robey, *Purchasing Power* (New York, 1938), pp. 10–11.

[4] Charles A. Rist, *History of Monetary and Credit Theory from John Law to the Present Day*, tr. by Jane Degras (New York, 1940), pp. 31–98.

single exception of Cantillon, failed to distinguish between the idea of bank credit as distinct, on the one hand, from paper money issued by the State, and, on the other, from commercial drafts and bills circulating among merchants. John Law's identification of an increase in credit with an increase in money was prolonged throughout the eighteenth century, "being as it were hallowed by the authority of Adam Smith and later Ricardo." [5] This was due to a failure to perceive the connection between the discount operations of banks and the issue of notes, as well as an inability to understand that inconvertible paper money is merely a substitute for metallic money and not an addition to it.

The distinction between money and credit is fundamental to all credit theory. It is based on the fact that paper money issued by the State is new money, definitive purchasing power which remains extant, a permanent addition to the currency supply, whereas bank notes (and, similarly, deposits) may not be incorporated into the currency but will be canceled, especially if their issue was created in the form of credits to commerce and industry.

The preoccupation of monetary theorists with the quantity of money has led them to neglect the qualitative basis upon which supplies of money are forthcoming. In the United States, in recent years, the view seems to have been adopted widely that the particular type of bank assets against which deposits are created is of no particular concern so long as these assets are "inherently sound" or "ultimately sound." No importance is attached to the functional concept of self-liquidating credits, nor to the particular points at which credit is injected into the economic system. Liquidity is conceived in terms of shiftability. It is believed that the development of open markets in securities, supplemented by the perfection of central banking, suffices to meet the requirements of liquidity so that the only really important consideration is the "ultimate soundness" of the debts held by the banking system. Ultimate soundness is measured by the probable solvency of the debtor or by the collateral which he is able to pledge.[6]

The indifference of monetary theorists to the qualitative basis upon which deposits are created also implies that deposit creation is a satisfactory substitute for savings. Perhaps the leading criterion of monetary theory is the maintenance of equilibrium between savings and investment. The mecha-

[5] *Ibid.*, p. 67.

[6] The prevalence of this view is reflected in various changes in banking laws and regulations during the last decade. See, e. g., the broadening of the definition of eligible commercial paper by the Board of Governors of the Federal Reserve System, Regulation A, October 1, 1937; also, changes made in the revised classification of bank assets for examination purposes, adopted by Federal and state supervisory bodies (*Annual Report of the Federal Deposit Insurance Corporation,* 1938, pp. 61–78); and the various amendments to the Federal Reserve Act, especially the Banking Acts of 1933 and 1935, and regulations thereunder, giving preferential treatment to government bonds as collateral for advances from Federal Reserve banks.

nism essential to this accomplishment is the creation or destruction of purchasing power by the banking system. There are various theoretical versions of the manner in which the process works. One commonly accepted view is that the competitive employment of bank credit with voluntary savings lowers interest rates and stimulates investment. Rationalization of this view is derived from the fact that the production cost of bank credit is determined by an entirely different set of factors from those which determine the production cost of voluntary savings. The production cost of bank credit "is the cost of operating the bank as a business concern, including allowance for losses and interest paid to depositors." [7] The production of bank credit "is limited or unlimited as the consequence of management" and depends upon the propensities of bankers, the desire for earnings, and the risks of loss on bank assets. On the other hand, in the absence of creations of purchasing power by banks, voluntary savings originate in abstention from consumption. The cost of production of such funds is the rate of interest necessary to induce such abstinence.

While the employment of newly created bank credit in competition with voluntary savings may be essentially "a mechanical process," monetary theorists have ignored the fact that the banks acquire additional assets in the process. Monetary theory has been interested, not in the asset basis upon which such credit is brought into existence, but in its total amount and cost. The conventional theorem that the capital requirements of borrowers ought to be financed from voluntary savings and that only current or operating capital requirements should be met with new bank credit has been rejected, since its observance is inconsistent with the effectuation of monetary policy.

Another version of monetary theory relates the creation of purchasing power by banks to the resulting expansion of incomes and to savings induced thereby. Thus, Keynes, in *The General Theory,* insists that, except in conditions of full employment, bank credits extended to entrepreneurs, additional to those already existing, permit new investment and increased money as well as real incomes. Furthermore, Keynes avers,

> the public will exercise a "free choice" as to the proportion in which they divide the increased income between savings and spending. . . . Moreover, the savings which result from this decision are just as genuine as any other savings. No one can be compelled to own the additional money corresponding to the new-bank-credit, unless he deliberately prefers to hold more money rather than some other form of wealth.[8]

Although Robertson employs somewhat different definitions of savings and

[7] Robert B. Warren, *The Search for Financial Security* (New York, 1940), p. 43.

[8] John Maynard Keynes, *The General Theory of Employment, Interest and Money* (New York, 1935), pp. 81–83.

investment, he asserts a rather similar proposition when he says: "the real value of a country's bank money is the same thing as the amount of real savings which the public has put in the past at the disposal of industry through the medium of banks, and its amount lies in the discretion of the public and not the banks." [9]

While these writers do not identify bank credit with savings (by definition, savings is the difference between incomes and amounts spent on consumption, whereas bank credit is a liability of the banking system, or an asset of the holders of deposit balances), they evidently believe that the result of bank credit creation is to expand savings correspondingly by an expansion in either monetary or real incomes. Under conditions of full employment, a part of the "savings" may be forced to the extent that rising prices reduce the value of money incomes. In either case, according to Keynes, the savings are "genuine."

In any event, creation of bank credit involves enlargement of bank deposits. These deposits must be held by someone somewhere in the economic system. The individual income recipient may exercise a free choice whether to save or to spend, but in the total sense, considering all income recipients together, no real choice is allowed, except, as Robertson argues, in so far as the disposition to hold deposits idle or to spend them determines their real value.

These views of the relation between bank credit creation and savings appear to have had some influence upon descriptions of the process of bank credit creation as it operated during the 1930s and has led to doubtful assertions regarding the nature of the growth of idle money in that decade.

In describing the growth in the volume of idle money during the 1930s, Thomas explained that,

> a large portion of the deposits now in banks represents savings being held there in the absence of other satisfactory available uses. Individuals, corporations, and other investors have passed on to the banks the responsibility of maintaining the flow of savings into investment channels.[10]

Likewise, the Secretary of the Treasury, in describing the institutionalization of the savings-investment process during the 1930s, said, "Individuals and non-financial corporations appear to have preferred to place their funds available for investment in bank accounts and insurance policies, instead of undertaking directly the investment of these funds in securities." [11]

In the passages quoted it is implied that somehow the public deliberately

[9] D. H. Robertson, *Essays in Monetary Theory* (London, 1940), p. 42.

[10] Woodlief Thomas, "The Banks and Idle Money," *Federal Reserve Bulletin*, March, 1940, pp. 195–96.

[11] *Annual Report of the Secretary of the Treasury* (1940), p. 95.

chose to place deposits with banks. The fact is that the volume of bank balances in the hands of the public must always equal the volume of deposits created by the banking system. Nevertheless, the growth in deposit balances during the 1930s was not caused initially by decisions of individuals to save in this form but resulted concurrently from the expansion in bank assets, which expansion was the result of policies of the banks in buying securities and of the Federal Reserve banks and the Treasury in facilitating the rise in bank reserves. The situation in the 1930s, therefore, is not accurately described by saying that individuals in some manner preferred to hold deposits, letting the banks buy the securities, instead of directly purchasing securities with deposits.

THE ROLE OF THE QUANTITY THEORY

The quantity theory of money has played a major role in the evolution of monetary theory. Although the familiar equation of exchange has been refined and modified to take into account institutional changes, the essential nature of the apparatus remains much as it was in the beginning. Money has always been treated as the independent variable and causation assumed to operate from the money side to the price or goods side of the equation. Whereas in early formulations the chief aim was to explain changes in the price level, attention has been redirected toward a consideration of the effect of changes in the volume of money upon interest rates, output, and capital formation.

Until the First World War comparatively little attention had been paid to the importance of the demand for money in determining its value. As a result of Fisher's emphasis on the velocity of money, the realization spread that the velocity of circulation is merely the converse of the idea of the demand for money, but that the latter is more significant. The lack of attention to demand persisted despite Marshall's attempt to restate the problem of variations in purchasing power in terms of a varying desire to hold money, and Friedrich Von Wieser's effort to state the same problem in terms of changes in the volume of money income.[12] Application of the marginalist analysis of value was later applied to money when it was questioned whether elasticity of the demand for money was always unity, and hence that prices were directly proportional to the value of money. But the objection was voiced that the estimates placed upon money by individuals partly depend upon, rather than determine, its objective value in terms of goods and therefore are not entirely subjective.[13]

[12] T. E. Gregory, "Money," in *The Encyclopaedia of the Social Sciences* (New York, 1933), X, 609.
[13] *Ibid.*

The dominant type of monetary theory since the First World War has been of the "marginalist" character. This is true of the cash balance and holding theories and the income theories. Recently, the so-called income and expenditure theories have dominated the controversy. They deal with the same general set of factors, the quantity of money available, the speed with which it is spent, and the physical volume of goods produced and sold for the flow of money expenditure.

While the approach is still essentially quantitative, it represents a considerable refinement of the crude type of quantitative relationships theretofore discussed. Gregory observed that it is the great merit of the income theories that they bring into the foreground the causal elements, such as change in the desire to hold money, which it has been shown may cause a change in prices without requiring a change in the supply of money; while an increase in the stream of money will have greater or less effect upon prices according to whether the increased resources placed at the disposal of consumers result in additional expenditures, or whether they are added to the "unspent margin," that is, neutralized because of the desire of the public to hold larger balances.

Hawtrey gave emphasis to the point that the quantity of credit alone was not the important consideration in price formation; rather it is the rate of credit issue in comparison with the rate at which goods are produced.[14]

Keynes in the *Treatise on Money* developed new equations to analyze the disposal of income by the consumer. Prices were treated as a function of psychological values assigned to goods by consumers in their choice between saving or spending. The result was to integrate the subject of money with the more general theory of value. This is in sharp contrast with the position of Mill, who thought natural values were determined by cost of production. Today, emphasis is placed on the degree to which the consumer will put his income to a particular kind of goods, and prices are said to change in proportion as changes occur in the demand for various kinds of goods. Thus the whole problem has been shifted back to a discussion of value, with the result that nowadays the price level is regarded as something which is continually changing, to the extent that consumption and savings are changing, and thereby it is treated as a function of consumer preference.

However, as Rist asserted, although contemporary theory recognizes that the value of money is determined by factors on both the demand and supply side, in practice it omits the factor of demand, which appears merely as the aggregate sum of the transactions effected. The theory of the value of money, instead of fitting into the general theory of value of commodities—in which

[14] R. G. Hawtrey, *Currency and Credit* (2d ed.; London, 1923), pp. 39–40.

demand is so important—seems to constitute a thing apart, as it were, outside the framework of general economic theory.[15]

Nevertheless, it would seem that to the extent that savings-investment theories do take into account the decision of consumers regarding the choice between expenditure, hoarding, and saving, they allow the factor of demand a place in the general theory. An exception is to be noted in Keynes's treatment of interest in the *General Theory*. Here the relevance of the propensity to consume is dismissed and the rate of interest is said to be determined by the quantity of money, given liquidity preference. This makes the quantity of money the determinant in the explanation of interest and, in turn, of investment and capital formation.

Until the recent revival of secular stagnation theories, the majority of writers was inclined to agree that in the long run there is a kind of central tendency for demand for goods to be sufficient to purchase all the goods that the economic system is capable of producing under given technical and physical conditions. The aim of the income-expenditure analysis, until Keynes's *General Theory,* however, had been concerned more with the shorter run behavior and particularly with cyclical excesses of supply or deficiency of demand, whichever it might be.

Since the First World War, less and less attention has been given to what was happening to the value of money as such, and more to the nature of business cycles, industrial instability, and fluctuating employment. The value of money was the aim of monetary theory in the nineteenth century because economists were mainly interested in problems of consumption.[16] Later, rising prices became associated with rising business activity, and hence attention was directed toward explaining the correlation between prices and business activity. But with the persistence of unemployment in the 1930s and the failure of investment in capital equipment to recover its predepression level, economists sought an explanation and a means of correcting this kind of "abnormal behavior." In the last ten years, especially, the problem has come to be expressed as one of controlling such factors as savings, consumer expenditures, and investment, not only with a view to eliminating cyclical fluctuations, but even of correcting secular trends. The causation in nearly all theories is assumed to operate from the money side to the goods side of the equation rather than the reverse.

In spite of progress in the form of refinement and qualification, contemporary monetary theory in explicitly assuming the independence of money and the dependence of other factors upon it commits itself to two basic postulates: first, the treatment of bank credit as though it were tanta-

[15] Rist, *op. cit.*, pp. 345 ff.

[16] Bhalchandra Andarkar, *The Theory of Monetary Policy* (London, 1935), p. 54.

mount to money; and second, the treatment of bank credit as though it conceives its own savings. Behind these postulates lies the hypothesis that bank credit is "free"; that is, that it can be withdrawn or injected into circulation more or less at will, and therefore that its effective supply can be controlled. Since banks are the chief issuers of credit and "money," and since they operate under economic and legal principles peculiar to themselves, there appears to be no justification for the arbitrary assumption of complete elasticity of the banking and credit mechanism limited only by State intervention.

THE NATURE OF THE ASSUMED CAUSATION

The bulk of the received doctrine has laid great stress upon the market rates of interest as the mechanism through which control in prices or investment is to be achieved. However, in recent years there has been evident a willingness to concede the relative unimportance of interest as a cost in the calculations of entrepreneurs and, at the same time, a tendency to lean more heavily upon the importance of raising capitalized values, enlarging money balances in the hands of the public, and inducing expenditure. Low interest rates may not logically be said to cause these conditions, but to be their reflection.

A somewhat extended controversy has centered around the entailed question whether lower interest rates exert their effect by stimulation of investment in working capital or in fixed capital. The doubt seems to have been resolved in favor of the view that interest is a much more important cost item in respect to fixed capital, i. e., investment in durable instruments. As a result, the theorizers have been led to advocate the inflation of bank credit for fixed capital purposes without deference to the traditional banking policy of restricting loans to working capital purposes. But such advocacy overlooks the difference in the condition of a banking system which finances long, as compared with one which finances short, and the problems of liquidity and solvency connected therewith.

Aside from this question, monetary theorists, with few exceptions, hold that there exists an interconnection between long and short rates, and that a policy of reducing short-term rates will be reflected in falling long-term interest rates, it being assumed that the markets for loanable funds are competitive on both the demand and supply sides.[17]

Whatever view is entertained regarding the *modus operandi* of the interest rate, writers of this school have not concerned themselves with the cor-

[17] See John Maynard Keynes, *A Treatise on Money* (New York, 1930), II, 352–57; and R. G. Hawtrey, *Capital and Employment* (London, 1937), pp. 114–15, who holds a somewhat different view of the relation between short and long rates.

relative effects of an easy money policy upon the banking position itself. All such policies require that the banking system be used as the independent instrument for effectuating reduced rates of interest and achieving increased investment. This intervention is predicated upon the purchase of debts by banks either from new borrowers or from the public.

However, due to uncomfortable doubts regarding the efficacy of the interest rate as a cost in stimulating investment, there has been a tendency to rationalize cheap money policies on other grounds, to stress the importance of enhanced capitalization, larger money balances in the hands of the public, and induced spending. This rationale introduces the multiplier concept and the acceleration principle to explain expansion of incomes and the derivation of larger output. This restatement of the case has involved a corresponding reorientation of the theory of interest. The rate of interest is now said to be determined by the quantity of money rather than by the demands for loanable funds by borrowers. But the problems associated with the inflation of bank assets, which are the necessary concomitant of an enlarged supply of money, remain as unsolved as they were before.

Despite the formal validity of the multiplier concept, the experience of the 1930s has convinced an increasing number of students of the correctness of the views of writers like Durbin and Robertson who held that the banking system can increase the quantity of money but cannot control its velocity except, perhaps, indirectly. The suspicion has been confirmed that the anticipations of the public may prove so refractory as to negate the influence of the enlarged supply of money. The effective supply of money has two components, M and V; it has been learned that the banks' influence is limited for the most part to M. In the 1930s the great expansion in the supply of money which the banking system provided was effectively compensated by a declining velocity of deposits, reflecting an intensification of the precautionary and speculative aspects of liquidity preference.

The expansion of income, which the multiplier implies, depends upon the existence of an increased propensity to consume, or certainty that there be no increase in the propensity to hoard money balances. The inescapable conclusion is that the effective prosecution of a policy of trying to increase incomes by monetary action requires inflation of the assets of the banking system, if the supply of money balances is to be enlarged to the extent required by the theory. A belated recognition of this truth is just beginning to creep into the current literature.[18]

In any event, if inflation of bank credit, either to stimulate cyclical re-

[18] See John H. Williams, "The Implications of Fiscal Policy for Monetary Policy and the Banking System," address before a joint session of the American Economic Association and the American Statistical Association, New York, December 28, 1941.

covery or to achieve secular prosperity, is to succeed, the solvency of the banking system must be preserved. This would seem to require, eventually, the realization of an enlarged rate of saving by the community so that the debt lodged in the banking system may be shifted to the public without involving the banks in losses. At least, an increased propensity of the public to spend on securities must materialize if the value of the debt held by the banking system is not to suffer depreciation in value owing to rising yields of fixed interest-bearing securities. Thus, monetary theories which depend upon the injection of bank credit contain an inherent contradiction except to the extent that they foresee ultimately an increased rate of savings.

THE NATURE OF THE DEMAND FOR CAPITAL AND THE AMOUNT OF CAPITAL REQUIRED

There remains what seems to be an unexplored field concerning the relation between the amount of physical capital needed, the amount of money capital, and the supply of money. Most writers have assumed that both cyclical and secular expansion involve changes which increase the demand for money capital, owing to the increased need for physical capital arising out of longer periods of production or increased roundaboutness of production, it being argued that inventions like steelmaking and electric power generation require the direct employment of larger physical installations of durable goods, and they also, in turn, induce an enlarged demand for capital in allied industries. A few writers have mentioned the possibility of capital-saving inventions, that is, of technological changes which involve a more economical use of the available capital, or a diminished amount of capital, owing to entirely new methods of producing output. The one-time fashionable secular stagnation theory of investment was conceived in terms of a reduced demand for capital owing to an alleged decline in the development of new capital-using industries and to retardation in the growth of population. On the other hand, its critics appeared to consider the demand for capital elastic because of the ever present possibilities of new invention, and implied that technological change involves increased quantities of capital.

The implication of the distinction between investment based upon capital-saving uses and that which requires enlarged capital have not been explored. From the standpoint of the banking system, if technological change involves the use of larger amounts of physical capital, longer periods of production, and more roundabout methods, there would seem to be a *prima facie* case for an enlarged supply of money if only to perform the increased amount of money work to be done. The same thing holds true where the amount of capital expands as a result of growth in population. On the other hand, if technological change involves capital saving and eventuates in the use of smaller proportions of capital relative to other factors, there would not appear to be any need for a larger supply of money-capital in order to achieve a larger output. Robertson is one of the very few who have concerned themselves with the ramifications upon the supply of money of either population or productivity changes. He believes that in the case of an increased effectiveness of labor, the benefits of increased productivity ought to be translated into enlargement of physical capital formation, rather than realized currently in greater consumption resulting from lower prices, and this attitude is consonant with his view of the importance of price rises in facilitating technological change. In the case of discontinuous leaps in investment, he found the inelasticity in the supply of savings to be an inhibiting factor, and he therefore favored expansion of bank credit. Acceptance of this view, however, is not inconsistent with the prescription that, once the gaps are bridged, the debt involved in their financing by banks ought to be shifted to the public.

THE FUNCTIONS OF BANKS

An impressive list of writers could be compiled whose monetary theories abstract from the banking system, and thus fall entirely outside its limiting framework, yet invariably the injection of money is assumed to be the function of the banking system. To Hawtrey, the function of the banking system is "to irrigate" the economic system with money; to Robertson, its function is to fill the gap between investment and savings; to Keynes, the banking system is the balancing factor in bringing about the equilibrium of savings and investment. These purposes are to be accomplished by the creation of money in the form of bank deposits by the banking system. Many writers imply or, in some cases, explicitly assume either "free" injections of credit, fiat money issued by the State, or unlimited elasticity of bank credit.[19] On the other hand, a few, including Schumpeter, Cassel, and Durbin, have clearly recognized the conditions upon which money is injected into the system or withdrawn from it.

The practice of making unrealistic assumptions regarding the conditions

[19] See J. R. Hicks, *Value and Capital* (Oxford, 1939), especially Chaps. XI–XIII; also Erik Lindahl, *Studies in the Theory of Money and Capital* (New York, 1939). Lindahl is one of few who clearly states his assumptions regarding credit. See pp. 161–62. Lindahl states in part: "The granting of credit is assumed to be entirely free and unrestricted. The terms of credit are the same for all and are not changed by an alteration in the rate of interest. The rate will, therefore, be the only factor determining the extent to which credits are granted." See also p. 238, where he discusses the removal of this assumption. Robertson's analysis in *Banking Policy and the Price Level* [(rev. ed.; London, 1932], p. 52) was based on the explicit assumption that "the community's money supply consisted entirely of the inconvertible of a single giant bank." See also p. 23 of the same work where the assumption is stated somewhat differently.

upon which credit is injected, whether explicit or implicit, no matter how useful for the purpose of theoretical exercise, promotes fallacious identification of credit with money, money with capital, and investment with savings, which tends to obscure and confuse the differentiation of more complex factors of causation. It is one thing to assume that banks can vary their assets and the supply of deposits within limits in the short run; it is another to assert that this proposition holds good in the long run without reference to the problems of liquidity and solvency, or to the motivations of bankers.

The assumptions made regarding the conditions under which variations in bank assets may take place has much to do with the conclusions reached in theorizing about the proper functions of banks. What may be perfectly good logic under the assumptions of an imaginary banking framework may have little or no relevance to real conditions existing in the contemporary world.

For example, one popular assumption is that the banking system resembles one very large single bank with which the public carries its deposit accounts and that these accounts are the only means of payment. Such an assumption removes all questions of interbank settlements and the need for bank reserves. It is then taken for granted that this bank can put into circulation deposits at will without limit merely by buying securities or making loans at rates of interest lower than those prevailing in the market. Sometimes it is assumed that injections may be made at any point in the system.[20]

The essential question is: How far can such a bank go in expanding its deposits? At first sight, there would appear to be no limit whatever except the demand for loans by borrowers or the willingness of the public to sell securities. The latter would depend upon the supply of outstanding securities and, in this way, upon their yields. The demand for loans, however, would not be restrained, since borrowers would merely issue additional debts. It is to be presumed, however, that even the officials of such a bank as this would be unwilling to make loans unless borrowers were able to repay old ones; in turn, the ability of borrowers to repay old loans would seem to set the limit upon expansion.

Postponement of repayment, owing to inability of borrowers, would amount to covering losses by artificial creations of the means of payment. Thus the theory of the single bank is a theory of fiat issue, and the process of issue, if carried to its extreme, would mean a complete suspension of the basis of the debtor-creditor relationship. Society would become deprived of the test of economic efficiency and would degenerate into an aimless, inefficient society unless production were to be controlled by direction of the

[20] See Andarkar, *op. cit.*, pp. 67–68.

State. In that case, it is apparent that indefinite extensions of bank credit involve the gradual absorption by the bank of the titles to the country's wealth with evenual abolition of private ownership and risk-taking. Both Ellis and Durbin perceived this.[21] At the extreme point, the bank would become synonymous with the State and cease entirely to perform, as a separate or independent institution, its function of underwriting risks and directing the use of credit.[22]

But it is apparent that the State could not afford to permit the bank to continue indefinite extensions of credit, i. e., indefinite dilutions of the means of payment, and that at some point it would intervene through the use of nonmonetary powers. This is obviously the lesson now being learned from the exigencies of war finance.

In summary, it is apparent that, at one extreme, there is a body of authoritative theory which regards the essential function of the banks as that of serving as an agent for inducing changes in investment, that is, capital formation, by enlargement of the supply of money; while on the other hand is a body of theory, of which Hayek is one of the chief exponents,[23] which holds that creation of bank credit is harmful and which therefore calls for neutral policy. Few of the writers mentioned deal specifically with the analysis of banking functions, or with the relation of the monetary aspect of their theories to the liquidity and solvency of banks. In the next section, therefore, attention will be given to an entirely different type of theory which deals more specifically with these questions.

QUALITATIVE CREDIT THEORY

Unlike monetary theory, qualitative credit theory has concerned itself with the relation between the lending functions of banks and their monetary functions. The chief characteristics of this type of theory may be said to include the following: (1) insistence upon the distinction between credit and money; (2) differentiation of the individual types of credit for which bank credit may be substituted; (3) the belief that the function of the banking system is to serve as a clearing mechanism to facilitate the exchange of goods rather than as an active agent for the promotion of price stability, capital formation, or deficit financing; and (4) separation of the money-supplying function of commercial banks from their investment or capital-formation function, (*a*) by limitation of book credit creation to

[21] Howard S. Ellis, *German Monetary Theory* (Cambridge, Mass., 1934); E. F. M. Durbin, *The Problem of Credit Policy* (London, 1935).

[22] Joseph A. Schumpeter, *Business Cycles* (New York, 1939), I, 116–18, remarks on the desirability of an independent banking system.

[23] F. A. Hayek, *Prices and Production* (2d rev. ed.; London, 1934), Lecture IV.

self-liquidating assets; (*b*) by prohibition of fixed asset financing except to the extent that banks hold deposits representing savings or possess capital funds of their own.

THE DIFFERENCE BETWEEN CREDIT AND MONEY

Various students of credit theory have insisted that the distinction between credit and money be preserved.[24] Willis explained that, since money is not a natural object, there is need of selection and, accordingly, in civilized societies, it is not recognized as such until it has been so designated by constituted authorities as standard money or legal tender. The term "credit," in his view, means the power to command goods and services without actually possessing money. When a person borrows at a bank, he does not borrow money but obtains the means of settling obligations without the direct use of money. Banking, therefore, is regarded as a means of offsetting or clearing claims expressed in money. This view readily admits that it is possible to get along without the use of any metallic standard, or standard money whatever, under specified conditions, but does not believe it desirable to do so, since one of the main purposes of standard money is that of serving continuously as a means of testing the ability of banks and different economic groups in the community to meet their obligations on demand.[25]

The banking mechanism, Willis said, is able to keep production within reasonable limits by insisting that customers be able to repay loans, and a nonpartisan administration of banking is presumed to refuse credit to those who are overproduced, and to those who are producing at an unusually high cost. Thus the function of banking in insisting that customers should always show probability of being able to repay their debts, that is, liquidate them by continuous production and sale, exemplifies the function of credit in regulating the output of goods, especially those goods whose value is not immediately tested by the requirements of consumption. In the final analysis, it is through determination of the access to credit that the banking system is thought of as eventually fixing the output of goods and determining interconvertibility of money and commodities on a basis which is, in effect, a regulation of supply. In this sense, the control of money is to be effected by the action of the bank in granting and assigning credit, that is, the right to demand money, among the different applicants for it. This is the field of credit as distinct from money. The function of money as such

[24] H. Parker Willis and George W. Edwards, *Banking and Business* (rev. ed.; New York, 1925), Chap. I; H. D. Macleod, *The Theory of Credit* (London, 1890), *passim.*; Rist, *op. cit.*, Chap. I; Robey, *op. cit.*, pp. 6–7.

[25] This statement of Willis's views is based upon "Money—Its History and Purposes," an unpublished address before the New York University Forum (Nassau College), Hempstead, N.Y., February 18, 1936.

is that of limiting the possibility of unduly extensive undertakings, or of undertakings whose products cannot, in all probability, be disposed of with success by their makers. Credit thus becomes a study of the conditions of production and of the probability that given fields of production can be matched against one another with success. Credit is, in other words, the process of regulating the volume of claims to money (deposit liabilities), and money itself is the ultimate medium by which these claims are tested.

The credit school of thought, as exemplified by Willis, holds that the desirable object to be attained in connection with the supply of money is that of rendering this supply neutral or passive with respect to the other aspects of economic behavior and to avoid having the credit mechanism itself become a source of disturbance. In practice, this means that the money supply should be limited by the legitimate extensions of credit by banks, legitimate in the sense that they are to be judged by the banker in the light of the ability of users of credit to liquidate their indebtedness to banks by continuous production and sale, and should not be divorced from this criterion and made to depend upon more or less arbitrary decision of the Government or other issuing authority. Nevertheless, no one of this school ever denied that the adjustment between money and credit, on the one hand, and goods on the other, has been imperfectly maintained. Imperfection has nearly always been due to: (1) erroneous information or judgment as to the volume of consumption, and hence as to resulting values; (2) extraneous interference on the part of the State for the purpose of fulfilling objects not regularly or strictly economic considerations, e. g. war; and (3) industrial changes and shifts growing out of alterations in technique of manufacture or type of industrial processes, as for example, invention of new mechanisms resulting in great changes in cost of production.[26]

THE PREDILECTION OF QUALITATIVE WRITERS IN THE MATTER OF SELF-LIQUIDATING ASSETS

Commercial banking theory has long been identified with the doctrine that a bank of deposit should finance only short-term, self-liquidating transactions of a commercial character. The term "commercial," however, has been interpreted in various ways. In a narrow sense, it denotes credit used for mercantile purposes, while broadly speaking the term comprehends all credit for the purpose of financing working capital in trade, industry, and agriculture. Among classical writers, Adam Smith was a leading exponent of the view that banks should confine themselves to the financing of trade as opposed to manufacture. However, modern "commercial loan" theorists

[26] Cf. address of H. Parker Willis, "Monetary Control," before the United States Department of Agriculture Graduate School, Washington, D.C., April 4, 1936.

have sanctioned the financing by banks of all types of working capital, at least to the extent that it is not permanently invested in the borrowing firm. In this connection, working capital is a concept which is divorced from the specific single transactions such as arise in the drawing of bills of exchange. However, qualitative writers have continued to emphasize that the functional test of self-liquidation should be applied in deciding whether or not the transaction is suitable for bank financing.

The corollary view is held that since banks are engaged in granting credit, they should not grant money capital; that is, they should not undertake to finance the fixed assets of borrowers, certainly not by means of credit creation. However, virtually all members of the Qualitative School have taken the position that a bank may undertake the financing of fixed assets to the extent that it possesses resources in the form of its own capital and to the extent that it controls savings deposits. Thus Dunkman said, "every bank has some real savings in the form of capital and surplus which may properly be used for the purchase of capital goods" and "it will also have some 'real' savings deposits" and in addition, "there may be a more or less fixed percentage of other deposits which are never withdrawn." [27]

Beckhart proposed a similar formula: "Book credits should result solely from the granting of self-liquidating commercial loans," and, if this policy is followed, "the permanent working and fixed capital required by business concerns would be supplied from savings and not from book credit extensions." [28] Capital assets, including investments, security loans, and real estate mortgage loans, would be permitted against receipt of "savings accounts" and "slow-moving accounts" (i. e., funds awaiting investment either as time or demand deposits, working capital funds of business concerns, and funds held with banks to enjoy the remittance privilege). James's rule is slightly different:

> The commercial banking system should extend such self-liquidating loans to business to an amount equal to the difference, at any moment of time, between the aggregate demand deposits and the amount of the minimum income balances. The rest of the portfolio can be composed of other types of assets.[29]

Qualitative theorists have employed various arguments in defense of this formulation of portfolio policy. Their reasoning is based upon the following considerations: (1) The banking system will possess greater inherent liquidity; (2) the rapid turnover of bank assets will permit frequent testing

[27] William E. Dunkman, *Qualitative Credit Control* (New York, 1933), p. 295.

[28] B. H. Beckhart, *Qualitative Credit Control*, pp. 3–5.

[29] Cyril F. James, *The Economics of Money, Credit and Banking* (2d ed.; New York, 1935).

of the basis of credit; (3) bank credit will exert small effect upon prices; (4) banks will avoid the risk that investment will not return sufficient earnings to justify it; and finally (5) such a policy will provide a well-ordered supply of the means of payment since credit will be adapted "to the value of exchangeable goods" (Dunkman).

THE LIQUIDITY OF THE BANKING SYSTEM

Qualitative theorists have argued that the restriction of the basis of created bank credit to self-liquidating assets would insure the banking system, as well as the individual bank, of the ability to contract the volume of credit in time of necessity. To this various critics have replied (1) that commercial loans, or self-liquidating loans, in the aggregate, are not liquid; and (2) that other types of bank assets are equally liquid by virtue of being traded on organized securities markets, or by central bank intervention.

The first point, that self-liquidating loans in the aggregate are not liquid, has been made by writers such as Anderson, Moulton, Mitchell, Currie, and Machlup.[30] However, the argument that other kinds of assets may be made equally liquid has not been underwritten by all critics of the self-liquidating theory. Thus, for example, Hardy and Machlup confined their criticism to demonstrating that neither working capital nor fixed capital loans are liquid in the aggregate or in times of crisis.

According to Moulton, it is impossible for a bank to compel a large number of loans to be paid, and therefore the fate of commercial loans is not greatly different, if at all, from collateral loans or investments in bonds and stocks.[31] Anderson contended in his early writings that the only commercial loans which possessed real liquidity were those which could be paid off without disappointing the reasonable expectations of the borrower.[32] Currie went so far as to allege that it is easier to contract security loans and investments, owing to the superior marketability of stocks and bonds over commodities, and because bank funds furnish only a portion of the market for stocks and bonds, while they furnish virtually the entire market for

[30] B. M. Anderson, *The Value of Money* (New York, 1917), p. 502.
H. G. Moulton, "Commercial Banking and Capital Formation," *Quarterly Journal of Economics*, XXVI (1918), 648 ff.
Waldo F. Mitchell, *The Uses of Bank Funds* (Chicago, 1925), *passim*.
Charles O. Hardy, *Credit Policies of the Federal Reserve System* (Washington, D.C., 1932), p. 329.
Lauchlin Currie, *The Supply and Control of Money in the United States* (Cambridge, Mass., 1935), pp. 38, 112.
Fritz Machlup, *The Stock Market, Credit, and Capital Formation* (New York, 1940), pp. 203 ff.

[31] Moulton, *op. cit.*, p. 648.

[32] Anderson, *op. cit.*, p. 502.

commercial loans.[33] In similar fashion, Anderson contended that the corporate organization of business, coupled with the growth of stock exchanges and a large body of active speculators, had given liquidity to credit instruments representing fixed capital, and, by reason of this circumstance, that modern banking derives its liquidity from the securities markets.[34] Incidentally, Anderson believed that the shift from a direct to a more indirect way of financing the business community meant that the function of risk-bearing and the creation of bank credit had been differentiated and the risk shifted from banks to others, e. g., to the speculators in securities.

Morton reached the conclusion that since the enactment of the Banking Act of 1935, liquidity and solvency have become practically the same thing, since "it now appears that institutional, legal, or conventional liquidity, in the form of rediscountability or convertibility, is the only feasible arrangement." [35] This is tantamount to the assertion that liquidity of the banking system can be maintained by the issuance of central bank credit.

Anderson, Mitchell, and Currie, as well as other believers in shiftability of bank assets, have been grossly in error in asserting the superiority of stocks and bonds over self-liquidating assets. Of course, the development of organized securities exchanges has given to a large variety of credit instruments marketability and mobility which they did not formerly possess. Nevertheless, the liquidity of banks' assets of this character depends upon the readiness of non-bank buyers to absorb such securities in the event that banks find it necessary to liquidate them. The ability to shift assets to non-bank buyers has not relieved the banks of risk; rather it has subjected them to a somewhat different kind of risk, viz., the risk that there will be found no large body of buyers ready at all times to absorb the securities offered by banks. Indeed, the banks have become subject to a money market risk, in addition to the credit risk inherent in a capitalistic society. Only to the extent that speculators operate with their own capital, and are therefore able to absorb losses, would this risk be reduced. Certainly this would not be true were these speculators as a group financed to a large extent by bank credit as they have been in the American system.

It does not appear that the advocates of self-liquidating assets ever denied categorically that all bank assets in times of crisis, when liquidation is attempted *en masse,* are liquid without central bank aid. Indeed, one aim of the original Federal Reserve Act was to give to self-liquidating assets the additional quality of shiftability.

There are important half-truths hidden in the arguments of the oppo-

[33] Currie, *op. cit.*, p. 112.
[34] Anderson, *op. cit.*, p. 517.
[35] Walter A. Morton, "Liquidity and Solvency," *American Economic Review,* XXIX, No. 2 (June, 1939), 283.

nents of the self-liquidating theory cited above. These are that, whereas formerly commercial loans to customers of banks were automatically tied to specific business transactions, the practice has fallen into disuse and loans have become more continuous, as Moulton noted. As regards shiftability, securities played a relatively insignificant role in the period of early capitalism, as Suviranta observed, and their marketability could not well be relied upon.[36] Later, as a result of the development of the corporation and of the stock exchanges, important categories of investment assets gained a high degree of marketability and have in this respect totally outdistanced the bulk of commercial assets. However, the thesis that in normal times all kinds of assets are liquid, while in crises none are, is "a photographic snapshot of two deliberately chosen moments of a cyclical period" which cannot show "the dynamic forces working beneath the surface." [37]

THE LIQUIDITY OF WORKING CAPITAL

The liquidity theory is not entirely concerned with raising funds in time of crisis. "It presents a much broader approach to the whole problem of banking policy and is intimately related to the process of capital formation." [38] The liquidity theory rests on the distinction between fixed and circulating capital, and this, in turn, is related by various writers to the liquidity and solvency of the banks and to the regulation of the money supply.

Advocates of self-liquidating loans, in recommending that commercial bank loans should be limited in terms of purpose to the fluctuating portion of a borrower's working capital, have implied that working capital is more liquid than fixed capital. Other writers objected that, from the standpoint of the system as a whole, neither working capital nor fixed capital is liquid, although it maybe true, from the individual point of view, that working capital can be released while fixed capital cannot be. The working capital of one entrepreneur can only be released if his assets are bought by a second. Therefore, it is said, the aggregate working capital for the system as a whole remains "invested" even though it may be turned over. Similarly, if production is assumed unchanged, the distinction between working capital and fixed capital, based upon the complete amortization of working capital within a production period as compared to partial amortization of fixed capital, is invalid. As raw materials are used they must be replenished, and, as fixed capital wears out, it must be replaced. This means that the proceeds from the turnover of working capital must be reinvested and not used for

[36] Br. Suviranta, "The Shiftability Theory of Bank Liquidity," in *Economic Essays in Honour of Gustav Cassel* (London, 1933), pp. 623–35.

[37] *Ibid.*

[38] James, *op. cit.*, p. 499.

the repayment of loans; proceeds from depreciation allowances must be reinvested to maintain the fixed capital equipment. Thus, working capital and fixed capital are alike in that they will be turned over but cannot be repaid as long as the scale of operations is maintained.[39]

However, the above argument overlooks the fact that in either seasonal or cyclical depression of business activity, the scale of operations is not being maintained. Under such conditions, the working capital loan is more easily liquidated, since it can more quickly and directly yield receipts which can be applied to repayment. Besides, in depression the decline in working capital is seldom catastrophic, since "goods were always being exchanged at one end of the line, in order to meet the demands of consumers, while cash was always being spent, at the other end, to purchase raw materials and pay workers." [40]

Even in depression, people must still eat food, consume fuel, and wear clothes (although the volume of their consumption may be reduced), and there is no reason at all why they should purchase either capital equipment or securities.[41] Even in the most severe depressions, such as that of 1929–33, production did not come to a complete standstill, and the economic system still continued to turn over goods in process and to move a considerable body of goods forward toward consumption, albeit a reduced volume. The ratio of the volume of working to fixed capital declined, but this was itself a reflection of the fact that working capital had been liquidated and that funds recovered from liquidation were used to retire bank loans. In addition, it was observed in Chapter V that during the 1929–33 depression, depreciation charges in excess of the actual consumption of fixed assets permitted recovery of funds and made them available for the repayment of loans.

THE RISK OF LOSS ON FIXED ASSETS

Qualitative theory avers that bank credit should not be extended for the financing of fixed assets. The reasons are based upon two major considerations: (1) Banks should not bear the risk that investment will not return sufficient earnings to justify itself; (2) unless such assets are financed with savings, the relationship between goods and credit, i. e., prices, will be disturbed.

In support of the first point, qualitative theorists have enjoyed agreement with a number of writers who do not necessarily subscribe to their other postulates. Thus, for example, Hawtrey maintained that "long term investments are liable to an indefinite capital depreciation, and consequently the banker needs short-term investments, not merely to help him in main-

[39] Machlup, *op. cit.*, p. 208.

[40] Cyril F. James, *op. cit.* (3d ed.), p. 568.

[41] *Ibid.*

taining cash payments, but to keep him solvent."[42] Cassel considered liquidity of importance because it enables banks "quickly to adapt their advances to the solvency of customers, to changes in conditions in the various branches of industry, and also to changes in the quality of the real security offered to them."[43]

From a price standpoint, the fact that losses involved in the liquidation of working capital may be smaller than those involved in the liquidation of fixed capital is an important consideration for the repayment of bank loans. As regards the "specificity" of goods, goods embodied in working capital will be more easily sold and turned over than will goods embodied in fixed investments. Furthermore,

> The loss of value is usually in inverse proportion to the number of uses to which goods can be put. Since fixed capital goods mostly consist of a type of capital that is least capable of being used for a purpose other than that for which it was originally intended, they are the ones that are most likely subject to capital losses.[44]

Robertson conceived of the function of banks as being that of providing the necessary "savings" through an expansion of bank credit. In Robertson's terminology the function of banks is, by suitable credit policy, to force or induce "lacking" so as to secure the application of lacking necessary to maintain investment. Qualitative writers have objected that this would imperil the banks by forcing upon them the assumption of risk arising out of the unproductiveness of the investment and the consequent need for revalorization of bank assets.[45]

The fundamental difference of opinion as to the function of banks and their proper policy is resolved into the question whether banks should be made active agents in equating investment with savings, or whether banks should only play an inactive part. It is evident that Willis, Dunkman, Beckhart, and other writers of their persuasion believe that the banking system should play only a passive part in this process, while Schumpeter, Keynes, Hawtrey, Robertson, and others conceive of it as playing an active role.

THE RELATION OF THE FINANCING OF WORKING AND FIXED CAPITAL TO PRICE DISTURBANCES

In order to prevent the banks from causing misdirections in investment and price instability, qualitative theorists have favored the restriction of

[42] Quoted in Dunkman, *op. cit.*, pp. 297 ff.

[43] Gustav Cassel, *The Theory of Social Economy*, tr. by S. L. Barron (new rev. ed.; New York, 1932), p. 429.

[44] Machlup, *op. cit.*, pp. 203, 256.

[45] Dunkman, *op. cit.*, p. 299.

bank financing to the volume of savings which are channeled through banks. This, Dunkman argued, would satisfy Keynes's fundamental description that:

> The conditions for equilibrium of purchasing power of money require that the banking system should so regulate its rate of lending that the value of Investment is equal to Savings.[46]

as well as Cassel's formula that,

> Demands for Capital must, by means of the rates of interest of the banks, be limited to the amounts of funds, supplied by current savings, so that no artificial purchasing power, with its accompanying rise of prices will be created.[47]

It is to be observed, however, that the essential difference between Dunkman, on the one hand, and Keynes and Cassel on the other, is that Dunkman believed that equilibrium could only be achieved by preventing the banks from expanding credit for fixed capital purposes, whereas most monetary theorists have advocated positive manipulation of bank credit in order to effect the equilibrium.

It is the belief of qualitative writers that loans based on goods which are intended to be sold will have less tendency to affect prices. The time between borrowing and repayment will be small, so that despite the fact that, from the point of view of the community as a whole, all extensions of credit result in a temporary increase in the amount of "money" over goods, the less the time between borrowing and repayment the less will be the effect on prices, and conversely.

> Therefore, when bank credit is extended for the purpose of acquiring capital goods for ownership, there is an increase in the demand for goods and in the total amount of credit in the community, which is not liquidated until the borrower offers something to sell. If what is offered for sale is the product of the use of the capital equipment itself, a relatively long time must elapse between the borrowing and repayment. . . . Credit, therefore, which is extended on the basis of capital goods has an inherent tendency to cause fluctuations in the level of prices.[48]

REGULATION OF THE SUPPLY OF MONEY

One of the fundamental principles underlying the liquidity theory is the principle that,

> working capital loans to business enterprises place the latter in temporary possession of a portion of the nation's circulating capital funds, and, in order that these funds may circulate smoothly and efficiently, the loan should be repaid at the time at which the borrower receives the proceeds

[46] *Ibid.*, quoted on p. 298. [47] *Ibid.* [48] *Ibid.*, p. 297.

> of the sale of his goods, thus rendering the funds available for a new loan.[49]

It is thus that the monetary counterpart of working capital is kept adjusted to the real volume of circulating capital.

Even Cassel, who is not ordinarily regarded as a qualitative credit theorist, asserted the importance of liquid bank assets to the proper regulation of the money supply. In his opinion, the covering of bank money by circulating capital is important because this "renders bank money especially suitable as a means of payment," [50] since by far the greatest employment of the means of payment consists precisely in payments for circulating capital, advancing in the process of production towards the consumer. It is also important "because in this way the community's supply of money is adapted to the changing volume of production." [51] Cassel argued that the cover for bank money should not only consider protective quality, but,

> the nature of the cover required . . . should provide a natural limitation on the supply of the means of payment. The total production of a community, but not the total wealth of a community, is suitable, but the supply of securities is not, because these represent fixed capital or mere promises to pay.[52]

Willis was one of the leading exponents of the view that the desirability of self-liquidating commercial assets rests broadly upon the regulation of the supply of money. Thus he said:

> A difference between this kind of credit operation on one hand and commercial credit on the other may be found in the fact that, whereas reimbursement or liquidation of commercial credit comes from the interchange of existing goods or goods which are on the point of being rendered consumable, investment credit may eventually be liquidated as a result of savings made through the increase of productive power. Both interest and principal will be repaid to those who have advanced current funds only in case of a real increase in wealth resulting from the productive operation.[53]

Where banks find it necessary to shift assets to the central bank because of overextensions of investment credit which became frozen,

> there is no provision for the ultimate regulation of the volume of credit which, in the last analysis, is dependent upon the actual amount of useful production. The action of a Reserve Bank in rediscounting, for instance, if not based upon the probability that the paper rediscounted will be paid out of the proceeds of human labor and consumption, is not it-

[49] James, *op. cit.* (2d ed.), p. 501.
[50] Cassel, *op. cit.*, p. 501.
[51] *Ibid.*, p. 433.
[52] *Ibid.*
[53] Willis and Edwards, *op. cit.*, p. 24.

self controlled by any definite principles and is regulated merely by the movement of values in the investment market.[54]

Naturally, most adherents to the theory of managed money do not view favorably the proposals of the qualitative school regarding the qualitative limitation of the basis of bank credit, for the obvious reason that such limitation is incompatible with the regulation of the supply of money in accordance with other criteria, such as the manipulation of the price level, the interest rate, or the financing of government deficits. Few writers in the field of monetary theory have taken any pains to refute the principle of self-liquidation, other than to assert that their own theories are superior, or that self-liquidating assets are not liquid anyway. It is apparent, however, that most of them believe that the ability of debtors to repay loans to banks is a function of the total supply of money. Thus, in Currie's view, the amount of circulating capital which "the banks may safely finance depends upon the relation of the total amount of money and the real income of the community." [55] Sayers avers that the question whether the transaction enables the debtor to repay, depends on the price which the sale of the commodity realizes, and this, he said, depends upon the supply of money.[56]

The self-liquidating loan thesis has been attacked on still other grounds. The contention has been made that credit cannot be limited to the working capital requirements of the community. Machlup, for example, argues that, if borrowers could have obtained funds, the effect of the new creation of credit is independent of the concrete use to which a particular credit is put, since the real beneficiary of the increase in the supply is a borrower who was previously excluded from the market, but who is now able to obtain funds and who remains *in concreto* unknown.[57] Under conditions of full employment, it is argued that credit will be more likely to find employment in fixed capital where interest as a cost factor is more important than in the case of working capital. Under conditions of less than full employment, an increase in working capital might take place with any increase in fixed capital if production could be extended within the limits allowed by the existing fixed capital equipment.

Thus, it is said, even if bank loans were limited to finance working capital or goods in process, the granting of such credit frees funds which were previously tied up in the running of the business, and the borrower can now undertake investments which he plans with funds of his own. Hence the concrete visible use to which new credit is put is not in any way identi-

[54] Willis, Chapman, and Robey, *Contemporary Banking* (New York, 1933), pp. 296–97.
[55] Currie, *op. cit.*, p. 36.
[56] R. S. Sayers, *Modern Banking* (London, 1938), pp. 219–20.
[57] Machlup, *op. cit.*, p. 251.

cal with the investment which the credit has *de facto* made it possible to realize. Furthermore, credit which the entrepreneur borrows for himself in the first instance may be relent to others in the form of trade credit, and make it possible for this firm to embark on investment. Besides, the entrepreneur may be rendered better able to buy more on a cash basis and so enable the firms which directly or indirectly supply him with materials to undertake investments; finally, new bank credit may release some other credit, and by easing the general credit market make possible investment elsewhere at some indeterminable point in the system.[58]

To this type of argument, the qualitative theorists have answered that inability to direct the flow of credit is not so much an objection to qualitative control as it is to quantitative control. Qualitative control is concerned with preventing inflation of credit through admission of goods to exchange at a higher valuation than the market may ultimately place on them. It is argued that if banks perform the credit analysis function properly and deny credit based upon an inflation of accounts receivable, that banks will prevent the reloan of the credit granted to secondary borrowers. Furthermore, it is argued that bank credit is not a homogeneous mass tantamount to money and competitive with all other supplies of funds. Under the prescription of qualitative analysis, bank credit by limitation would not be of this neutral or even fungible character; while in the aggregate the supply of bank credit would be limited by specific criteria not operative with respect to other supplies of loanable funds.[59]

FUNCTIONAL SEGREGATION OF BANKING

Qualitative writers all seem agreed that it is desirable to restrict the creation of book credit by banks to self-liquidating transactions, but they are not opposed to permitting banks to engage in non-self-liquidating transactions, such as the financing of fixed assets, provided the lending banks control savings deposits or capital funds of their own in sufficient amounts. Thus the position is taken that extension of bank credit should be functionally separated from the investment of savings.[60] In Beckhart's words, "Credit inflation can be avoided only if the functions of the banks, the lending and the capital formation functions, are each confined to their proper sphere and do not encroach one on the other."[61] Willis said that "it

[58] *Ibid.*, p. 257.

[59] Dunkman, *op. cit.*, pp. 320–21.

[60] It is this separation of function which some monetary theorists do not believe it is possible to distinguish. For example, Thomas says, "It is not possible to distinguish between Banks' functions as creators of money and as investors of savings, because both functions operate together." (Thomas, *op. cit.*, p. 196).

[61] B. H. Beckhart, *Qualitative Credit Control*, p. 22.

is highly desirable, in a planned society, that banking and credit should not be allowed to operate simultaneously in investment and commercial credit extensions." [62] Garlock is one of the few qualitative writers who appears to have made a positive recommendation for functional specialization of banking.[63] From a practical standpoint, it does not seem possible that the functional separation of commercial and investment credit, or of self-liquidating and non-self-liquidating credit, can be realized without actual legal and physical segregation of banks, even assuming that clear criteria can be formulated by which to test the quality of prospective loans.

As long as deposit creation is carried on in the same institutions which make loans for fixed capital purposes, even though limited to the savings deposits and capital funds of the given bank, the various loan markets will continue to be competitive and, as Machlup argued, it will not be possible to say what the eventual employment of created credit will be. The fact is that banks for years have extended more noncommercial and more non-self-liquidating credit than they have granted self-liquidating credit, and there can be little question that, from the standpoint of the lender, both kinds of credit are competitive. Furthermore, from the standpoint of the banking system as a whole, all deposit credits, including time and savings deposits, at some point in the past were issued by banks against the acquisition of assets. The banking system is the original source of *all* deposit credits; the primary deposits of one bank were at some earlier point the derived deposits of another bank. Therefore, the distinction between primary and derived deposits which is made by qualitative writers in order to differentiate the active and passive aspects of bank operations is not valid for the system as a whole. As long as the system operates upon the basis of fractional reserve requirements, and as long as the behavior of the individual bank is guided proximately by its reserve position, i. e., by what other banks are doing, the total quantity of deposits outstanding in the system will not be subject to a sequence which places the receipt of deposits temporally ahead of the utilization of funds.

The only way, therefore, in which to effectuate a complete separation of functions, in this author's opinion, would be through an institutional segregation of banks into those which have the power to create book credit in the form of demand deposits subject to transfer by check, and those which may only receive deposits. It would be necessary to limit credit extension of the former class of banks to self-liquidating loans, while the latter class of banks would be free to advance funds for fixed capital purposes. Under

[62] Willis, Chapman, and Robey, *op. cit.*, pp. 774–75.

[63] Fred L. Garlock, *Country Banking in Wisconsin during the Depression*, United States Department of Agriculture Technical Bulletin No. 777, July, 1941, p. 107.

these conditions, individual borrowers could only acquire additional deposit balances when some other holder consented, or was forced, to give them up, unless the borrower could show evidence of engaging in self-liquidating transactions. If this separation were effected, the self-liquidating loan market might be shut off from other loan markets on the supply side, since there would be no competition with voluntary savings except for a special class of risks. Under these conditions, overissue of bank credit might be prevented, since credit would be limited in aggregate volume to an amount commensurate with the demand for money as a means of payment.

Owing to their preoccupation with the coördination of the current supply of money with the circulation of goods, qualitative theorists have failed to consider the possible usefulness of banks as agents of dynamic change. In any event, they do not give adequate consideration to the part which banks should play during periods of change, other than those of a seasonal nature. Limitation of assets to those which are self-liquidating may provide an ideal policy for a stationary society in which operations are essentially repetitive, but it does indicate what banking policy is called for under conditions of growth or cyclical instability.

On the other hand, it has already been shown that monetary theorists have an entirely different conception of the functions of banks, because they regard them as instruments for financing development, for balancing the disequilibrium between savings and investment, etc. Such theories, with few exceptions, regard as inconsequential the purpose for which credit is to be created. It seems clear that if there is to be no discrimination in the functional employment of credit in individual transactions, steps must be taken to strengthen and fortify the banking system against the results of overexpansion. It will be indicated that these steps entail, not only central bank intervention to provide artificial liquidity, but the strongest kind of nonmonetary measures to sterilize the inflationary potential induced by creations of money, and to facilitate the shifting and absorption of losses which otherwise will destroy the foundation of the banking system and precipitate its failure.

Chapter VII

THE CHANGING CHARACTER OF COMMERCIAL BANKING

THE NATURE of commercial banking in the United States has undergone such radical changes since the First World War that today the adjective "commercial" seems strangely inappropriate. These changes were not altogether the result of the business depression of 1929–33, since they were operative long before that; [1] nor were they confined to the United States.[2] This chapter endeavors to examine some of the reasons for these changes and as far as possible to show their implications to the future administration of the banking system.

In the course of this chapter it will be shown that the decline in the commercial character of banking was due in much less degree to the effect of technological change upon the requirements of the business system for working and fixed capital, than to changes in the techniques by which borrowers raised their money capital. Alterations in financial technique, in turn, are found to have resulted in part from technological change, but also from the great increase in the total supply of bank credit and its injection at new points in the economic system. The increase in the noncommercial nature of banks assets signifies a fundamental revision in the basis of bank credit creation for which adequate provision must be made if the banking system is to be kept in working order in the future.

[1] B. M. Anderson writing in 1917 said: "In traditional discussions of banking, the impression is given that commercial paper is the normal and dominant type of banking assets. . . . The great bulk of banking credit in the United States, even of 'commercial' banks, is not commercial credit. Much of it, in the smaller places, especially, represents in fact, whatever form, long time advances to agriculture and industry." See B. M. Anderson, Jr., *The Value of Money* (New York, 1917), p. 501.

[2] See League of Nations "Money and Banking 1938/39," I, *Monetary Review,* pp. 83–84, for comparisons of major asset groups of commercial banks expressed as percentage of the total balance sheet of banks in various countries 1913, 1925, and 1929. See also: J. Douglas Gibson, "The Changing Character of Bank Assets," *Canadian Banker,* XLV, No. 1 (October, 1937), pp. 145–54.

THE COMPOSITION OF THE ASSETS AND LIABILITIES OF COMMERCIAL BANKS[3]

The most cursory inspection of Table 4 for all commercial banks reveals that radical changes have taken place in the nature of bank credit during the twenty-year period 1920–40. The table reveals a great relative increase in the proportion of banking resources devoted to securities investments, especially government obligations; a relative contraction of loans and discounts by which their ratio to total resources was cut more than in half; and a relative growth in the proportion of cash and due from banks.[4] On the liability side of the balance sheet, it is apparent that bank capital has become less important in financing the assets of banks, while deposits have become correspondingly more important.

THE DECLINE IN LOANS

The total loan volume is made up of several categories which in Table 5 on page 101 for national banks have been divided into loans commercial in form, loans noncommercial in form, and real estate loans.

The most significant change occurred in the commercial loan category. Whereas the total loan volume rose during the 1920s owing mainly to the tremendous growth in loans based on securities and real estate loans, com-

[3] Presentation of the statistical movements of various types of bank assets as well as analysis of their implications are to be found in such works as the following:

H. Parker Willis and J. M. Chapman, *The Banking Situation* (New York, 1934).

Pearson Hunt, *Portfolio Policies of Commercial Banks in the United States, 1920–1939* (Cambridge, Mass., 1940) Harvard University Graduate School of Business Administration, "Business Research Studies," No. 24.

Temporary National Economic Committee, Hearings, *Investigation of Concentration of Economic Power,* Part IX, "Savings and Investment," pp. 3746 ff.

Board of Governors of the Federal Reserve System, *Federal Reserve Charts on Bank Credit, Money Rates, and Business,* and *Banking Studies* (1941), p. 177.

American Bankers Association, *The Earning Power of Banks* (1939), and *Changes in Bank Earning Assets* (1936).

Allyn Abbott Young, *An Analysis of Bank Statistics* (Cambridge, Mass., 1928).

Comprehensive data relating to the changing composition of bank assets in foreign countries are available in the publications of the League of Nations. See *Commercial Banks 1913–1929,* pp. 14–24; *Commercial Banks 1929–1934,* pp. xxxv–xlii; and "Money and Banking 1938–39," I, *Monetary Review,* 82–95.

[4] Absolute changes in billions of dollars in various asset items of all commercial banks were as follows:

	1920	*1929*	*1937*	*1940*
Cash and due from banks	8.1	9.0	15.0	24.6
Loans and discounts	28.1	35.6	17.5	17.4
Investments in securities	8.5	13.6	22.1	23.8
Miscellaneous assets	2.5	3.5	2.3	2.0
Total assets	47.2	61.7	56.9	67.8

TABLE 4

PERCENTAGE DISTRIBUTION OF ASSETS AND LIABILITIES OF ALL OPERATING COMMERCIAL BANKS IN THE UNITED STATES AND POSSESSIONS, SELECTED YEARS, 1920–40 [a]

As of June 30

	1920 [b]	*1929* [b]	*1937* [c]	*1940* [c]
Assets:				
Cash and amounts due from banks	17.2	14.7	26.4	37.1
Obligations of United States Government	7.9	8.0	25.7	24.3
Other securities	10.1	14.0	13.2	10.1
Loans and discounts	59.6	57.7	30.7	25.8
Fixed and miscellaneous assets	5.2	5.6	4.0	2.7
Total	100.0	100.0	100.0	100.0
Liabilities:				
Total deposits	77.4	79.3	86.9	89.7
Miscellaneous liabilities	10.9	6.6	1.3	0.8
Total capital accounts	11.7	14.1	11.8	9.5
Total liabilities plus capital accounts	100.0	100.0	100.0	100.0

[a] Source: *Annual Report of the Federal Deposit Insurance Corporation* (1940), p. 43.

[b] Based on figures published by the Comptroller of the Currency for "All Active Banks" in *Annual Report* (1940), p. 320.

[c] See *Annual Report of the Federal Deposit Insurance Corporation* (1940), Table 118, p. 140.

mercial loans began to decline in the early 1920s, slowly at first, but rapidly after 1929, and reached a low plateau in the 1933–35 period from which they had recovered moderately by the outbreak of the Second World War. For national banks, loans commercial in form declined from 75 percent of loans in 1920 to 48 percent in 1939.[5] Moreover, approximately one quarter of the loans commercial in form were presumed in 1939 to be of a non-commercial character, since their maturities were over one year in duration.[6] Such "term" loans expanded rapidly during the latter half of the

[5] In order to measure the volume of commercial loans, many writers employ the "all other loan" series (prior to 1938) and the "commercial, industrial, and agricultural loan" series (since 1938) of the official classifications of the Comptroller of the Currency and the Board of Governors of the Federal Reserve System. Hunt's series, however, seems superior, in that it includes additional loan classifications.

[6] See *Federal Reserve Bulletin,* July, 1939, "Term Loans by Banks to Commercial and Industrial Concerns," pp. 560–62. This article summarizes the results of a special analysis based on reports from member banks in 101 leading cities submitting condition statements and, therefore, covering about four hundred banks holding approximately 70 percent of the commercial, industrial, and agricultural loans of all member banks. Of ap-

TABLE 5

LOANS AND DISCOUNTS OF NATIONAL BANKS, SELECTED YEARS, 1920–39 [a]

As of June 30

	1920	1929	1939
In Millions of Dollars			
Loans commercial in form	10,264	7,909	4,096
Loans noncommercial in form	3,118	5,114	2,624
Real estate loans	230	1,413	1,829
Total loans	13,611	14,436	8,549
In Percentages of Total Earning Assets			
Loans commercial in form	75.4	54.8	47.9
Loans noncommercial in form	22.9	35.4	30.7
Real estate loans	1.7	9.8	21.4
Total loans	100.0	100.0	100.0

[a] Source: Pearson Hunt, *Portfolio Policies of Commercial Banks in the United States 1920–1939* (Cambridge, Mass., 1940), Harvard University Graduate School of Business Administration, "Business Research Studies," No. 24, Exhibit C.

1930s. They represent the extension of commercial or industrial credit for intermediate capital purpose repayable on an installment basis over periods running typically five years. The rise of this type of loan reflects, not only an effort by banks in their search for earnings to compete with the capital market, but also, from the borrowers' standpoint, the desire to obtain cheap financing without the onerous burden of registration of publicly offered securities. This development is of major significance in indicating the possibilities of revision in the traditional practices of commercial banks in lending only on short term. The term loan indicates one possible way in which the bank lending machinery may be adjusted to accommodate large-sized corporations which, during recent decades, have resorted to new techniques for obtaining money capital.[7]

proximately $3,900,000,000 of commercial, industrial, and agricultural loans outstanding on April 19, 1939, about $1,000,000,000 had a maturity, when originally made, of one year or more. (In addition, about $170,000,000 of loans secured by real estate were made by these banks to commercial and industrial businesses for periods of one year or more.) It is noteworthy that about 70 percent of the total dollar amount of such loans had original maturities of three years or more.

[7] Reasons for the rise of term loans are to be found in the following:

Association of Reserve City Bankers, *Term Loans of Commercial Banks* (1938).

Hearings, Committee on Interstate and Foreign Commerce, United States House of Representatives, 77th Cong., 1st Sess., *Proposed Amendments to the Securities Act of*

Since 1929 the commercial banks have undertaken on an increasing scale the extension of consumer cash loans directly through the establishment of personal loan departments, through the discounting of sales finance paper, and indirectly by loans to other consumer-financing agencies. These types of loans have not been separately classified by the reporting agencies, but special investigations indicate that direct and indirect extensions of consumer credit have been substantial.[8]

The decline in total loans was due, of course, only in part to the decline in commercial loans. After a tremendous expansion in the 1920s, loans to brokers, and other types of loans collateraled by securities, underwent a

---

1933 and to the Securities and Exchange Act of 1934, Part II, Committee print, November 7–19, 1941, pp. 527–44.

H. G. Moulton, *Financial Organization and the Economic System* (New York, 1938), p. 323.

[8] It is estimated that at the end of 1940 aggregate consumer debt in the United States was $27,600,000,000, of which 70 percent represented long-term debt held against real estate and home construction. Of the remainder, credit extended for a period of longer than three months for purchasing goods at retail and which is repayable on a deferred payment basis amounted to $5,000,000,000, of which $3,100,000,000 was in the form of retail installment credit and $1,900,000,000 represented cash loans to consumers made by banks and other cash-lending agencies. Cash loan credit by commercial banks at the end of 1940 was reported at $581,000,000 as compared with approximately $30,000,000 at the low point in 1933. Total cash loan credit by all agencies rose from about $400,-000,000 to $1,900,000,000 at the end of 1940. These data are based on figures from the Bureau of Foreign and Domestic Commerce, *Survey of Current Business,* September, 1941, pp. 9–10; and the National Bureau of Economic Research, *The Volume of Consumer Installment Credit, 1929–1938,* Bulletin No. 79, September 1, 1940, pp. 9–12.

According to the 1939 *Census of Business,* "Sales Finance Companies and Bank Holdings of Installment Paper," p. 40, personal loan departments of commercial banks had outstandings in the amount of $310,000,000 at the end of 1939. In addition there were $541,000,000 of installment indebtedness representing discount of sales finance paper, not including direct loans to sales finance companies, personal finance companies, and industrial banks. It is indicated that the sum of personal loans and installment paper, $824,000,000, was 7.4 percent of the sum of the total of "loans commercial in form" plus "all other loans," $11,058,000,000. This was roughly 5 percent of total loans, discounts, and overdrafts. If anything like these proportions obtained in previous years, it would seem that fluctuations in consumer loans might account for significant changes in Hunt's commercial loans series. For growth in commercial bank credit extended by personal loan departments, see National Bureau of Economic Research, *op. cit.,* p. 9. The volume of commercial banks' indirect financing of consumer installment credit was undoubtedly considerable. Chapman found that at the end of 1937, 181 large banks situated in the principal commercial centers of the country had a total of $505,000,000 in outstanding loans to sale finance companies, personal finance companies, and other consumer credit agencies, and a total of $254,000,000 at the end of 1938. See John M. Chapman, *Commercial Banks and Consumer Installment Credit* (New York, 1940), p. 25. It is clearly apparent that a large part of the so-called commercial and industrial loans and, in years prior to 1938, "all other loans," consisted of direct or indirect extension of consumer credit. Furthermore, changes in the volume of borrowing by various consumer financing agencies from commercial banks at times exercised a marked effect upon the volume of reported "commercial and industrial" loans.

severe deflation in 1929–33 which carried them to a low level from which no significant recovery has been experienced. Real estate loans recovered somewhat from their depression lows but have not regained their former volume.

It would be enlightening to know what portion of the loans was extended for working capital purposes as well as the portion which was self-liquidating in nature. Unfortunately, the published data do not permit such estimates to be made, since no relevant criterion of classification is observed. However, there is no doubt that there has been a decline in the volume of self-liquidating loans and in loans for working capital purposes, and a larger relative allocation of bank credit to non-self-liquidating purposes including fixed asset financing. This transition has been furthered since the advent of the "term" loan method of financing the permanent working capital requirements of large corporations. The decline in the self-liquidating character of loans was evident in the early 1920s in the growing volume of real estate loans and loans collateraled by securities.[9]

THE RISE OF INVESTMENTS

Additionally, it is to be noted that bank investments in securities grew steadily during the entire period 1920–40. The growth in the 1920s was represented mainly by corporate and foreign bonds and in the 1930s by government bonds almost exclusively, as indicated in Table 6, page 105 for national banks.

FACTORS RESPONSIBLE FOR THE DECLINE IN BANK BORROWINGS BY INDUSTRY[10]

Among the more important separate reasons which have been cited to explain the decline in the volume of commercial and industrial loans are the following:

1. Technological change: the vertical integration of industry; growth in

[9] Moulton had estimated that even as early as 1918 about 50 percent of all loans of national and state banks and trust companies was devoted to investment uses, and that, including indirect investment, about two thirds of all credits extended by commercial banks went for fixed capital rather than working capital. See H. G. Moulton, "Commercial Banks and Capital Formation," *Quarterly Journal of Economics*, Vol. XXVI, 1918. Anderson, who applied much more severe criteria as to what constituted "commercial" character, found that banks extended over two and one-half times as much credit at a given time to the security market as they did to commerce. His data indicate that over 60 percent of the total credit extended by banks was noncommercial in character. See Anderson, *op. cit.*, p. 509. Both writers applied very strict criteria which, if employed today, would mean that commercial loans are virtually nonexistent.

[10] A partial list of works dealing with this subject includes the following:

Hunt, *op. cit.*

Gurden Edwards, *Changes in Bank Earning Assets* (New York, 1936).

unit size of individual firms; improvements in transportation and communications; and reduction in seasonal variations.

2. Corporate policy with respect to the purchase and holding of inventories, as well as the sale of finished goods.

3. New methods of corporation finance and accompanying changes in policy: the development of securities markets; the accumulation of earnings and their reinvestment within the corporation; the accumulation of depreciation reserves in excess of maintenance and replacement expenditures.

4. The development of specialized methods for financing working capital; installment sales finance; discounting of receivables; the growth of consumer credit.

5. Competition of non-bank lenders: the rise of government financial institutions, especially in the field of agricultural finance, and the Federal agency financing of small business.

American Bankers Association, *The Earning Power of Banks* (New York, January, 1939).

Lauchlin Currie, "The Decline of the Commercial Loan," *Quarterly Journal of Economics,* XLV, No. 4 (August, 1931), 698–709.

Lauchlin Currie, *The Supply and Control of Money in the United States* (Cambridge, Mass., 1935), Chap. IV, "The Monetary Theory versus the Commercial Loan Theory of Banking"; also pp. 121–23.

George N. Edwards, *The Evolution of Finance Capitalism* (New York, 1938), pp. 241–44.

W. von Tresckow, *Merchants of Debt: a Study in the Changing Character of American Banking and Its Effect on Securities* (New York, 1936).

O. M. W. Sprague and Randolph Burgess, "Money and Credit and Their Effect on Business," in *Recent Economic Changes* (New York, 1929), II, Chap. X, 657–707.

Melvin T. Copeland, "Marketing," in *Recent Economic Changes* (New York, 1929), I, Chap. V.

R. S. Sayers, *Modern Banking* (London, 1938), pp. 236–45.

H. G. Moulton, "Commercial Banking and Capital Formation," *Journal of Political Economy,* Vol. XXVI, 1918.

H. G. Moulton, *Financial Organization and the Economic System* (New York, 1938). See especially Chap. XXI, "The Changing Character of Commercial Banking."

H. G. Moulton, *The Formation of Capital* (Washington, D.C., 1935), Chaps. VI, VII, and VIII.

H. G. Moulton, G. W. Edwards, J. D. Magee, and Cleona Lewis, *Capital Expansion, Employment and Economic Stability* (Washington, D.C., 1940), especially Chap. III.

Rufus Tucker, "The Growth of Large Corporations and the Formation of Capital," in *Capital Formation and Its Elements* (New York, 1939), pp. 86 ff.

League of Nations, "Money and Banking," *Commercial Banks* and *Monetary Review,* various years.

Albert R. Koch, *The Financing of Large Corporations, 1920–39* (preliminary ms, New York, 1941).

Charles L. Merwin, Jr., *Financing Small Corporations, 1926–1936* (New York, 1942).

J. Douglas Gibson, "The Changing Character of Bank Assets," *Canadian Banker,* XLV, No. 1 (October, 1937), 145–54.

TABLE 6

INVESTMENTS OF NATIONAL BANKS, SELECTED YEARS, 1920–39[a]

As of June 30

In Millions of Dollars

	1920	*1929*	*1939*
United States Government	2,270	2,804	8,770
State, etc.	338	757	1,694
Railroad	416	592	535
Public utility	283	694	478
Other	879	1,809	1,076
	4,186	6,657	12,553

In Percentages of Total Investments

	1920	*1929*	*1939*
United States Government	54.2	42.1	69.9
State, etc.	8.0	11.4	13.5
Railroad	10.0	8.9	4.3
Public utility	6.8	10.4	3.8
Other	21.0	27.2	8.6
	100.0	100.0	100.0

[a] Source: Pearson Hunt, *Portfolio Policies of Commercial Banks in the United States 1920–1929,* Exhibit C.

6. Contraction of foreign trade and the development of new techniques of financing.[11]

Since the tendencies in bank borrowing have not been uniform for all lines of business it is necessary to examine the available information con-

[11] Special reasons have been assigned to explain the decline in the volume of bill financing, especially in European countries. Thus, the League of Nations in *Monetary Review, 1938/39* cited the following reasons: (1) increased self-financing of industry during the postwar years; (2) tendency toward elimination of the wholesale merchant as intermediary, through the process of integration of trade and industry (wholesale merchants were the chief users of such instruments); (3) increased use of telegraphic transfers for making payments between centers which formerly settled by means of bills, a change induced partly by the first two factors and partly by the fourth; (4) development of the overdraft in the place of the bill of exchange, particularly in the Anglo-Saxon countries other than the United States, for purposes of short-term accommodation; and (5) imposition of exchange control in a large number of countries. Some of these factors would also seem to have bearing upon the United States. However, here the bill of exchange and the acceptance never attained the importance which they had abroad. The use of commercial paper was the more common practice, especially prior to the Federal Reserve Act. Reasons for the decline in the volume of commercial paper outstanding seem to be the same as those which explain the decline in the volume of commercial loans. See A. O. Greef, *The Commercial Paper House in the United States* (Cambridge, Mass., 1938), pp. 145–50.

cerning the amount of borrowing by different lines of business before undertaking to evaluate the importance of the factors cited.

THE IMPORTANCE OF BANK BORROWING BY DIFFERENT CLASSES OF INDUSTRY

The bulk of bank borrowing for many years has been by firms engaged in manufacturing and trade, not by those in rail transportation or public utilities. From an early date the railroads and public utility companies were financed by the issuance of stocks and bonds and, to a much lesser extent, by bank loans. Manufacturing corporations, on the other hand, have been much more dependent on bank borrowing. This has been due to different technological characteristics as well as to different trade practices. The two principal elements in working capital explain this. First, the comparatively small volume of inventories carried by public utility and railroad companies rendered them less subject to seasonal variation on this account than was true of manufacturing. Also, railroads and public utilities employed greater proportionate quantities of fixed instruments than did manufacturing. Secondly, the railroads and public utilities have not extended credit to their customers except to a minor extent, whereas in manufacturing, custom and competition encouraged the practice of extending large amounts of trade credit. This has required the carrying of a large volume of receivables in the form of either open accounts or notes. It is because of the nature of its working and fixed capital requirements that manufacturing in the past has been more suited to bank financing than other lines of economic activity.

MEASUREMENT OF THE BANK LOANS OF DIFFERENT CLASSES OF BORROWERS

One of the greatest obstacles confronting an analysis of the relation of commercial banking to the financing of industry has been the lack of data concerning the borrowings of different classes of commercial and industrial borrowers. The bank loan statistics have not been classified by trade or industry, or by size, or by other relevant criterion, so it is necessary to seek this information elsewhere.[12]

On the other hand, the data on business corporations until quite re-

[12] Since this was written, it is of interest to note that on April 14, 1942, the Board of Governors of the Federal Reserve System was reported to have sent questionnaires to member banks seeking information as of May 15, among other things, on the loans extended to thirteen different classifications of business. See New York *Herald Tribune*, April 14, 1942, financial page. The results of this inquiry were published in the *Federal Reserve Bulletin*, August, 1942.

cently have not been published in a form which permits measurement of the amount of bank borrowing. Scattered evidence indicates that the notes payable mainly represent indebtedness to banks in the case of large corporations, but this may be less true of the small corporations.[13] Most tabulations of corporate financial data do not show a division of current liabilities into its component elements. Even where such a breakdown is available, the notes payable item is rarely divided into payables to banks, to trade, and to others.

Fortunately, dollar series on notes payable for large manufacturing corporations and for large trade corporations, covering the years 1920–39, as well as a similar series for small corporations for the years 1925–36, have been compiled.[14] These data are given in the Appendix, but they have also been plotted in Chart 1, where they are compared on logarithmic scale with a series on commercial loans.[15]

It is apparent that the relationship between the behavior of the notes payable series and the commercial loan series is not very intimate although there is a general tendency for all to decline.[16] It is to be observed that notes payable of the manufacturing sample often moved in a direction opposite from trade, indicating that generalizations with regard to the reasons for the decline in commercial bank loans may be misleading. The failure to find any close correspondence between the behavior of these particular series of notes payable and the total volume of commercial loans is also due in large part to the fact that the commercial loan series is not pure, since

[13] The *Statistics of Income* data in 1926 were divided between accounts and notes payable, but this division has not been made since then. The Securities and Exchange Commission requires corporations submitting annual reports to show bank debt separately on Form 10K, but these materials are not available except for very recent years. The published summaries in *Statistics of American Listed Corporations* do not show such a breakdown. The Federal Trade Commission has published data for a sample of 350 large manufacturing corporations as of December 31, 1939, which shows separately notes payable to banks and notes payable to others (see Koch, *op. cit.*, p. 77, n. 7.

[14] Koch's sample of large manufacturing corporations represents 29 percent of the total assets of all manufacturing corporations and 45 percent of the total assets of all corporations with assets over $10,000,000. In retail trade, his sample represents 8 percent of total assets of all trade corporations with assets over $10,000,000. Koch, *op. cit.*, pp. 1–11.

Merwin's sample of small corporations represents about one tenth of the number of small corporations and about one fifth the volume of business of corporations in those fields whose assets are under $250,000. See Merwin, *op. cit.*, p. 18.

[15] Hunt, *op. cit.*

[16] After making a similar comparison between commercial loans and the combined notes payable of manufacturing and trade, Koch remarked: "Changes in the bank loans of big corporations do not determine the course of all commercial loans of national banks. The borrowings of small and medium-sized corporations, partnerships, and individuals, including farmers and brokers, must be very large." Koch, *op. cit.*, Chap. IV, p. 16.

Chart 1

COMMERCIAL LOANS AND NOTES PAYABLE

(In Thousands of Dollars)

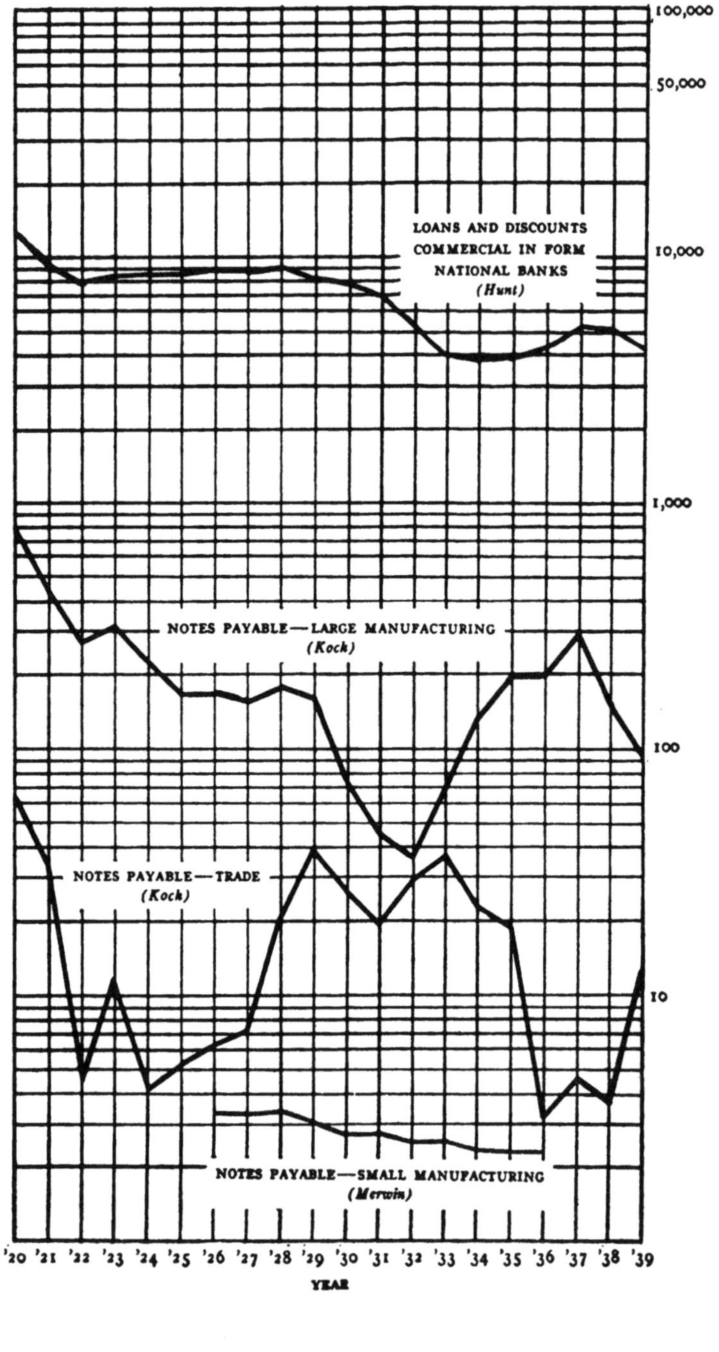

it includes a certain volume of agricultural loans and personal loans to consumers.[17]

Furthermore, the series, loans commercial in form, is only approximately representative of commercial loans, owing to classification revisions, which renders misleading certain year-to-year changes.[18]

In Table 7 the relative importance of notes payable for large manufacturing corporations, large trade corporations, and small corporations is brought out by comparing their notes payable for each year with total assets. It is manifest that bank loans for a considerable number of years comprised a very minor element relative to other means of financing large corporations in both trade and manufacturing, but that they were relatively more important in the case of small corporations.[19] In all three cases, how-

[17] Thus, of the $4,096,000,000 of loans "commercial in form" reported by Hunt as of June 30, 1939, for national banks, $3,139,000,000 represented "commercial and industrial loans," according to the official classification of the Federal Deposit Insurance Corporation, while $680,000,000 were "agricultural loans (excluding loans on farm land)." The volume of agricultural loans of banks declined between 1920 and 1934 by more than did the volume of total loans. Whereas the ratio of personal and collateral loans to farmers to total loans was 12.6 percent in 1920, it was only 3.9 percent in 1934. Similarly, whereas the ratio of agricultural loans, including loans on farm real estate, to total loans was 17.3 percent in 1920, it was only 6.4 percent in 1934. See Norman J. Wall, *Agricultural Loans of Commercial Banks,* United States Department of Agriculture, Technical Bulletin No. 521, July, 1936, p. 28. Apparently, therefore, the decline in Hunt's series for "loans commercial in form" was influenced progressively by the greater decline in agricultural loans. This decline was accounted for, not only by a loss in agricultural purchasing power, but by refunding of bank loans into long-term mortgages obtained from sources other than commercial banks, by writing off uncollected loans, and, in recent years, by a shift in new financing to Federal and federally sponsored agencies. (*Loc. cit.*) Sayers has observed that in the United States, agriculture was notoriously dependent on banks for a large part of its capital, but there occurred a relative decline in agriculture and the growth of specialized institutions which financed it. See Sayers, *op. cit.*, p. 240.

[18] Thus, before 1938, Hunt's series of "loans commercial in form" included "all other loans," but in 1938, by official reclassification, "all other loans" became a separate classification from the new one, "commercial, industrial and agricultural loans." After 1938 Hunt excluded the new series "all other loans" from his loans "commercial in form." As of June 30, 1939, for national banks, "all other loans" amounted to $1,884,-000,000 as compared with $4,096,000,000 in loans "commercial in form" for that year.

[19] Sloan found that for 514 corporations, current liabilities in 1926 and 1927 were distributed as follows:

IN PERCENT

Year	*Bank Loans*	*Accounts Payable*	*All Other*	*Total*
1926	16.5	49.0	34.5	100.0
1927	18.6	47.7	33.7	100.0

Of these 514 companies, only 190, or roughly two out of every five, had any bank loans whatever at the end of 1927. With regard to the 190 companies having bank loans, the distribution of current liabilities was as follows:

Year	*Bank Loans*	*Accounts Payable*	*All Other*	*Total*
1926	38.3	41.7	20.0	100.0
1927	44.7	37.3	18.0	100.0

Table 7

RATIOS OF NOTES PAYABLE TO TOTAL ASSETS, 1921–29 [a]

Percentages

	Large Companies		*Small Companies*
	Manufacturing	*Trade*	*Five Groups Combined*
1921	3.6	6.3	
1922	2.3	0.9	
1923	2.4	2.2	
1924	1.7	0.7	
1925	1.1	0.8	10.1
1926	1.0	0.8	10.3
1927	0.9	0.8	10.1
1928	1.0	2.0	9.8
1929	0.9	3.2	7.9
1930	0.4	2.1	7.8
1931	0.3	1.5	8.5
1932	0.2	2.4	9.0
1933	0.4	2.9	9.1
1934	0.8	1.7	8.6
1935	1.2	1.6	8.3
1936	1.2	0.2	8.2
1937	1.6	0.3	
1938	0.8	0.2	
1939	0.5	0.8	
	—	—	—
1921–39	1.1	1.5	

[a] Source: for large companies, Albert Koch, *The Financing of Large Corporations, 1920–39* (New York, 1941), Appendix D, Table IV–7, p. 39 and Table IV–8, p. 40; for small companies, see Appendix A compiled by the author from Charles L. Merwin, Jr., *The Financial Characteristics of American Manufacturing Corporations,* Temporary National Economic Committee, Monograph No. 15 (Washington, D.C., 1940), Appendix F, Tables 1-A to 1-E.

ever, the importance of bank financing appears to have been diminishing, although it is noteworthy that in trade, bank financing during the period 1928 to 1935 rose greatly in importance.

Over the period 1921–39, the notes payable of large manufacturing corporations declined both in dollar amount (see Chart 1) and relative to accounts payable and other current liabilities. Although they have increased in importance since the depression, they are still small relative to their level

---

The bank loans of these 190 companies were equivalent to about 13 percent of current assets at the end of 1927, whereas the aggregate of bank indebtedness of the 514 concerns was only 4 per cent of current assets. See Laurence H. Sloan, *Corporation Profits* (New York, 1929), pp. 271, 274.

in the first half of the 1920s. In the period 1933–37 "term" loans played an important part.

In trade, the behavior of notes payable was quite different. The level was low during most of the 1920s but rose absolutely and relatively during the first half of the 1930s. Notes payable of small manufacturing companies in the period 1925–36 fell off steadily, both absolutely and relatively.

THE FREQUENCY OF BANK BORROWING

Very little information is available regarding the numerousness of bank loans among various branches of industry. However, it is known that there has been a decrease in the number of large companies with no notes payable. Table 8 compares for each year the percentage of companies with no notes payable with those companies whose notes payable were between 0 and 45 percent of total notes and accounts payable, and with those whose notes payable were between 45 percent and 100 percent of total notes and accounts payable.[20]

TABLE 8

STANDARD STATISTICS COMPOSITE OF 400 CORPORATIONS DISTRIBUTED BY SIZE OF RATIO OF NOTES PAYABLE TO TOTAL OF NOTES AND ACCOUNTS PAYABLE, 1927–38[a]

Percentages

	No Notes Payable	*0 to 45 Percent of Total Payables*	*45 Percent to 100 Percent of Total Payables*
1927	64	14	22
1928	69	12	19
1929	65	15	20
1930	77	14	19
1931	68	13	19
1932	70	14	16
1933	70	16	13
1934	68	18	15
1935	65	18	17
1936	63	20	17
1937	58	15	27
1938	70	12	18

[a] Source: Charles L. Merwin, Jr., *The Financial Characteristics of American Manufacturing Corporations,* T.N.E.C. Monograph No. 15, pp. 79–80.

[20] Charles L. Merwin, Jr., *The Financial Characteristics of American Manufacturing Industries,* Temporary National Economic Committee, Monograph No. 15 (Washington, D.C., 1940). See also: "Standard Trade and Securities," Standard Earnings Bulletin Supplements, *Composite Financial Statements* (Standard Statistics Co., N.Y.), which were published annually up to 1939. However, the published data do not reveal the breakdown between notes and accounts payable.

Table 8 shows that approximately two thirds of the companies did not use any notes payable to finance their working capital, indicating that most large corporations have not relied on commercial banks during the period under study. It is apparent that the proportion of companies with no notes

TABLE 9

RATIO OF NOTES PAYABLE TO NOTES AND ACCOUNTS PAYABLE FOR STANDARD STATISTICS COMPOSITE OF 400 CORPORATIONS, BY INDUSTRY AND BY SELECTED PERIODS, 1927–38 [a]

Industry	*Number of Companies*	*Percent of Notes Payable to Notes and Accounts Payable*			
		1927–29	*1930–33*	*1934–38*	*1927–38*
Advertising, printing and publishing	7	5	14	8	10
Autos, trucks	13	6	2	3	3
Auto parts	27	25	20	17	20
Auto tires	10	39	13	31	30
Beverages	4	21	52	33	36
Building supplies	22	11	13	17	14
Chemicals, fertilizer	19	8	6	9	8
Containers	3	0	0	13	6
Electric equipment	10	3	9	20	12
Food products	27	9	16	45	33
Household products	16	25	27	34	29
Leather, shoes	7	54	20	35	35
Machinery	25	12	15	20	16
Medicines, drugs	5	36	16	12	19
Metals	21	34	70	41	49
Miscellaneous manufactures	24	31	37	26	31
Office equipment	9	3	8	26	15
Oil products and refining	25	9	12	25	17
Paper and its products	3	40	3	15	17
Railroad equipment	10	14	33	11	19
Shipping and shipbuilding	7	32	25	1	17
Steel and iron	17	3	13	15	11
Sugar products and refining	8	44	51	28	40
Textiles, apparel	30	60	53	65	60
Tobacco products	16	58	26	58	47
Mainly manufacturing	365	22	24	27	25
Nonmanufacturing	35	36	54	26	42
Total	400	23	25	28	26

[a] Source: Charles L. Merwin, Jr., *Financial Characteristics of American Manufacturing Corporations,* T.N.E.C. Monograph No. 15, Table 40, p. 82.

payable varies a good deal over the business cycle, as well as year in and year out. In the depression years, the percentage of companies out of debt to banks increased, but in the recovery leading up to 1937 a larger proportion of companies again were "in the banks," and it is particularly striking that in 1937 the lowest percentage of companies with no notes payable was recorded, meaning that there were more companies indebted to banks in that year than in any other year covered. However, the precipitous change in 1938 indicated again that corporations were freeing themselves from dependency on banks, as well as on trade credit for working capital.

In Table 9 is shown the ratio of notes payable to the total of notes and accounts payable for the same sample of corporations—by industry and by periods.

THE RELATIVE IMPORTANCE OF BANK DEBT TO OTHER TYPES OF CURRENT DEBT

There does not appear to have been much change in the importance of notes payable to other types of current debt. Actually, a slight rise in the percentage of notes payable to the total of notes payable and accounts payable appears to have taken place, from 23 percent in 1927–29 to 28 percent in 1934–38. However, the industrial breakdown reveals that this rising trend was observable in nine out of the twenty-five industries, whereas in three industries there was a declining trend. Six industries showed a higher ratio in depression than in prosperity or recovery, and seven had a lower ratio in depression than in either of the terminal periods.[21]

In Table 10, movements in the percentage ratio of notes payable to notes and accounts payable are compared with the movement in the ratio of current debt to total debt, for both manufacturing and nonmanufacturing groups.

In both manufacturing and nonmanufacturing, current debt decreased in relative importance during depression and conversely. In manufacturing, however, bank loans did not change much relative to current debt, whereas in nonmanufacturing the proportion of bank loans became greater when current debt declined.[22] This seems to reflect the opposite movement in the

[21] Charles L. Merwin, Jr., *The Financial Characteristics of American Manufacturing Industries*, T.N.E.C. Monograph No. 15, p. 83.

[22] Koch found that there was little net change in either the dollar volume of accounts payable or their importance relative to the other components in both manufacturing and trade, whereas other current liabilities were a consistently increasing element of current debt in both groups since 1920. See Koch, Chap. IV, p. 12.

TABLE 10

COMPARISON OF NOTES PAYABLE AND CURRENT RATIOS, FOR STANDARD STATISTICS COMPOSITE OF 400 CORPORATIONS, SELECTED PERIODS, 1927–38 [a]

	1927–29	*1930–33*	*1934–38*	*1927–38*
Manufacturing:				
Ratio notes payable to notes and accounts payable	22	24	27	25
Ratio current debt to total debt	41	34	46	41
Nonmanufacturing:				
Ratio notes payable to notes and accounts payable	36	54	26	42
Ratio current debt to total debt	43	28	38	36

[a] Source: for current debt to total debt, Charles L. Merwin, Jr., *Financial Characteristics of American Manufacturing Corporations,* T.N.E.C. Monograph No. 15, Table 52, p. 104; for notes payable to notes and accounts payable, *ibid.,* Table 40, p. 83.

absolute amount of notes payable in manufacturing and trade which appeared in Chart 1.

The implication of these findings is that corporate borrowers were able to finance themselves in ways other than by the incurrence of current debt either in the form of indebtedness to banks or indebtedness to other corporations. The other ways include borrowing in the securities markets as well as reliance on internal sources of funds, such as retained earnings and nonfinancial balance sheet items.[23]

THE EFFECT OF TECHNOLOGICAL CHANGE UPON THE CAPITAL REQUIREMENTS OF INDUSTRY

A number of investigations based upon the experience of the 1920s attribute the decline in the volume of commercial bank loans to diminished working capital requirements, particularly inventory requirements, arising out of technological change.[24] The thesis is that substantial economies were

[23] See *infra.*

[24] Arthur S. Dewing, *The Financial Policy of Corporations* (3d rev. ed.; New York, 1934), p. 472. A study of the balance sheets of 169 corporations representing sixteen industries of all sizes showed that on the basis of a composite mean average, the ratio of fixed capital to current capital rose from 2.05 in 1919 to 4.35 in 1931. Thus, it was said, whereas before 1920 corporations and all economic organizations possessed relatively large amounts of current capital, during the 1920s the proportion of fixed capital underwent significant increase. This was attributed to the fact that the period of the 1920s involved the transformation of plant facilities to a peacetime basis and the more

realized from the integration of manufacturing into larger units, both vertically and horizontally, and that these economies implied a smaller relative need for inventories in manufacturing and trade. Improvements in transportation facilities and the speeding up of deliveries, it was argued, relieved the need for carrying as large inventories as otherwise would have been the case. Presumably, the increasing prevalence of the large-sized unit was important in reducing the amplitude of seasonal fluctuations and in rendering the production process more continuous. Furthermore, as firms become larger in size they enjoy economies in the investment and disinvestment of short-term funds. The balances required to meet expenditures will be smaller for one big firm than for twelve small firms one-twelfth the size of the big firm.[25]

More recent studies which examined the period of the 1930s, in addition to the 1920s, have cast doubts upon the validity of the thesis outlined in the preceding paragraph.[26] They show that, whereas in the 1920s manu-

---

economical use of plants, which naturally required increased expenditure for fixed capital.

See also National Bureau of Economic Research, *Recent Economic Changes* (1st ed., New York, 1929). Writers for the National Bureau of Economic Research appear to have been partially responsible for the "reduced inventories" thesis which became so fashionable. On the basis of a sample study of 241 manufacturing and mining companies, 1922 to 1927, in which sales and inventory relatives were compared, it was argued that "at the end of 1927 inventories of raw materials, goods in process, and finished goods in the hands of industrial companies were about 20% less than they would have been if hand-to-mouth buying, changes in production methods, and improvements in transportation conditions had not occurred."

See "Marketing" by Copeland, *ibid.*, I, 350–51, 356–60. Also see "Money and Credit and Their Effect on Business" by Sprague and Burgess, *ibid.*, II, 682–84, for a somewhat different explanation.

[25] Sayers, *op. cit.*, p. 239.

[26] Analysis of data supplied by the Robert Morris Associates revealed that the ratio of sales to inventories in thirty-two trades, including manufactures, middlemen and retailers, was rising during the 1920s in most cases, and "there can be little doubt that less working capital was required at the end of the prosperous twenties than at the start." However, for years subsequent to 1929, Hunt found that the ratios "are very erratic" and that "no general trend can be established for trade as a whole or for any one trade." Hunt concluded that, on balance, there has been a tendency for banks to lose loan volume because of more efficient handling of working capital, but "it is clear that this tendency has not been the principal cause of the decline in the volume of bank loans for commercial purposes." Hunt, *op. cit.*, pp. 26–27.

It was found that for large financial corporations, 1920–39, "the amount of working capital . . . has held an even relationship to sales" and that "in spite of improvements in transportation, communication, and industrial organization, the aggregate inventory requirements of our samples of large manufacturing and trade corporations have not changed during the past two decades. The increased standards of living of the American people and the shift in consumer buying to more durable goods has probably resulted

facturing and trade may have required less working capital per unit of sales, recent evidence does not show that these tendencies have persisted nor that they are of sufficient magnitude to have been the principal cause of the decline in commercial loans.

PHYSICAL CAPITAL REQUIREMENTS IN RELATION TO BANK LOANS

It is a significant fact that the absolute and relative decline in the volume of commercial loans has taken place during a period when the total capital requirements of the economy appear to have remained fairly constant relative to output. The belief has been commonly held that the development of capitalism has meant increasing employment of capital per unit of output. However, this does not appear to have been the case. Neither does it appear that the capital requirements per unit of output have declined owing to capital-saving inventions.[27]

If total capital has increased *pari passu* with output, even though it has not exceeded it, it cannot be regarded as a factor responsible for the decline in commercial loans. Considering the fact that the capital stock consists of two principal components, fixed instruments and inventories, the question becomes one of finding out whether the relative composition of the stocks of capital has undergone any change. Here there does appear to have been a gradual, if slight, relative reduction in inventories as compared with fixed capital, although recent studies indicate that in manufacturing, if not in

---

in longer periods of production, requiring larger dollar volume of inventories. Relative to sales these companies kept as much inventory on hand during the thirties as they did during the twenties." Koch, *op. cit.*, p. 4.

In the case of small corporations there is no definite evidence that "inventory holdings moved decisively either upward or downward" during the period 1926–36 although it contributed slightly more than its share to the decline in total assets of a sample of small corporations in five industrial groups. Charles L. Merwin, Jr., *Financing Small Corporations, 1926–1936*, pp. 72–73.

[27] Alvin Hansen, *Fiscal Policy and Business Cycles* (New York, 1941), p. 356. Hansen says that during the last fifty years or so the physical capital stock of the economy has increased approximately in proportion to real income. "If this be so, it follows that in terms of the time element in production which is the very essence of the capital concept, our system of production is little more capitalistic now than fifty or seventy-five years ago. It requires, in other words, a period of employment of our productive resources no longer than formerly to reproduce the total capital stock." "Considering the economy as a whole, including fields of economic activity other than manufacturing, there is no evidence that the advance in technique has resulted in recent decades, certainly not in any significant measure, in any deepening of capital. . . . Although the deepening process [in Hawtrey's sense, the employment of more capital per unit of output] is going on all the while in certain areas, elsewhere capital saving inventions are reducing the ratio of capital to output."

other lines, neither the sales to inventory ratios nor the sales to working capital ratios have changed very much during the last two decades.[28]

Table 11 compares capital assets of all nonfinancial corporations with inventories for the period 1926 to 1938. It reveals very little change in the dollar value of such assets, but there is evident a tendency for the reported value of inventories to decline absolutely and relatively to fixed assets in depression.

TABLE 11

CAPITAL ASSETS AND INVENTORIES OF ALL NONFINANCIAL CORPORATIONS, 1926–38 [a]

In Millions of Dollars

	Capital Assets	*Inventories*	*Ratio*
1926	84,094	20,016	4.2
1927	89,694	19,937	4.5
1928	92,962	20,076	4.6
1929	98,627	20,990	4.7
1930	102,202	18,309	5.6
1931	97,665	14,891	6.6
1932	93,919	12,221	7.7
1933	91,246	13,458	6.8
1934	88,063	14,177	6.2
1935	87,160	14,678	5.9
1936	87,635	16,519	5.3
1937	90,535	18,468	4.9
1938	80,860	16,529	4.9

[a] Source: Data 1926–36 excerpted from compilation available in T.N.E.C. Hearings, *Investigation of Concentration of Economic Power*, Part IX, "Savings and Investment," p. 4042. Years 1937–38 were compiled from *Statistics of Income, 1937*, Part II, and *Statistics of Income, 1938*, Part II.

In the economy as a whole, Kuznet's findings in *National Income and Its Composition* seem to indicate very definitely that, for the period 1918 to 1938, net changes in business inventories constituted a contracting share of the gross capital formation total, and that it is the decline in the percentage accounted for by business inventories "that is fully responsible for the decline in the share of business capital formation." [29] Elsewhere he stated: "Similarly the share in national income of net flow to inventories declined fairly consistently. . . . It is possible that this downward move-

[28] Koch, *op. cit.*, p. 4.

[29] Inventories in this connection were measured, not as the change from one year-end inventory to the next, but so as to reflect the actual accretion of commodities to, or actual draft of commodities from, the commodity stock comprising inventories.

Simon Kuznets, *National Income and Its Composition, 1919–1935* (New York, 1937), p. 44.

ment is a declining phase of a long cycle in inventory holdings (associated with a downward sweep of the price level) . . .[30] These results are summarized in Table 12.

TABLE 12

PERCENTAGE SHARES OF TYPE OF PRODUCT COMPONENTS OF CAPITAL FORMATION IN NATIONAL INCOME AT 1929 PRICES, 1919–38 [a]

	Producers' Durable Goods Including Business Construction	*Change in Business Inventories*
1919	3.0	4.9
1920	3.2	7.2
1921	0.7	-0.1
1922	1.3	0.5
1923	3.3	4.0
1924	3.2	-1.3
1925	3.9	2.2
1926	4.3	1.5
1927	4.2	0.5
1928	4.2	-0.5
1929	4.9	2.8
1930	3.3	-1.3
1931	-0.3	-1.9
1932	-4.3	-5.7
1933	-4.4	-3.0
1934	-2.1	-3.6
1935	-0.6	2.0
1936	1.9	3.8
1937	3.2	3.2
1938	0.7	-0.4
Average:		
1919–23	2.3	3.3
1924–28	4.0	0.5
1929–33	-0.2	-1.8
1934–38	0.6	1.0

[a] Source: Simon Kuznets, *National Income and Its Composition 1918–1938* (New York, 1941), p. 272.

Data on the dollar value or volume of inventories covering long periods of years are not plentiful nor are they reliable. Nevertheless, in Tables 13 and 14, unadjusted dollar inventories, 1926–38, for nonfinancial corporation, compiled in *Statistics of Income,* are presented for comparison with dollar inventories, 1918–38, compiled by Kuznets. These data are plotted in Chart 2.

[30] Simon Kuznets, *National Income and Its Composition, 1918–1938* (New York, 1941), p. 273.

INVENTORIES OF MANUFACTURING AND NONFINANCIAL CORPORATIONS, 1918–38
(In Billions of Dollars)

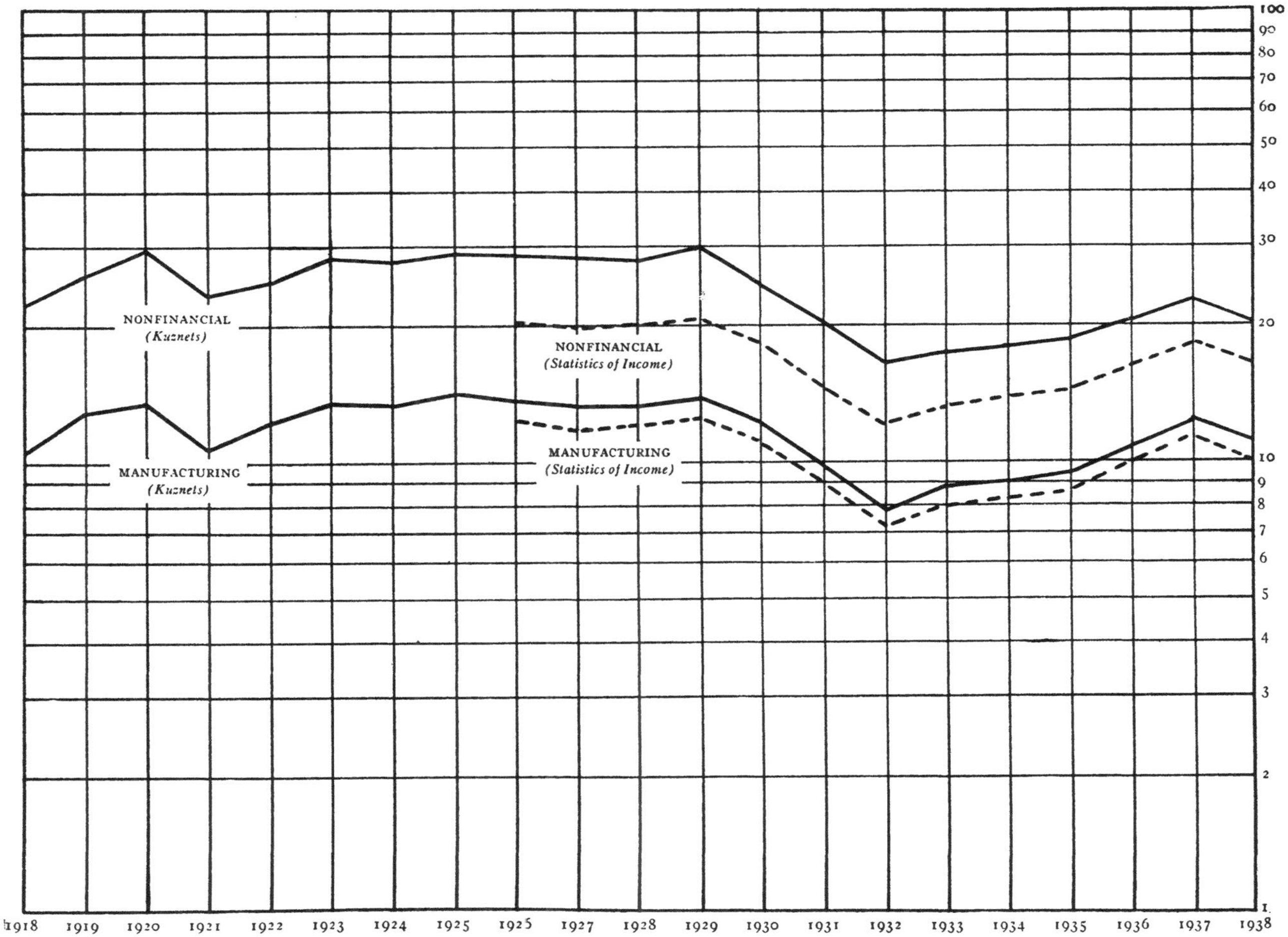

TABLE 13

INVENTORIES OF ALL NONFINANCIAL CORPORATIONS AND MANUFACTURING, 1926–38

Statistics of Income Series

Millions of Dollars

	All Nonfinancial Corporations [a]	*Manufacturing* [b]
1926	20,016	12,284
1927	19,937	11,884
1928	20,076	12,011
1929	20,990	12,614
1930	18,309	11,157
1931	14,891	9,003
1932	12,221	7,310
1933	13,458	8,084
1934	14,177	8,319
1935	14,678	8,705
1936	16,519	10,029
1937	18,467	11,454
1938	16,529	10,192

[a] Source: Excerpted from T.N.E.C. Hearings, *Investigation of Concentration of Economic Power,* Part IX, "Savings and Investment," Exhibit 587, p. 4042. Data for 1936–38, compiled from *Statistics of Income.*

[b] Excerpted from *Statistics of Income,* various years.

The absolute dollar valuation of total inventories for manufacturing since 1918 does not appear to have undergone much net change, although the predepression level had not been regained on a permanent basis by the end of 1938. The decline in the volume of inventories in trade, however, according to both series, is pronounced, as is also the case with transportation, so that the explanation of the tendency for aggregate inventories in the system to decline must lie mainly in the behavior of the nonmanufacturing groups where, it is apparent, there has been a relative and absolute reduction in inventories.[31]

[31] It is of interest in this connection that while dollar inventories rose during the First World War, they apparently did not undergo great change in physical amount. Terborgh, in a study of the behavior of inventories 1916–23 for all manufacturing concerns for which both opening and closing inventories were reported in Moody's *Manuals,* found, after deflating the series for prices, that: "It appears that in the aggregate the physical volume of manufacturing inventory changed very little in the period 1915–1918 and rose only moderately during 1919. The gain during 1920 was substantial, by either of the alternative measures for that year, but does not appear to have been followed by any significant net liquidation in 1921. The period closed with physical inventory at a high point." This study, aside from suggesting that physical inventory requirements may not respond as greatly as commonly supposed to expansion in output, also attests that inventories at the start of the period considered above in the text were at a high point cyclically, so that there is no conclusive evidence of a downward secular decline, certainly not more than can be explained by price changes. See George Terborgh, "Man-

TABLE 14

INVENTORIES, VARIOUS LINES OF BUSINESS [a]

As of December 31

Current Valuation in Millions of Dollars

Year	*Transportation*	*Trade*	*Miscellaneous*	*Service*	*Mining*	*Manufacturing*	*Construction*	*Totals for Groups Shown*
1918	775	9,970	71	63	550	10,320	390	22,139
1919	741	12,490	83	85	1,017	12,906	471	27,793
1920	1,147	12,742	95	112	1,100	13,484	588	29,268
1921	1,019	10,202	72	103	761	10,705	573	23,435
1922	869	10,678	78	129	607	12,118	587	25,066
1923	1,081	11,809	89	134	731	13,721	708	28,273
1924	939	11,706	104	139	807	13,270	778	27,743
1925	906	12,157	40	154	749	14,005	899	28,910
1926	950	12,075	15	194	691	13,727	998	28,650
1927	1,033	11,779	24	187	740	13,284	977	28,024
1928	1,008	12,022	18	188	561	13,362	800	27,959
1929	1,129	12,372	10	202	754	13,920	992	29,379
1930	982	10,169	6	255	483	12,264	581	24,740
1931	897	8,731	7	210	515	9,864	423	20,647
1932	749	7,080	8	152	422	7,950	424	16,785
1933	779	6,889	2	148	445	8,852	404	17,519
1934	636	7,160	6	173	435	9,152	483	18,045
1935	631	7,456	4	165	373	9,550	555	18,734
1936	699	8,042	6	178	334	10,986	642	20,887
1937	832	8,536	2	184	402	12,547	643	23,146
1938	699	7,942	2	184	332	11,162	641	20,962

[a] Source: Simon Kuznets, *National Income and Its Composition 1918–1938* (New York, National Bureau of Economic Research, 1941), II, 903–10.

The absolute decline in inventories from the average of the 1920s to the 1930s may afford a partial explanation of the absolute reduction in bank loans, but it does not explain the decline in bank loans relative to inventory requirements. As already mentioned, commercial loans began to decline during the twenties when inventories were actually rising.[32] This is not to

ufacturing Inventories during and after the World War," *Federal Reserve Bulletin,* July, 1941, pp. 613–17.

[32] In this connection, see Lauchlin Currie, "The Decline of the Commercial Loan," *Quarterly Journal of Economics,* XLV, No. 4 (August, 1931), 698–707. Currie found in a study of the period 1922–28 that for 729 companies, the proportion of inventories financed by bank loans (as measured by notes payable) was extremely small. At the end of 1928, bank loans were only 8.4 percent of inventories and 3.8 percent of current assets. During the period, a steady decline occurred in notes payable both absolutely and relatively. This characterized twenty-five out of thirty groups of companies, the exceptions being department stores, paper, coal mining, and copper. Currie's series showed an actual increase of inventories for the sample of about $1,000,000,000, while bank loans declined by about $253,000,000.

deny that in some lines of activity there has been a reduced absolute and relative need for inventories as compared with fixed assets or output, but the changes which have taken place for the system as a whole appear to be inadequate to explain changes in bank loans. Moreover, a peculiar fact is that in trade, where there is some evidence to indicate a more efficient utilization of working capital, the volume of bank loans in the late 1920s and the early 1930s actually increased.

THE INFLUENCE OF CHANGED FINANCIAL TECHNIQUE UPON THE DECLINE IN COMMERCIAL LOANS

Since changes in fixed and working capital requirements do not adequately account for changes in bank borrowings, it seems logical to suppose that the explanation lies in the adoption of new financial techniques. Here several factors appear to have been at work: (1) the growth in the average number of corporations and their size which, together with the development of the organized securities markets, gave borrowers access to new sources of loanable funds; (2) increased reliance upon "internal" sources of financing, such as the withholding of earnings and the accumulation of depreciation reserves in excess of actual outlays for maintenance and replacement; (3) increased reliance in some lines of business upon trade credit; and (4) the adoption of policies which aimed at independence of banks and the reduction in short term debt.

THE GROWTH OF CORPORATIONS

Growth in average size of corporations has been associated with increase in the number of corporations and their proportionate contribution to the total national output.[33] This was of particular significance in manufactur-

[33] T.N.E.C Monograph No. 27, *The Structure of Industry*, pp. 52–57. In terms of wage earners, the average establishment was one-third larger in 1937 than in 1914; in terms of product (in dollars of equal purchasing power) more than twice as large; in terms of quantity of product, over four-fifths larger. As measured by value or volume of output, the greater part of the growth in size occurred between 1919 and 1929.

T.N.E.C., Senate, 75th Cong., 3d Sess., Hearings, *Investigation of Concentration of Economic Power*, Part I, "Economic Prologue," p. 94. See also Exhibit 54, p. 93, and p. 228. The number of corporations increased from 1910 to 1930 by about 90 percent, while the number of firms increased only 45 percent; that is, the number of corporations increased about twice as fast as the business population. Partnerships underwent a steady and sharp decline during the 1920s. From 1924 to 1933 there was a decline in the number of partnerships from 321,158 to 214,881, while the number of corporations increased from 417,421 to 504,080. (These figures are to some extent unreliable owing to variation in number of firms reporting in the tax returns.)

Manufacturing concerns organized on a corporate basis in 1904, both large and small, accounted for 73.7 percent of the volume of production; by 1914, 83.2 percent; and by 1929, 92.1 percent. George W. Edwards, *op. cit.*, pp. 241–44.

ing, where, until the end of the nineteenth century, firms were mainly organized in the form of individual ownership, or partnership, and, to some extent, small corporate units. On the other hand, railroad and public utility companies at an early date adopted the corporate form of organization, which from the beginning enabled them to borrow through sale of stocks and bonds.[34]

Evidently, the growth in the large-sized corporation exercised a direct effect on the method of financing, particularly upon the relation between the individual borrowing concern and its bank. While the small corporation continued to borrow from banks there was an increasing tendency for the large corporations to utilize the sale of securities in the capital market and to reduce bank loans. In this way the obligations of corporations were converted from short-term bank loans to long-term bonds and stocks.[35]

Sprague and Burgess, on the basis of their study of developments during the 1920s, described the situation as follows;

> A larger proportion of the assets of business enterprises has come to be financed by means of the resources of owners and long term obligations; a smaller proportion through current obligations to banks and merchandise creditors. At the same time, there has been a wide diffusion of ownership through the sale of securities in many enterprises that were formerly closely held by a few individuals, in addition to those that had long been available for purchase by the public. . . . But, with all the diversity in policies exhibited in recent changes in corporate financial structure, there is to be noted general agreement in a desire and purpose to reduce the volume of current obligations.[36]

[34] George W. Edwards, *op. cit.*, pp. 282–84.

[35] *Ibid.* Edwards found a reflection of this in the fact that the current debt of large industrial corporations rose from $8,544,000,000 in 1913 to $16,750,000,000 in 1932. Between 1920 and 1930 funded debt rose from $4,800,000,000 to $10,400,000,000, whereas between 1921 and 1932 the ratio of unfunded debt to total debt dropped from 74 percent to 51 percent.

[36] Sprague and Burgess, *op. cit.*, II, 681–83. Sprague and Burgess based their findings on a study of a large number of corporations made by the credit department of the Federal Reserve bank of New York. For small samples of companies in the wholesale grocery, cotton goods manufacturing, shoe manufacturing, wholesale drygoods, lumber, and drug maufacturing industries, bank loans declined from $51,614 in 1922 to $39,688 in 1927. In the same period the ratio of total debt to current debt increased in all but shoe manufacturing. There was also an apparent tendency for the ratio of capital funds to both total debt and current debt to rise, reflecting a preference for permanent methods of financing business. Among the reasons cited for this development were the following: "Improvements in methods of production, in general involve the employment of increasing amounts of capital in fixed forms; seasonal peaks in industry are being reduced, and business organizations of large size are occupying a widening area in the field of production and merchandising . . ."

DISADVANTAGES OF BANK BORROWING

Currie argued that the growth of large companies with access to the stock and bond markets was only a partial explanation of the decline in the bank loan.[37] The chief explanation, he said, lay in the disadvantages inherent in the practice of borrowing which, in the eyes of the larger industrialists, far outweighed the temporary advantages of small savings in interest charges. The short-term loan held the disadvantage that, not only must interest be paid, but the loan itself was expected to be liquidated at a near date. Furthermore, the larger and more successful companies were not content with the elimination of debt but, in addition, acquired working capital far in excess of seasonal needs and held deposits and temporary investments in securities, not as a temporary employment of idle funds, but as a permanent condition. In Currie's opinion, inability to raise funds in other ways was the main reason for bank borrowing. This, he believed, was indicated by the fact that the companies which were growing most rapidly, and therefore appeared to require larger loans, actually reduced them to a nominal figure, while companies whose earnings were poor, or declining, were carrying heavy bank loans and, in some cases, actually increasing them.

INTERNAL FUNDS

Hunt found that "probably the factor of reinvested funds is of major significance among the forces causing changes in commercial bank portfolios." The trend, he said, "all points toward the truth of the general conclusion that businesses have reduced bank loans by the reinvestment of earnings and the sale of long term bonds or stocks," and that "it appears certain that a significant part of the decline of bank loans for commercial purposes is

[37] Lauchlin Currie, "The Decline of the Commercial Loan," *Quarterly Journal of Economics,* XLV, No. 4 (August 1931), 698–709. Currie contended that the rate of interest in this period (1922–28) was nearly as high as that on bank loans, while call money rates were low, making it improbable that companies could reduce costs by substituting long-term bonds for short. Currie maintained that the theory which makes temporary savings of interest the main motive for borrowing assumes static conditions and, implicitly, that the borrower's own capital and long-term borrowing can continuously be employed, and that there are no cyclical variations in output and profits. However, this does not altogether fit the case of seasonal bank borrowing, which is a theory which assumes that capital and credit are not continuously employed, and that therefore it is advantageous to resort to temporary bank borrowings to finance seasonal or cyclical variations on a basis which does not require permanent issuance of bonds, involving a fixed recurring expense, which continues whether the capital is employed or not. In the case of permanently employed fixed capital, the entrepreneur has to compare the estimated marginal efficiency of his capital with whichever is the lower, the existing long-term rates or the average of the expected future short-term rates (plus costs of reborrowing). See F. A. Lutz, "The Structure of Interest Rates," *Quarterly Journal of Economics,* November, 1940, p. 60.

due to business policies which have emphasized the retirement of short term debt." [38]

Koch's study of the financing of large manufacturing concerns demonstrates quite clearly that concerns of this class depend for their financing largely upon funds raised internally from operations or by borrowing in the securities markets, rather than from banks, although he notes the recent tendency of big corporations to increase the amount of intermediate credit obtained in the form of "term loans" from banks.

Undistributed earnings and depreciation accruals, when earned, make up the major portion of funds from operations. However,

> the volume of total funds from operations of large concerns in all major classifications has been considerably smaller in the thirties than it was in the twenties. In addition, there has been no clear-cut tendency for this volume in the case of large manufacturing and trade corporations to increase relative to fixed capital outlay.[39]

Contrary to others, Koch found that the importance of outside financing during the late twenties was overemphasized "because of the mass of purely financial transactions with which it was intertwined." On the whole, he concluded that the trend in security sales relative to fixed capital outlays and funds from operations has not changed materially since 1920. Relative to short-term debt, however, security sales increased during the twenties but have since decreased, especially between 1934 and 1939.[40]

SMALL CORPORATIONS

The behavior of small corporations in respect to borrowing and sources of funds, however, is quite different from that of large corporations. Analysis of ratios of net worth to total debt for various years and by size of corporations shows clearly that the larger companies have a relatively high proportion of net worth. Similarly, in comparing ratios of current to total debt, it is clear that the larger the company, the smaller the relative amount of current debt. Other things being equal, it is to be expected that as the average size of the establishments increased, the business system would be found to have a relatively larger portion of its liabilities in the form of either stock outstanding or long-term debt and a relatively smaller proportion in current liabilities. This seems to be related to a definitely and progressively declining turnover of merchandise with increase in size. Higher current ratios

[38] Hunt, *op. cit.*, pp. 27–29. On the basis of data obtained from the Robert Morris Associates, Hunt compiled ratios of net worth to debt, net worth to fixed assets, and notes payable to total assets, for fifty-four and fifty-three trades for the period 1920-29.

[39] Koch, *op. cit.*, pp. 7–8.

[40] *Ibid.*, p. 10.

are found to be associated with lower turnovers.[41] It is not surprising, therefore, that bank loans have been declining relative to other types of earning assets as the average size of corporations has grown.

While the data are meager on small companies, one study has recently come to hand which throws considerable light upon the reasons for the decline in commercial bank loans.[42] Merwin found for samples of small companies in five industry groups that, aside from owner's equity, which consisted of retained earnings as well as stock flotations, and represented anywhere from two thirds to three fourths of the funds invested, short-term credits were the most important financing medium. Such credits consist of accounts payable to raw-material suppliers and notes payable "probably largely to banks." During the period covered by his study, 1926–36, accounts payable became relatively more important, and notes payable less important as a source of funds, while at the same time the total assets and liabilities of the firms decreased. The decline in notes payable and the rise in relative importance of accounts payable were attributed to several factors, of which shrinkage of dollar inventories was only one. Shrinkage in inventory was largely due to the fall in commodity prices and was presumed inadequate to explain fully the decline in notes payable to banks.

Among the other factors of some importance was the shift from bank to mercantile credit. Merwin attributed this to several factors. On the demand side were: (1) the decline in raw material prices; (2) considerations of convenience, including freedom from bank control. On the supply side were: (1) cheap money rates; (2) competition among raw-material suppliers; and (3) tightening of bank credit in the depression. Expansion in mercantile credit occurred despite less liberal terms in some lines.

Merwin found not only a tendency for small firms to shift their short-term financing from banks to mercantile sources, but also, as the increase in their ratio of cash to notes payable indicates, a tendency to reduce the scope of their net debtor relationship to banks. He explained that at the same time that the small firms reduced their ratio of receivables to accounts payable they also effected a downward revision of their net creditor relationship to their customers. Over the period 1926–36 the firms studied piled up cash holdings that were almost as large as their bank debts, and took more credit grants from raw-material suppliers than they extended to their own customers.[43]

[41] For substantiation of these relationships, see Charles L. Merwin, Jr., *The Financial Characteristics of American Manufacturing Industries,* T.N.E.C. Monograph No. 15, Tables 50, 33, and 44.

[42] Charles L. Merwin, Jr., *Financing Small Corporations, 1926–1936,* pp. 71-79.

[43] *Ibid.*, p. 3.

BANK BORROWING—ITS MOTIVATION

In the first part of this chapter it was indicated that the decline in bank loans was not attributable to a change in the amount or nature of the physical capital requirements of the business economy. At least from the quantitative standpoint, such changes have not been of sufficient magnitude to explain the metamorphosis which occurred in the volume of direct borrowing from banks. It was therefore necessary to consider a somewhat different set of factors concerned with the techniques employed in financing fixed and working capital requirements of industry. Various investigations have indicated several reasons why commercial and industrial loans have declined: As corporations become larger in size they rely more heavily upon financing outside of the banks; for short periods, funds derived from internal sources provide a source of funds of varying importance; the greatest percentage decline in bank borrowing has taken place in the class of small-sized firms where a shift to dependence on suppliers was noted; the increased reliance of small business upon its trade and manufacturing suppliers has not been accompanied by an increased reliance of the latter upon banks; and finally, in the case of both small- and large-sized establishments, and generally in all lines of business, the piling up of cash (deposits in banks) has reduced the net debtor relationship of business to banks and rendered the business economy less directly dependent for its immediate requirements upon banks than ever before.

Virtually all studies based upon a "supply and use" or "sources and applications" of funds analysis, such as those by Koch, Merwin, Mack, and Hersey, referred to in preceding pages, have stressed the increased importance of internal sources of funds, especially during the last two decades. There can be no doubt that business has gradually increased the proportion of financing for all purposes through charges to current operations and, likewise, the proportion of fixed assets and inventories purchased with funds provided internally. This is a trend which Woodward finds it logical to expect as the total capital equipment rises and as a growing part of expenditures on it each year are accounted for by expenditures to preserve it.[44] This is to be contrasted with the situation prior to the First World War when new investment was financed to a much greater extent by borrowing either from banks or through the capital market.

The reasons for outside borrowing from banks or others are not entirely clear, although it is evident that the demand for loans by business firms is proximately a function of their cash position. The net sources or applica-

[44] Donald B. Woodward, "Changes in Capital Financing," *Journal of the American Statistical Association,* Vol. XXXIII, No. 201, March, 1938.

tions of funds from retained income and nonfinancial balance sheet items represent the difference between money received as sales dollars and cash expenditures for purchase of goods necessary to the production and sale of stock in trade. Causal importance logically runs from retained receipts to changes in cash, changes in the asset securities, borrowing, and proprietary shares. However, there does not appear to be any invariable relation between the need for funds, when need is interpreted to mean net requirements for the operation of a business exclusive of transactions of a financial nature, and changes in borrowing or capitalization.[45]

Under the present organization of business and the accounting practices in force, the individual corporation has acquired a great deal of flexibility in the techniques by which it may cover its cash requirements and, while borrowing is a function of the total need for funds, its amount and timing are no longer a direct function of specific applications of the sums borrowed. Factors of convenience, ability, relative cost, etc., all condition the amount and kind of borrowing.[46]

[45] Ruth P. Mack, *The Flow of Business Funds and Consumer Purchasing Power* (New York, 1941), p. 204. On the basis of an analysis of the sources and uses of funds of fifty-four corporations, 1934–39, Mack concluded that "there appeared to be a palpable relation between the amount of borrowing and the amount of net negative retained receipts over a period of five years. . . . However, an attempt to correlate short term borrowing with changes in inventory, or long term borrowing with unusually heavy purchase or equipment which exceed the amount of current depreciation, fails to disclose any clear pattern." *Ibid.*, pp. 205, 208.

[46] Sloan said the question was one of profitability: "It must be true that on the average and in times of normal prosperity, business finds it more profitable to supply its own working capital than to borrow it from banks." Sloan, *op. cit.*, p. 278.

Currie stressed the desire for independence from banks and the factor of inability to obtain credit elsewhere. "The Decline of the Commercial Loan," *Quarterly Journal of Economics*, Vol. XLV, No. 4 (August, 1931).

Hersey, on the basis of a study of fifty-eight large companies in six industries (representing about one eighth of all manufacturing and mining), concluded that "the short term financing with notes payable or by drawing down cash or equivalent tends to act as a cushion to absorb for a while an increase in funds needed for fixed or working asset expansion or renewal which can not be met from currently retained cash receipts from operations." Long-term financing comes into play only as the need for funds persists or expands beyond the capacity of shorter term financing to provide them, or else as corporations find it desirable and possible to finance at long term in order to strengthen their short-term position. Arthur B. Hersey, "Sources and Uses of Corporation Funds," *Journal of the American Statistical Association* (June, 1941), XXXVI, No. 214, 265–74.

Mack suggested that borrowing is not linked positively to ability to borrow. Mack, *op. cit.*, p. 208.

Koch held the view that, in so far as the large manufacturing is concerned, the bank loan "serves the function of convenience rather than necessity and when these corporations borrow they do so because they desire to maintain close banking connections to facilitate possible larger borrowing in the future." Koch, *op. cit.*, Chap. IV, p. 14.

THE IMPORTANCE OF INCREASED CASH HOLDINGS

The volume of cash holdings of large corporations has grown steadily since 1928, although this growth was temporarily arrested, but not reversed, in the 1929–33 depression.[47] In general, the increased cash holdings of business firms relative to total assets and to various types of debt enabled the business system to gain a position of greater independence with respect to specific sources of funds. This was indirectly the result of the tremendous expansion in bank credit which enabled the flotation of corporate securities during the 1920s and government securities during the 1930s.

From the standpoint of an individual firm in the economic system, or a group of firms, cash balances can be acquired from two possible sources: from other non-bank holders; or from new creations of deposits by banks. From the standpoint of the economic system, excluding the banks, cash balances can be acquired from one source only, namely, their creation by the banking system.[48] Assuming no change in the volume of bank credit, an increase in the cash balances of an individual firm must be at the expense of a decrease in the deposit balances of other firms, or non-bank holders, or else because of more intensive use of the total deposits in existence.

These general principles hold true regardless of the immediate source from which the individual firm may derive its increased cash balances. It makes no difference whether the source is internal funds or outside borrowing. Consequently, the ultimate explanation of the increased cash holdings of the business community must be sought in the factors which explain the distribution of total stock of deposits and in those which explain its rise.

The growth in the total stock of deposits 1920–40 was accompanied by a change in the distribution of the stock among various economic classes and consequently in alterations in their respective debtor or creditor relation to banks. Hart's findings [49] corroborate the natural supposition that business concerns, although continuing to hold something like the same proportionate share of the total stock, by reducing indebtedness to banks, were able to convert what was in 1929 a debtor position into what had become by the end of 1937 a definitely net creditor position. This is shown in Table 15.[50]

[47] Murray Shields, *Interest Rates . . .* (New York, 1941). See chart p. 42 showing movement of cash balances of 161 large corporations.

[48] See Chap. V, *supra*.

[49] A. G. Hart, *Debts and Recovery* (New York, 1938), pp. 60–71, 296.

[50] Koch found that "not only have big business concerns relied very little on bank loans for funds during the past twenty years, but, as a group, they have been the creditors rather than the debtors of banks during these years." Since most cash is held in the form of bank deposits and since most notes payable are owed to banks, the ratio

Individuals, as an economic group, apparently have always been creditors of the banks, but it is noteworthy that their creditor position during the years 1929–37 was enhanced. Governmental bodies, despite their larger absolute holdings of deposits, became more deeply indebted to the banking system, as would be expected in an era of deficit finance. Life insurance companies, and presumably other financial institutions, not only acquired larger relative ownership in the total stock of deposits, but at the same time improved their customary position as a net creditor of the banking system. This was partly a reflection of the institutionalization of the savings-investment process, and partly of the inability of the institutions to find attractive outlets for funds under their control.[51]

TABLE 15

DEBTOR-CREDITOR RELATION BETWEEN BANKS AND VARIOUS ECONOMIC CLASSES, 1929–37 [a]

Excess (+) or Deficiency (–) of Deposits Compared with Debts to Banks

In Billions of Dollars

	1929	*1930*	*1931*	*1932*	*1933*	*1934*	*1935*	*1936*	*1937*
Federal and local government bodies	–3.73	–3.69	–4.21	–4.63	–5.79	–8.36	–11.26	–13.47	–12.89
Life insurance companies	0.14	0.15	0.16	0.25	0.39	0.53	0.72	0.83	0.77
Corporations and unincorporated businesses	–12.66	–12.34	–12.00	–9.40	–4.79	–1.70	0.00	1.45	0.50
Individuals, etc.	11.26	10.96	12.53	10.19	8.10	9.21	12.04	13.23	14.50
Totals	–4.99	–4.92	–3.52	–3.59	–2.09	–0.32	1.50	2.04	2.86

[a] Source: A. G. Hart, *Debts and Recovery* (New York, 1938), p. 296. Data were based upon the Annual Reports of the Comptroller of the Currency. Figures relate to all commercial banks, and exclude mutual savings banks and private banks.

THE SHIFT IN THE POINT OF CREDIT INJECTION

The expansion in the volume of consumer credit and in government credit resulting from the monetization of these types of debt by the banking sys-

of cash holdings to notes payable furnishes rough indication of the creditor-debtor relationship between banks and big business. He found that cash holdings of a large manufacturing sample increased consistently from a low of 1.4 times notes payable in 1921 to a high of 31.4 times in 1932. From the high it dropped to a low of 3.8 times in 1937, only to rise again in 1939 to 19.4. The annual average of the ratio for 1937–39, 11.3, was over five times the 1921–23 average of 2.0. See Koch, *op. cit.*, Chap. IV, p. 20.

[51] Interpretation of these changes is based upon Table 15 as well as upon data concerning the distribution of the ownership of the total stock of deposits, presented in Chap. IV.

tem exercised a marked influence on the manner in which the business community was financed, since it shifted the point at which credit was injected into the system and withdrawn from it. The cash which business firms acquired was absorbed to an increasing extent through gross income and did not involve an increase in the liabilities of business firms, since it represented retained earnings and non-cash expenditures. On the other hand, the indebtedness of individuals and government, principally the latter, was increased and caused the shift in net debtor position already referred to.

This shift in the point of entry has been temporal as well as spatial. To the extent that a new volume of credit was added to the system by means of consumer and government debt, the requirements of business concerns, especially in the field of trade, for accounts receivable financing was reduced and this, in turn, seemingly tended to work back to manufacturing and other suppliers, in turn reducing the demand for bank credit in the form of industrial and commercial loans. The economic system came to be financed nearer the point of final consumption and, to this extent, required less financing at other points.

THE RISE IN THE TOTAL SUPPLY OF FUNDS

The so-called internal sources of funds from retained earnings and non-cash expenditures cannot logically be regarded as a source of funds for the economy as a whole. Nor do such things as non-cash expenditures afford a continuing source of funds in the long run if customary accounting practices are followed in calculating costs and fixing selling prices.[52] It is necessary to take into account the underlying sources from which the total supply of funds of the economic system are derived. It is here that the relation of the banking system to the financing of the economic system has undergone a fundamental change which surrounds and blankets all the changes with regard to immediate sources and uses of funds by the units in the business system. The reduced direct dependence of the business world upon the banks is related to the growth in total bank credit and its injection into the

[52] It is of some importance in this connection that, whereas in the 1933–34 period business was able to accumulate funds, and 1935–37 to finance capital outlays by drawing on working capital, i. e., without resort to outside financing, in 1936 the diminution of working capital combined with the incidence of the undistributed earnings tax, and the demonetization of the public debt in 1937, drove the businessmen to the banks for funds. Similarly in 1940 and 1941, with the heavier tax program on account of the war and the demands caused by expanded outlays of industry, bank loans again began to swell, showing that internal sources were not sufficient. See Woodward, *op. cit.*, p. 17. For an explanation of the rise in bank loans during 1936 and 1937 in the face of retarded business activity and inactive capital markets, see J. Brooke Willis, "Commercial Bank Lending and Its Relation to Capital Financing," *Financial Reporter*, November 4, 1937.

system via channels other than direct loans to industry. The reasons for the rise in noncommercial and nonindustrial assets of banks, therefore, provides a partial explanation of the decline in bank loans, since it was the rise of these assets which occasioned the rise in cash balances.

In the long run, changes in the volume of deposit liabilities of the banking system result from changes in the earning assets of banks, that is, in the volume of debts financed by the banking system, although there have been periods, notably the eight years 1932–40, when the increase in bank reserves was of comparable importance in causing changes in the volume of deposits. However, in reviewing the banking history of the United States since the Civil War, we see that the feature of chief significance was the parallel growth in deposits and earning assets.[53] Naturally, the volume of reserves grew, but at a rate inconsequential to the long-run expansion of deposits. This has been true especially since the establishment of the Federal Reserve System, which permitted more efficient use of a given volume of reserves, owing to their mobilization and centralization and to the perfection of the clearing technique. The result was that deposit banking, until the last decade, was conducted on a relatively smaller aggregate of reserves than ever before. This is not to underestimate the importance of bank reserves in inducing change in the loan and investment policies of banks, but merely to indicate that the offsets to deposits in the banking system, in the long run, have consisted of debts and not money or central bank credit.

The period 1920 to 1940, however, reveals a growing divergence between the deposits and the loans and investments of banks. This is due to a number of factors, principally the rising volume of cash reserves which, by itself, accounted for more than half of the net expansion in deposits in the years 1933 to 1940. Analysis of the factors causing changes in deposits during selected intervals of years, 1920 to 1940, throws further light on this question.[54]

[53] Moulton has indicated in simple and striking fashion the close correlation between the earning assets of national banks and their issue in the form of notes and deposits for the years 1863–1937. See H. G. Moulton, *The Formation of Capital,* p. 87, and *Financial Organization and the Economic System,* p. 314.

This parallelism is sufficiently close to lead one student to measure the long-term rate of growth of deposits by the rate of growth in earning assets. See Gardner Means, "Bank Debts," in *The Internal Debts of the United States,* ed. Evans Clark (New York, 1933), p. 338. Means calculated the rate of growth of loans and investments at about 5 percent a year during the 1920s. From 1922 to 1927 the rate of growth was about the same as it was between 1908 and 1915. After adjustment for changes in the price level, he found that the rate of growth in the twenty-year period 1908–27 was a straight line on logarithmic scale. Since it was slower than during either the period 1875–97 or 1897–1907, he concluded it was not at an abnormally rapid rate. *Ibid.*, pp. 338–41.

[54] The statistics employed in the following paragraphs are based upon the analysis of factors causing changes in deposits which is given in the Appendix.

In the period 1920–24 deposits grew faster than loans and investments. This was due to the gold inflow. In the next four years, 1924–28, loans and investments grew more rapidly than deposits, due to a considerable increase in the capital funds of the banks. For the entire period, deposits grew faster than reserves, owing mainly to the transfer of deposits from the category of demand to the time category, which permitted the available credit base to support a great expansion of deposits matched by loans and investments.

During the first period, 1920–24, the reserves of the banking system underwent a substantial increase owing to the acquisition by the banking system of about $2,800,000,000 of funds from gold imports. In the second period, 1924–28, reserves were increased chiefly because of rediscounts at Federal Reserve banks. This growing volume of reserves was the potential factor to the expansion in the superstructure of bank credit and was, as Brown said, more important as a permissive factor than the actual quantitative changes which took place in it.[55] The banking system proved in this era to be a "one-way" banking system. Credit expansion proceeded without interruption because reserves either were acquired from outside the system, or were provided internally by central bank creation.

Since 1929 bank deposits have experienced the greatest contraction and subsequently the greatest expansion in the history of American banking. The factor of greatest single importance in the contraction, 1929 to 1933, was the decline in bank loans. Reductions in holdings of corporate and local government securities were also responsible, but it is noteworthy that holdings of government securities increased. On net balance for the period, there was little or no change due to the monetary gold stock, whereas the Reserve banks, by purchasing securities, actually provided an item of about $1,500,000,000 as an offset to the decline in deposits.

Means estimated that between June 30, 1931, and March 31, 1932, a period of eight months, roughly $2,000,000,000 of deposits were destroyed by the action of the banks in selling securities, and an additional $5,000,-000,000 by the willing or unwilling repayment of loans by borrowers, the remaining cancellation of deposits being accounted for by more than $600,-000,000 of currency withdrawn into circulation in exchange for deposits. and a little less than $600,000,000 of gold withdrawn for foreign account, and in addition the substantial item of $1,421,000,000 lost through bank suspensions.[56]

Analysis of the expansion since 1933 has been divided into two periods which were characterized by essentially different forces. In the period 1933–

[55] William Adams Brown, Jr., *The International Gold Standard Re-interpreted*, 1914–1934 (New York, 1940), I, 579.

[56] Means, *op. cit.*, p. 376.

36 the increase in bank holdings of United States Government securities was the most important single factor, offset to a small extent by an actual decline in bank loans. The remainder of the deposit expansion was largely accounted for by the increase in monetary gold stocks and the creation of reserves by the Reserve System. The inflow of gold caused the major portion of the increase in bank reserves and created a climate favorable to the expansion of bank investments, in view of the lack of satisfactory loan outlets.

In the succeeding four years, 1936–40, the expansion in deposits continued without abatement, but here the principal factor accounting for the rise was the growth in gold stocks and its analogous increase in bank reserves. True, there was a further rise in securities holdings, principally United States Government securities, as well as an expansion in loans which had begun in 1935, but the magnitude of these factors was dwarfed beside that of the change in gold stock. The inflow of gold was, of course, the reflection of the tremendous flow of capital towards the United States, a large part of which eventually found a temporary resting place in securities and bank deposits, and, to a lesser extent, of the excess of merchandise exports over imports.

Viewing the expansion phase, 1933–40, as a whole, roughly one-half the rise in deposits was caused by the rise in gold stocks and about one-half by the expansion of bank loans and investments, of which government bonds were the principal factor of influence. As already noted, this period represents a real departure from earlier periods in which the changes in deposits were almost entirely to be accounted for by changes in the earning assets of the banks. At no time has bank capital played a very important part as compared with other factors in explaining changes in deposits. It is true that before 1929 there was a moderate growth of bank capital, while afterward there was a substantial contraction in bank capital owing to writedowns and suspensions of banks. In the expansion period after 1933, bank capital grew by something like $1,000,000,000, accounted for in considerable part by government purchases of preferred stocks of the banks and accumulation of earnings. This is a subject whose qualitative aspects will be considered in the next chapter.

REASONS FOR THE RISE OF NONCOMMERCIAL ASSETS

In many respects the rise of noncommercial assets of banks reflects independent causation and was not merely the substitution of new types of bank assets for old. In so far as the 1920s were concerned, suffice it to say, the rise in loans to brokers, in loans secured by securities, and in real estate loans was caused, not only by relaxation of credit standards generally, by the liberalization of the banking laws, but also, in general, by the speculative mania of the period. Securities investments likewise were encouraged by the laxness of the laws and by the development and abuse of the security affiliates of banks.

A number of writers have called attention to the fact that securities investments rose relatively to loans in the depression years, e. g., following 1929. Securities investments, in their view, seem to be regarded as a kind of compensating form of asset designed to offset cyclical changes in other assets.[57] It is said that commercial banks are more easily able, within the limits of the standards of liquidity under which they operate, to increase the volume of investments than to increase the volume of their advances, especially during a period when commodity prices are falling rapidly, such as was the case during the early 1930s, whereas they cannot lend unless there is a large, unsatisfied fringe of borrowers.

This seems to have been the case in 1929–32, when banks enlarged their investments in government securities as loans declined. However, the reasons for the rise of investments, particularly in the last decade, does not lie only in the lack of traditional outlets for bank funds. Except for brief periods, the volume of investments has moved without inverse relation to the volume of loans. A principal reason for the rise in investments was the desire of individual bank managements for earnings.[58] In a period of cheap money, such as the last ten years, the desire for earnings necessitated a tremendous volume of purchases owing to the extremely low yields available if the purchasing bank was to confine its holdings to short-term issues, as seems generally to have been the practice with government securities. Despite the large purchases of bonds, declining yields prevented income from investments from rising. (Such income increased moderately during 1933 to 1937.)

Since the era of deficit financing, government bonds have been available in abundance on terms designed to appeal particularly to bank buyers. The flotation of issues by the Treasury has relied heavily upon the technique of oversubscription to new issues by banks; the commercial banking system functioned as the underwriter of new issues on a scale never before attempted with any other class of security. This, combined with a diminished supply of high-quality corporate issues, led to the concentration of bank holdings in government bonds, encouraged further by certain tax advantages and shiftability features, viz., their eligibility for use as collateral at par

[57] In this connection see Lauchlin Currie, *The Supply and Control of Money in the United States*, p. 122; Sayers, *op. cit.*, pp. 232–36; R. G. Hawtrey, *Capital and Employment* (London, 1937), p. 92; League of Nations, *Commercial Banks 1929–1934* (Geneva, 1935), p. xlii.

[58] The loss of loan outlets was partially responsible for this. Cf. Shields, *op. cit.*, p. 43.

behind advances from the Federal Reserve banks and the general understanding that the Federal Reserve System open market account was prepared as a matter of policy to support the market. Fortunately or not, depending upon the point of view, the expansion in bank reserves, resulting in major part from gold imports, occurred at the very time when deficit financing was undertaken on a grand scale. This rise in reserves was carefully nurtured by the Administration; at least, except for intermittent half-hearted attempts at control, the reserve base was allowed to expand so that the banks would be induced to buy government bonds.

The rise in the Federal lending agencies, financed either directly by the Treasury or through guarantees, and thus indirectly by the banking system, also contributed to the growth in deposits as well as to a decline in commercial loans. Whereas recent studies show that the great proportion of Federal loan credit has definitely been noncompetitive, and whereas, in the urban and rural mortgage field, government credit actually supported the private lending institutions by refunding their holdings and making them more liquid, it still remains true that a certain portion of the Federal loans were of a directly competitive nature.[59] This is particularly true in respect to agricultural finance, where government-owned or subsidized farm credit agencies became twice as important quantitatively as private mortgage lenders. The rise of government loans to finance the holding of commodities and the rise of the production credit associations were important factors in reducing the volume of the agricultural component in the category "commercial, industrial, and agricultural loans" and the older category, "all other loans."

The monetization of government debt and consumer debt resulted in a vast increase in the supply of deposits, which, it is important to note, were injected into the system indirectly, finally becoming lodged in the hands of various economic classes in the community and swelling the customary proportion which had been observed between cash balances and other assets, and converting what had been a net debtor position of the business community with respect to the banks into a net creditor position. In these circumstances, it is not surprising that the volume of commercial and industrial borrowing from banks would fail to recover its predepression levels.

IMPLICATIONS OF THE MONETIZATION OF DEBT

It is evident that the banking system in the last decade absorbed an increasing proportion of the total debt outstanding in the community. From

[59] Cf. Neil H. Jacoby, "Government Loan Agencies and Commercial Banking," address before the American Statistical Association, December 28, 1941.

1913 to 1929, the fraction of total debt held by the banking system remained approximately constant at one-sixth, but since 1929 it has increased.[60]

CHART 3

GROWTH IN DEBT COMPARED TO DEBT FINANCED BY BANKS

(In Billions of Dollars)

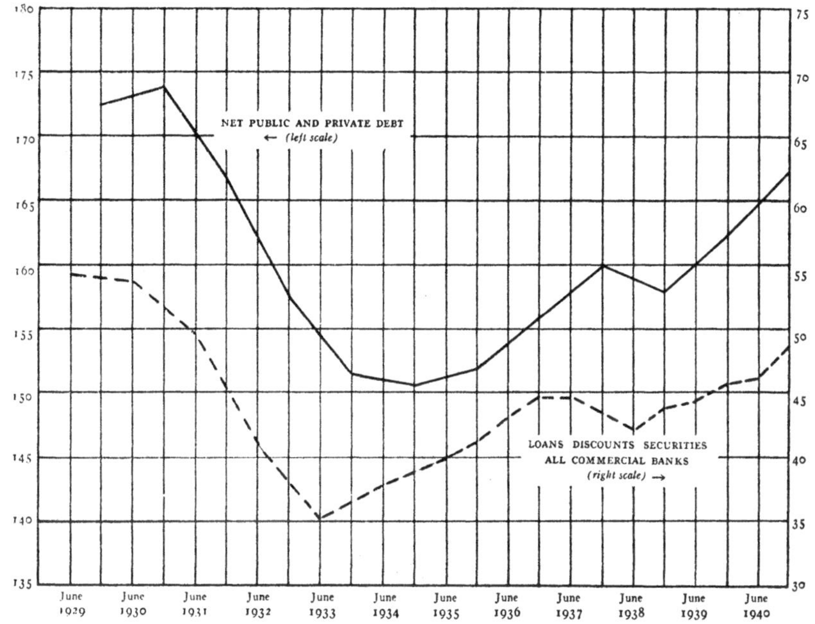

[60] The ratio of total debt to debt held by banks was computed as follows:

RATIO OF TOTAL DEBT TO BANK CREDIT

	1914	*1919*	*1929*
Debts in the United States, long-term plus short-term, in billions of dollars	89	177	276
Loans and investments of commercial banks (i. e., debt held by banks)	16	31	48
Ratio of total debt to debt held by banks	5.6	5.7	5.8

Sources: Data on loans and investments were obtained from League of Nations, *Commercial Banks 1913–1929*, p. 332. Estimates of long- and short-term debt were obtained from *The Internal Debts of the United States*, ed. Evans Clark (New York, 1933), pp. 13, 301. Total long-term debt was given as follows, in billions of dollars:

1913–14	38
1921	75
1929	126

Total short-term debt was given as follows:

1913	51
1921	102
1929	150

Chart 3 and Table 16 compare the volume of outstanding debt with the corresponding volume of bank holdings of debt since 1929. It is apparent

TABLE 16

COMPARISON OF THE GROWTH OF DEBT IN THE UNITED STATES, WITH THAT PART FINANCED BY THE BANKING SYSTEM, 1929–40 [a]

In Millions of Dollars

	Net Public and Private Debt	*Loans, Discounts, and Securities of All Commercial Banks*
1929, June		49,204
December	172,998	
1930, June		48,686
December	173,735	
1931, June		44,743
December	166,596	
1932, June		35,977
December	157,161	
1933, June		30,274
December	151,059	
1934, June		32,816
December	150,313	
1935, June		34,782
December	151,825	36,105
1936, June		38,631
December	155,814	39,594
1937, June		39,594
December	159,609	38,471
1938, June		37,251
December	157,996	38,786
1939, June		39,429
December	162,144	40,709
1940, June		41,214
December	167,254	43,997

[a] Source for net public and private debt: Robert B. Bangs, "Public and Private Debt in the United States, 1929–1940," *Survey of Current Business* (United States Department of Commerce), November, 1941, pp. 18–21. Net public and private debt measures the indebtedness of final borrowers in the United States. Total legal debt obligations outstanding were corrected by eliminating intermediary debt (i. e., debt which is offset by receivables arising from the relending of borrowed funds) and debt issued by, but held within, a "unit" having economic coalescence. See p. 20, *Survey of Current Business,* November, 1941.

Source for loans, discounts, and securities of all commercial banks: Federal Deposit Insurance Corporation; data were based on Comptroller's series for all active banks, but adjusted to remove mutual savings banks.

Prior to December, 1935, figures for loans, discounts, etc., for all commercial banks are available only as of June 30 of each year. Figures for net debt are available only as of dates nearest the year-end.

that absolute changes in debt were matched approximately by absolute changes in the volume of debt financed by banks.[61]

The distribution of debt between banks and other holders is a factor of great weight in determining the maximum debt burden which can be supported by the economic system. Obviously, there would be no problem at all if the debt were held by the same units which issued it. The problem of servicing debt arises when debt is held by economic classes other than those who issue it. A distinction must be drawn between non-bank holders and bank holders. For example, where government debt is held by non-bank holders, its servicing involves the transfer of purchasing power from taxpayers to bondholders. Even so, if the debt were held by the same persons who paid the taxes, the distribution of the total income of the community would remain unaffected. The transfer problem becomes most serious when the debt is held by the banking system since, under this condition, the service payments involve transfer of purchasing power from the non-bank public to the banks. This process may prove deflationary before actual amortization of the debt is attempted, since the sums transferred must be withdrawn from current incomes. This requires either restriction of consumption or dissavings. Besides this, any losses arising from fluctuations in market valuations, as a result of changing expectations of the debtor's ability to pay, or changing anticipations regarding the future level of interest rates, must be absorbed by the banking system.[62]

In earlier sections it was shown that an increasing proportion of the debt monetized by the banking system is noncommercial and non-self-liquidating. This change would be of less significance if the noncommercial, or "investment," assets of the banking system had not increased at a faster rate than resulting deposits were converted into savings. Chart 4 compares a series representing "investment" assets with a series representing capital funds plus savings deposits for national banks 1915–39.[63] It reveals the extent to which the banking system financed "investment" (i. e., non-self-liquidating) operations by deposit creation without subsequent transformation of

[61] It is of signal importance that between 1932 and 1940 the Federal debt held by individuals and corporations (other than banks and insurance companies) changed hardly at all. Actually, these groups sold marketable forms of debt on net balance between 1934 and 1940. See *Annual Report of the Secretary of the Treasury* (1940), pp. 92–108.

[62] Wide distribution in the ownership of debt is advantageous for other reasons, such as protection against unilateral modification of the contract, etc. See Institute of International Finance of New York University, *Some Aspects of the Mounting Public Debt*, Bulletin No. 119, February 24, 1942.

[63] The series "investment assets" represents the sum of bonds owned, real estate loans, loans on stocks and bonds. It is equivalent to all loans noncommercial in form, plus securities investments in Hunt's tabulations. See Appendix for further explanation and supporting data.

Chart 4

"INVESTMENT" ASSETS OF NATIONAL BANKS COMPARED WITH CAPITAL FUNDS PLUS SAVINGS DEPOSITS

(In Billions of Dollars)

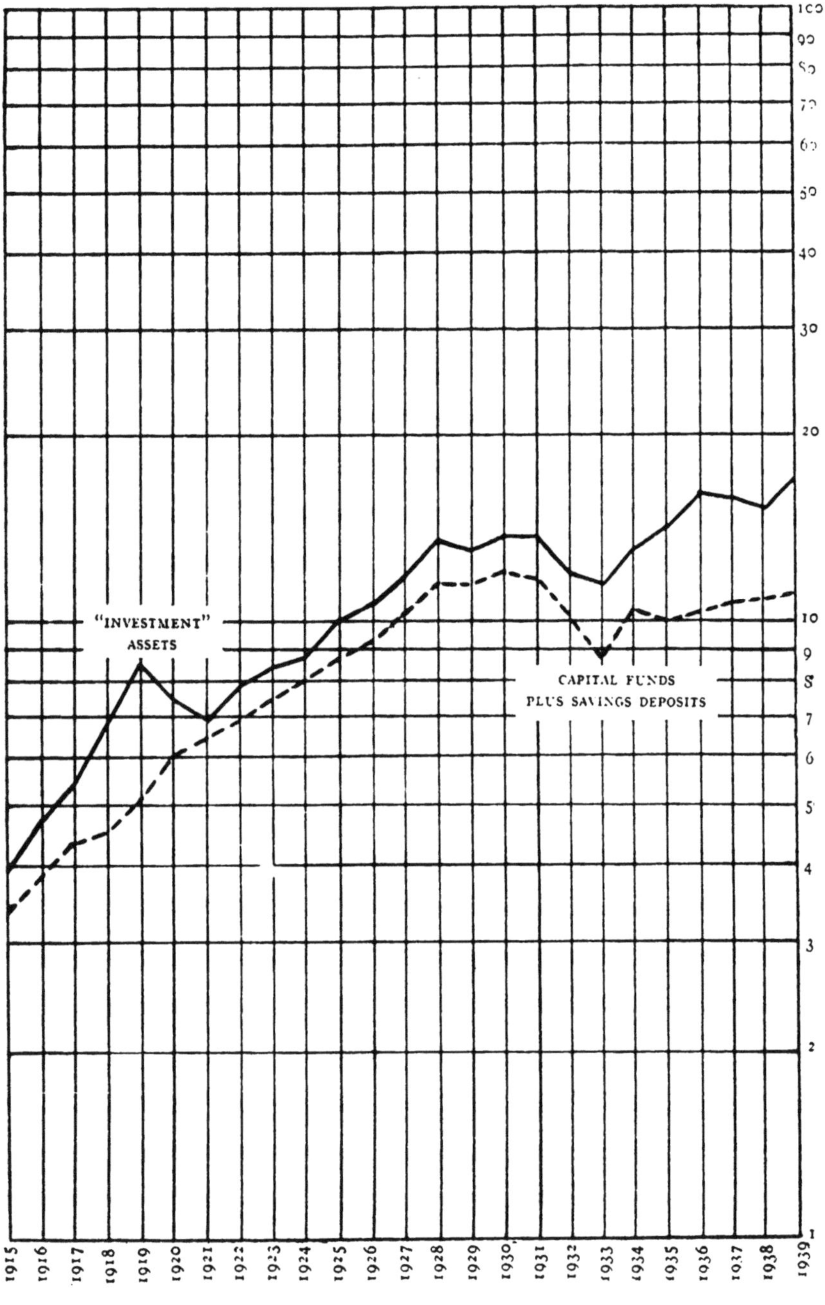

deposits into savings, in other words, the extent to which the banking system exceeded its function as a passive intermediary in the savings-investment process.

Prior to the First World War the magnitude of "investment" assets was approximately the same as that of the banks' own capital plus savings deposits. There were two subsequent periods in which the series diverged sharply, during the First World War, and since 1929. Moreover, during the 1920s, the prewar relationship was never regained although an incipient tendency was evident in the early 1920s. Thereafter, the series gradually diverged until the relationship became completely divorced after 1929.[64]

The gap between investment assets and saved funds controlled by banks was most pronounced in the two eras of government deficits, reflecting the fact that deficits were financed by creation of bank credit. It is quite evident that the growth in capital funds and savings deposits in the wake of such periods was insufficient to match the inflated debt holdings of the banks.

According to qualitative theorists, banks are justified in making capital loans and buying investments to the extent of their capital funds plus savings deposits. It is apparent that the banking system as a whole has not observed this criterion, nor can it possibly do so until the conditions which give rise to the acquisition of noncommercial assets are rectified. As suggested in the preceding chapter, the successful operation of a banking system based upon self-liquidating assets depends upon the restriction of credit creation to a basis representing self-liquidating debts. This would seem to require segregation of those banks which function as intermediaries in the investment of savings from those which have the power to write up book credits transferable by check.

This observation is not meant to imply that qualitative criteria serve no useful purpose. On the contrary, it has been one aim of this chapter to bring out the implications of the abandonment of such criteria. The earlier sections of the chapter showed that alteration in the kind of debt monetized by the banking system involved a shift in the point at which credit is injected in the economic system, and that the debtor-creditor relationship between various economic classes had changed in such a way as to render the business community more independent of bank influence. Severance of the relation between the conditions upon which credit is issued and the purposes to which it is finally devoted means separation of the money-issuing

[64] It is probable that the series would have diverged more sharply during the 1920s if allowance were made for the fictitious nature of time deposits. Many deposits, which were held in this category in order to earn interest, were not true savings deposits. Banks encouraged or condoned the practice in order to enjoy low reserve requirements to which time deposits were subject. Also, if account were taken of real estate owned by banks and other investments, the divergence would have been greater.

function of banks from their credit-issuing function. It also means, as explained in earlier chapters, that the banking system must depend for repayment of the debts it holds upon sources of income or accumulated savings which are unrelated to the income-producing power of current credit. For this reason, the banking system has lost whatever inherent liquidity it may once have possessed. The qualitative nature of debts financed by the banking system is important, not only because of considerations of liquidity, but also because of questions of solvency, that is, of the ability of the community to service the debt incurred.

There is no doubt that the expansion of debt in the 1920s was in excess of the capacity of the economic system to service it.[65] Debts often proved unproductive in the sense that the assets financed failed to produce income. This led to numerous bankruptcies, debt moratoria, revisions of contracts, and policies of cheap money to permit easy refunding on new terms. The fact that the rise in debts since the bottom of the depression has consisted mainly of government obligations does not remove the possibility that a considerable part of this debt may prove unproductive. Much of it is already unproductive, since the expenditures which give rise to it are not matched by income-producing assets but rather, in wartime, by an actual destruction of wealth.

Writing down of government debt through repudiation or receivership could not avoid consequences more serious than those which attended the 1929–33 depression. Furthermore, it is but natural to anticipate future policies to keep commodity prices high and interest rates low in order that national income may be sufficient to support the debt. Such policies, in turn, depend upon bank financing and expansion of credit, and thus produce a vicious circle of bank asset inflation.

[65] Debt was the subject of inquiries conducted by the Twentieth Century Fund. See Evans Clark, ed., *op. cit.* See also the findings of Hart, *op. cit.* A different approach to the relation of the growth of debt to the growth in production was undertaken by Bassett Jones, *Debt and Production* (New York, 1933). Jones found that debt (as measured by all interest-bearing securities excluding refunding issues, plus bank loans, but not including investments by banks, plus public debt) increased from 1880 very nearly according to the compound interest law, but that the accrual, or growth factor, was not exactly constant and increased slowly with time. He argued that production does not and cannot physically grow according to any such law; that since 1910–15 its rate of growth has decreased, and consequently, since the gain per unit was unable correspondingly to increase, fixed charges or accruals on the debt could not be paid in full.

Chapter VIII

BANK CAPITAL

THE PURPOSE AND FUNCTION OF BANK CAPITAL

FROM THE STANDPOINT of economic function, the capital account of a commercial bank has a variety of purposes. First, it serves as a source of funds with which to meet the initial expenses of organization, including the acquisition of building, fixtures, etc. Secondly, it may serve also as a supplementary source of funds for loans and investments, although today this is of minor importance. Thirdly, the capital account represents the owners' equity or net worth upon which the bank trades in issuing its own credit. At the same time the capital account alleges that the value of the assets exceeds the contractual claims of creditors. In this sense it constitutes a financial fund, subject to fluctuation in value, from which losses can be covered before impairment of depositors' claims.

Since the beginning of banking regulation in the United States, statutory requirements of minimum capital on organization have been intended to give to the State the power to prevent financially irresponsible persons from embarking upon deposit banking projects. By fixing the mimimum subscribed capital prerequisite to the acquisition of a charter, it has also been possible to limit the number of banks coming into existence. Ordinarily, this objective can be accomplished simply by refusing charters, or by licenses, as was the case on the reopening of the banks in 1933, but even then capital ratios were employed as a criterion.

Perhaps one of the most significant features of modern deposit banking, as distinguished from other types of financial institutions and other lines of business, is the small proportion which the capital account bears to the total resources, or to the "borrowed" funds. In earlier chapters it was pointed out at length that the typical individual commercial bank accumulates its assets principally by receiving cash and claims on other banks (primary deposits) and by actively expanding deposits (derived deposits) as a result of its lending and investing activities. Sales of capital stock and accumulation of earnings constitute only a minor source of funds and, on the average, represent today no more than, roughly, 10 percent of the total resources.

The principal function of the capital in any going bank, therefore, is to serve as the means by which losses may be absorbed. This statement applies with equal force to the banking system as a whole. The only real protection to the depositor against loss depends on the ability and readiness of someone other than himself to absorb losses. The losses themselves are an inescapable fact in any society no matter what its political organization or complexion. This is why banking laws surround the capital account with a multitude of restrictions and why the supervisory authorities, especially the Federal Deposit Insurance Corporation, have insisted more vehemently upon the need for adequate bank capital, a matter which will be considered later in this chapter.

Theoretically, a bank could operate without any capital whatever if it never experienced any losses either from depreciation in assets or from failure of current income to exceed expenses. Since these ideal conditions are never fully realized in practice, the optimum capital bears a direct relation to the potential losses which may be incurred in the course of time.

In contemporary banking the deposit liabilities comprise virtually the entire liability of the individual bank and of the system. There exist small miscellaneous liabilities in the form of bills payable, acceptance liability, and rediscounts but, except for these, total liabilities are synonomous with deposits. Deposits are in major proportion demand deposits. A minor fraction are "time" deposits payable on thirty days' notice and not subject to check but, nevertheless, current as regards withdrawal rights. Deposits are legally a right to demand payment in legal tender and their valuation, therefore, is incapable of appreciation or depreciation in terms of dollars.

This characteristic of deposit liabilities raises two basic problems in the conduct of the banking business, of critical importance both in the management of the individual bank and in the administration of the system. The first problem concerns the liquidity of the bank or banks; the second, their solvency. For the individual bank liquidity is a question of the availability of bank reserves, whereas solvency depends upon the adequacy of bank capital, that is, the amount by which the liquidating value of assets exceed liabilities.

Function of Bank Reserves

Bank reserves are a particular type of bank assets, ordinarily cash or its equivalent.[1] For the individual bank, the purpose of cash reserves is to

[1] Broadly speaking, the reserves of an individual bank include the whole list of assets ranked qualitatively according to the degree of their convertibility into cash. For the system, in a broad sense, reserves likewise comprise the entire list of assets, but their liquidity becomes a function of the ability of debtors to surrender deposit claims in return for cancellation of debt.

serve as a means by which the individual bank can make legally acceptable payments to the depositor public or to other banks. For the banking system, reserves may likewise serve as a means of payment when the banking system is called upon to redeem deposits held by the public or by persons in foreign countries. However, given a closed system, and assuming no demand for currency by the public, the banking system, as a system, has no need for cash reserves. But the individual banks in that system, nevertheless, still require reserves in order to make payments to one another or to clear accounts with each other. The cash reserves of the system, under these conditions, are the medium in which interbank accounts are to be settled; and the given aggregate of reserves, whatever the material of which it consists, undergoes a continuous process of being repeatedly used over and over again as its ownership is transferred from bank to bank. In this process and under the conditions assumed, legally required minimum reserves serve no purpose other than to prevent individual banks from expanding their credit by making loans and investments beyond the limits imposed by the specified relation which reserves must bear to deposits.

In reality, the cash reserve position of the individual bank is determined, first, by its relation to other banks in the system, which in turn is the result of the rate at which funds are paid into or away from the given bank; and secondly, by factors which affect the aggregate volume of reserves of the entire system, such as gold movements, demand for currency, and action by the central bank to create or contract the aggregate volume of reserves through rediscount or open-market operations.

If the aggregate amount of reserves for the system is assumed to be given, its distribution among the individual banks in the system is determined by the asset policy of the individual units and is fixed in the clearing process, the results of which are recorded on the books of the central bank.

For the individual bank, therefore, reserves serve a monetary function and are the means by which an individual bank can divest itself of deposit liabilities and shift these liabilities to other banks in the system.[2] From the point of view of the individual bank, deposits are canceled against reserves, but from the standpoint of the system, both the reserves and the deposit liabilities remain extant. Cash reserves of individual banks do not directly determine their power to absorb loss. They provide protection for this purpose only in the sense and to the extent that their adequacy may obviate the need to liquidate other assets under pressure and thereby avoid the incurrence of losses.

For the individual bank, reserve policy has to do with the proportion of assets which a bank holds in liquid form, that is, in legal tender or its equiva-

[2] See Chap. II, *supra*.

lent. The reserve problem is a problem of liquidity or convertibility. In the individual case, it concerns, in part, the amount of cash or legal tender holdings; in part, the amount of salable assets; and, in part, maturing self-liquidating assets. But for the system, leaving the central bank out of consideration, reserve strength concerns the ability of the system to liquidate assets through sale or ability to command repayment. Except for the power to issue legal tender currency or to divest itself of currency holdings, the only way the system can pay off its deposit liabilities is by contraction of the assets by which the deposit liabilities were derived. In liquidation such as that caused by depression, the bulk of deposits must be paid by offset unless the central bank is prepared to discount any class of asset, or the Government is prepared to issue fiat currency, to an indefinite extent. Certainly the latter devices provide no real solution of the difficulty and can only temporize with the causes responsible for it.

However, in contemporary practice, the central bank sometimes may alter the given volume of reserves by creating additional reserves through open-market purchases or rediscounts and thereby may relieve the pressure upon banks to liquidate assets. This kind of relief when extended to individual banks, or to the system, constitutes a means of loss avoidance since it involves the transfer of assets from member banks to the central bank at fictitious or artificially determined prices and valuations. It is in reality a deliberate attempt to refute the reality of loss and to temporize with its absorption.

The function of the central bank in regard to reserves ought to be confined basically to perfection of the system by which the ownership of the given volume of reserves can be rapidly and continuously shifted and redistributed in accordance with the demands of the clearing process. Secondly, it ought to be concerned with the creation of reserves for the alleviation of individual banks in the banking system where factors outside the control of an individual bank or banks, such as gold movements and currency hoarding, disturb the balanced distribution of reserves or threaten to upset the mechanics of its operation because of temporary shortages. In all these cases, the artificial creation of reserves can only be validated if, in the course of time, the forces originally giving rise to the disequilibrium reverse themselves or provide their own compensation. The actual creation of reserves treats results, not causes, and can only be undone by cancellation which, to be successful, requires correction of the circumstances which rendered necessary the creation of reserves.

Function of Bank Capital

The problem of bank capital is an entirely different kind of problem in so far as the individual banking unit is concerned. It is not a question of the liquidity of assets, it is a question of the adequacy of the total assets in relation to the fixed contractual liabilities; that is, it concerns the solvency of the institution. Even if the assets of an individual bank were 100 percent liquid, they might not necessarily be sufficient in amount to satisfy the claims of the depositors on liquidation. Since deposit liabilities are fixed contractual dollar claims payable on demand and not subject to value change, whereas the assets are due in the future, and therefore subject to variation in value depending upon the market prices of securities and the ability of borrowers to repay, it is always essential that the value of the assets exceed the liabilities to creditors. The amount of this excess measures the extent to which capital is really available. For the individual bank, the optimum capital is a function of the relation or proportion between total assets and total liabilities. Capital, unlike reserve, is not analogous to, or synonymous with, any particular asset or group of assets.

A liquidation of deposits by the general public *vis à vis* the banks requires, in the final analysis, liquidation of assets by the banks. Cash reserves are an asset not subject to shrinkage in value as measured in the money of account, but their exhaustion will force the system to rely upon the dollar values to be realized from the liquidation of other assets in amounts sufficient to satisfy, that is, to offset, or match the claims of depositors. The system must rely upon its ability to compel repayment by borrowers, or to sell its securities to non-bank buyers probably on their terms, otherwise it is forced to borrow or discount with the central bank. If the process of liquidation involves contraction in asset values, that is, loss, there must be present an excess of assets over liabilities sufficient to absorb such losses as may occur. This is a question of the sufficiency of capital accounts.

When losses occur, neither the capital of the individual bank nor the capital of the banks in the system can escape loss absorption unless those losses can be shifted. From this there is no escape if the changed state of affairs is incapable of rectification. The function of bank capital is to facilitate this revaluation without impairment of depositors' claims.

For the individual bank, the relation between reserves and capital lies in the fact that inadequate cash liquidity may require the sale of other assets, in turn contraction in asset values, loss and diminution of capital. Thus the older theory of banking asserted that since banks operated on a slender margin of capital, liquidity should be achieved through self-liquidating assets, or by portfolio arrangement by which the rate at which funds were received by the individual bank could be synchronized with the rate at which they were paid out. Where this was not achieved, the individual bank was expected to depend for the adjustment of its position *vis à vis* other banks in the system upon liquidation of assets through sale or rediscount, or by borrowing from other banks, any one of which might or might not involve loss and consequently impairment of stated capital.

For the system, the relation between reserves and capital is more clearly apparent. Here, the system must undergo forced liquidation at the expense of contraction in asset values and destruction of capital unless losses are either shifted to depositors, as occurs when banks fail, or to some outside agency, as when the central bank rediscounts or purchases securities at agreed-upon values.

Some theorists would solve the problem by having the central bank or the State contribute the liquidity by having unlimited rediscount or loan facilities available. For the system this means creation of reserves, not merely redistribution of the existing amount of reserves, for the purpose of accomplishing the transfer of assets from the banks. But this process itself means that values are being preserved by monetization of assets through central bank or State issue. At best, this practice can only serve as a temporary stop-gap which, to be successful in the long run, requires the ultimate restoration of the values of the assets involved. On any other assumption, there still remains the question of loss absorption. In this case, the creation of reserves serves as a kind of temporary alternative for loss absorption. A given quantity of reserves has no inherent power to absorb losses; and, therefore, creation of reserves is not to be regarded as a substitute for loss absorption since it treats results, not causes. It involves repercussions and ramifications which can be traced only with great difficulty, but which, in the first instance, mean shifting the loss to the central bank and, in all probability, eventually to the public.

The facilitation of a general liquidation of the banking system through the creation of reserves by the central bank has results vastly different from a general liquidation of the banking system which is accomplished either by the repayment of loans or sale of investments to the non-bank public. In the latter case, bank deposit liabilities are canceled against assets—credit is thereby extinguished. In the former case, the depositors succeed in converting their deposit claims into currency issues of the central bank or of the State, while their indebtedness to commercial banks is shifted from the banks to the central bank or to the State—credit remains latent, only its technical form having been changed.

It would appear to be desirable that the incidence of losses resulting from mistakes in credit extension should fall upon the institutions which make them, and that they should be taken currently when and as incurred, and not postponed, as is the case where the central bank comes to the rescue. The loss absorption function of bank capital is important, not alone to protect the deposit creditors of particular banks, but also to fix the incidence of losses. In this way the amount of loss incurred measures the correctness of the policies of given institutions.

THE NATURE OF BANK CAPITAL REQUIREMENTS

Bank capital was probably one of the first aspects of the banking business to which government addressed itself; yet it remains one of the most neglected points of regulation. As the special charter system was gradually discarded and replaced by general banking laws a minimum capital requirement came to be a prerequisite to a bank charter and was the principal statutory provision to which administrative authorities were compelled to adhere in deciding whether or not to grant charters.

Throughout the history of the United States, under Federal as well as state laws, the statutory control of bank capital has assumed certain characteristic features which have remained substantially unaltered to the present date. The principal features are as follows:

First, in every case the law specifies some absolute minimum, or minima, of capital on organization.

Secondly, in the Federal law, and in most state laws, the basic minima are graduated according to the population of the place in which the bank is located.

Thirdly, with a few exceptions to be noted, neither the statutes nor the administrative authorities have attempted to fix the amount of capital required of banks already in existence. Penalties for impairment of capital, of course, serve indirectly to encourage preservation of original capital investment.

There seems to be almost universal agreement among students of banking that the absolute and arbitrary capital requirements on organization have failed signally to check excessive competition and a generally overbanked condition. This has been attributed to the fact that the minima were set too low and, since the supervisory authorities in granting charters refused to be guided by any other criteria, it resulted in the establishment of too many banks with small capital accounts. Obviously, some requirement regarding original capital is needed, even where other conditions are imposed upon the establisment of new banks, and the proper amount must always be, to a large extent, the subject of arbitrary determination by someone. This weakness could have been readily corrected by raising the minima, as was done in 1933 in the case of national banks, and by the exercise of more strict review by supervisory officers of applications for charters in the light of the need for new banks and the adequacy of the existing facilities. An absolute minimum requirement is not, therefore, a serious structural defect; indeed, it has much to commend it as a guide to the supervisory authorities.

However, in grading capital according to population of the places in which banks are to be located, the legislatures have committed a patent absurdity which ought long ago to have been corrected in a forthright manner, but which instead has been allowed to survive because of the mistaken notion that the optimum size of bank capital is a function of population. The legislators for many years have reasoned that the grading of capital requirements according to population was intended to establish a proportion between capital and the amount of business likely to be performed by the bank after organization. This argument obviously assumes that the volume of business done by a bank will be determined by the population of the place in which the bank is located. But if the intention is to relate required capital to the volume of business, why should it not be related directly to it? Furthermore, it may be reasoned *a priori* that population will determine the volume of business of an individual bank only if that bank has a monopoly of the business in its community. Manifestly, population fails as an index for individual banks in places where there is more than one bank.[3]

Barnett is among the few writers who have made any mention whatever of the weakness of capital requirements based on population. He said:

> The grading of the amount of capital according to population of the place in which the bank is located is evidently a very crude way of securing a proportion between capital and volume of business. The elaboration of the scale is of some service, but there remain differences in the volume of business transacted in places of the same size and the more important differences in the amount of competition which different banks must meet.[4]

A more realistic defense, or rather explanation, of capital requirements graded according to population was that it afforded a means of encouraging the formation of banks in smaller cities and towns. This is confirmed by the fact that in most state laws the grades are not numerous nor do they apply to places of large population. (Under the National Bank Act there is no grading for cities of more than fifty thousand population. The grading ceases at an earlier point in many state laws.)

It is to be noted that the argument that capital requirements graduated

[3] It is shown at a later point in this chapter that population of the places in which banks are located is inversely related to the ratio of capital to assets for aggregates of banks in these places.

[4] George E. Barnett, *State Banks and Trust Companies*, National Monetary Commission, S.Doc. 659, 61st Cong., 3d Sess. (Washington, D.C., 1911), p. 50.

according to population afford a means of encouraging the formation of banks in small places contradicts another argument used in its defense, namely, that capital requirements based on population tend to check excessive competition. In effect, the graduation according to population is a means of circumventing the limitation upon the number of banks which would have been effective had the maximum scale of capital been universally applicable. What limits competition is not the graduation according to population but the absolute requirement itself.

Of course, even the population requirement fails to avoid the necessity of establishing some basic minimum for the lowest class of population. Throughout our history this amount seems to have been an arbitrary matter for which there has been uniformity only in the case of national banks, whereas variability has characterized the state laws.

As mentioned earlier, there have been and are some exceptions to the general pattern of absolute minima graded according to population. The principle of requiring capital to be related to the indebtedness of a bank predates bank supervision. In the first charters granted in a number of states by special acts of legislatures, provisions are to be found which operated to limit the amount of debt a bank could incur in relation to its capital. These restrictions varied from about 10 percent to 30 percent of capital to liabilities.[5] With the adoption of general banking laws, this type of restriction was generally discarded, though it remained an elastic administrative principle. However, for about fifty years, general banking laws in several states have based the capital required for each bank directly upon the amount of business done by the bank. Requirements based on population were supposed to accomplish this, but it is obvious they never have. The criterion selected has been either asset or deposit volume of the individual bank.

One of the earliest attempts to apply this principle is found in the Iowa savings bank law of 1874 which set an absolute minimum requirement of $10,000; but further stipulated that such banks might receive deposits only to the amount of ten times their capital. If deposits were received in excess of this limit, the bank was required to increase its paid-up capital. Kansas experimented with a similar requirement between 1897 and 1901. In this case, the requirement was much more severe. It provided that the total investments of any bank, exclusive of United States bonds, should not exceed four times the capital and surplus actually paid in. The Kansas bank commissioner described the purpose of this law in the following language:

[5] *Annual Report of the Superintendent of Banks, State of New York*, Part I (1940), Legislative Document (1941), No. 24, p. 14.

> The provision, which produced the greatest opposition, was the section which limited the total investments of every bank to four times its capital and surplus. The theory upon which the adoption of this section was urged was that a bank's capital should bear some proper proportion to the volume of business transacted by it; and there being no possible way by which the amount of deposits could be restricted, the idea of restricting the investments appeared to be not only possible but wise. It was argued in support of the proposition that it would result in an increase in the capital of small banks, thereby giving greater protection to depositors; that it would not be a difficult matter to procure additional capital when, for each $1,000 thus invested, the bank could invest $4,000, and above all, that banks should be content with receiving an income on $4 for every dollar invested. The operation of this section has resulted in nearly every 100 banks increasing their capital or surplus. Many have carried their entire net earnings to surplus, thereby adding to the strength of the bank and the security of depositors.[6]

Finally this law was repealed in 1901 in favor of the then generally accepted type of absolute minima graded according to population, but a vestige of the former principle was retained in the stipulation that no bank might accept deposits in excess of ten times its paid-up capital and surplus.

Several other states (California, Nevada, Oklahoma, South Dakota, Texas, Nebraska, and Rhode Island) adopted similar methods of determining the amount of required capital, most of these rules stipulating a 1:10 ratio of capital and surplus to deposits. (In South Dakota the ratio was 1:15. In Oklahoma the commissioner had the power to fix the proper ratio. Texas adopted a sliding scale which related the ratio to the absolute amount of capital. Nebraska provided that loans and investments, exclusive of reserve, banking house, and fixtures, should not exceed eight times capital and surplus.)

In spite of the evident dissatisfaction with this kind of capital requirement, it has survived to the present day in a number of state banking laws and since the banking crisis of 1933 has been adopted by an additional number of states. Apparently, the laws of as many as eighteen states now specify some sort of relation between deposits and capital.[7] Typically the required

[6] Quoted by Barnett, *op. cit.*, p. 51.

[7] This number is somewhat higher than that usually cited. A digest of the significant provisions of these laws is contained in the Appendix based upon information obtained from an unpublished survey of the Federal Deposit Insurance Corporation, and from comparative analysis of state laws cited by various other investigators, and by checking the currency of laws in doubtful states. Enumeration and description of the various laws will be found in the following places:

Roland I. Robinson, "The Capital Deposit Ratio in Bank Supervision," *Journal of Political Economy*, February, 1941, p. 47, n. 13.

ratio was 10 percent, though certain states deviate from this standard.[8] Only a few of the laws are strictly enforced, while in most of the states enforcement is discretionary with the banking supervisors.[9]

In twenty-seven of the states which have no laws regulating capital to deposits ratios, the banking authorities are said by the Federal Deposit Insurance Corporation to make some attempt to encourage a 10 percent ratio, and to coöperate with other supervisory authorities in this endeavor, but in eight states there is apparently little or no encouragement by the authorities toward the maintenance of an adequate ratio.[10]

It is of some significance that experiments of this kind of capital requirement were confined almost exclusively to the states, prior to the adoption of Federal deposit insurance. However, sporadically, the Federal authorities had earlier evinced some interest in it, an illustration of which is to be found in the remarks of the Comptroller of the Currency in his *Annual Report* for the year 1914, a time when the average ratio of total deposits of national banks to capital and surplus was about 4.6. He said:

> The view is held by many practical bankers and experienced economists that it is not sound banking for an active commercial bank to be allowed to receive deposits in excess of ten times its capital and surplus. I am

---

Institute of International Finance of New York University, *Ratio of Capital Funds to Deposits of Commercial Banks in the U.S.*, Bulletin No. 112, October 14, 1940.

American Bankers Association, *Compilation of State Statutes Requiring Surplus at Time of Organization of Banking Institutions, Accumulation of Surplus by Banking Institutions, Ratio between Capital and Surplus and Deposits*, prepared by the legal department, April 15, 1936; mimeographed.

Frank P. Smith and Ralph W. Marquis, "Capital and Surplus as Protection for Bank Deposits," *Bankers Magazine*, March, 1937, pp. 215–26.

[8] The 10 percent standard was required in nine states. In some states the ratio was from 10 percent downward. In Minnesota the legal ratio was only 4 percent.

[9] The laws of California, Nevada, and Wisconsin are strictly enforced. In Colorado and Nebraska enforcement is said to be lax, while in Arizona the law is not enforced at all. In Minnesota, which requires a ratio of only 4 percent, the banking commissioner encourages a 10 percent ratio. In Texas, New York, and Indiana the law provides that enforcement is entirely at the discretion of the banking supervisors. In Texas the supervisors decide each case on its own merits. In New York the Banking Department in practice is somewhat lenient in requiring maintenance of the 10 percent ratio; The Indiana Banking Department applies the law only when it fails to bring about an adequate capital ratio through negotiations with the bank. Under the Indiana law banks are exempt from the 10 percent requirement if their cash plus government bonds is equal to 50 percent of their deposits. In Iowa authorities regard the condition of the bank and capability of management rather than a fixed ratio. Michigan's law allows the commissioners to change the requirements for individual banks. No definite information is available regarding North Dakota's enforcement of the law, but it is believed that the law is not enforced. The preceding statements are derived from information obtained from the Federal Deposit Insurance Corporation.

[10] Information furnished the writer by the Federal Deposit Insurance Corporation and based upon advices from the Corporation's supervising examiners, January, 1939.

firmly impressed with the correctness of this view, and respectfully recommend to the Congress that the national bank act be amended so as to provide that no national bank be permitted to hold deposits in excess of ten times its unimpaired capital and surplus . . .

Such a limitation need not interfere with the growth and development of the bank. When its deposits approach an amount equal to ten times capital and surplus, or whatever other limitation may be fixed, arrangements may be made to increase its capital. A bank whose deposits amount to ten times its capital and surplus, if efficiently managed, should be so profitable that there would be no difficulty in providing for an increase of capital by sale of additional stock. . . . A commercial bank whose capital and surplus amounts to less than one-tenth of its deposits is . . . doing business on too small a capital and upon too narrow a margin of safety, and does not furnish its creditors the protection to which they are entitled against unexpected losses and contingencies which are liable to, and do, so frequently arise.[11]

There have been comparatively few changes in respect to the other statutory requirements surrounding the capital accounts of banks. After the inauguration of a plan of Federal deposit insurance under the Banking Act of 1933, the double-liability provision, which formerly affected all stock issues of national banks as well as most state banks, was discarded. In 1935 several new provisions were enacted which required the banks to accumulate surplus by continuing to set aside one tenth of net earnings before the payment of dividends until and unless surplus equaled 100 percent of stock capital. Also, it was required that national banks on organization must have a surplus in an amount equal to 20 percent of capital. The stricter requirements regarding surplus are designed to strengthen and enlarge the capital account but can do so only gradually. However, since the complete breakdown of the banking system in 1933 there has developed an increasing interest on the part of the supervisory authorities in the matter of bank capital, and since that time there has been some evidence of insistence upon more stringent capital requirements than are called for explicitly in the statutes.

In 1934 the Comptroller of the Currency stated that the Comptroller's office was in a position to require national banks to maintain adequate capital. In 1933, on the occasion of the re-opening of the banks, the Federal supervisory authorities had already been guided by capital ratios in the licensing of banks eligible to reopen, in the strengthening of the capital structure of the banks through purchase of preferred stock by the Reconstruction Finance Corporation, as well as in the admission of state banks to

[11] *Annual Report of the Comptroller of the Currency*, I (1914), 21.

membership in the Federal Reserve System, while since that time permission to retire preferred stock has been made conditional upon the observance of a specified capital ratio (ordinarily 1:10).[12] Furthermore, the Federal Deposit Insurance Corporation in 1939 went so far as to assert that it would enforce the 1:10 rule in the case of new banks based upon the prospective volume of business.[13] This represented the first time that the Federal authorities attempted the application of this type of capital requirement to new banks.

In recent years the Federal Deposit Insurance Corporation has been the principal agency to insist upon more adequate bank capital and the leading advocate of the theory that required capital ought to be related to the volume of bank assets. This position has been gradually evolved, has undergone considerable modification, and evidently has not yet become fully oriented. The Corporation at first expressed the capital ratio in relation to deposits, but soon afterward wisely recognized that it was more logical to specify a relation to assets. Thus at the present time the ratio is defined as the ratio of net sound capital to the appraised value of assets.[14] The guiding rule is that "each bank should have a sound capital, having due regard to the character and quality of assets, so as to give reasonable assurance of the maintenance of a margin of protection to depositors and other creditors." [15] In testing the adequacy of capital, the Corporation considers the following factors: (*a*) quality of assets with reference to fixed and substandard assets: (*b*) managerial ability; (*c*) possible liabilities arising out of fiduciary operations; and (*d*) local economic conditions.

The Corporation and its spokesmen have at various times taken the position that one of the chief objects of supervision is to assure adequate capital, and that if a large number of banks are constantly on the brink of insolvency, they tend to abdicate their functions as suppliers of credit, especially in times of uncertainty, in order to avoid risk and in an effort to preserve solvency.[16] It has also been asserted that the bank with small capital is being subsidized by the other banks in the insurance system.

[12] See American Bankers Association, *The Answers of the American Bankers Association in Reply to Part 9 of the Questionnaire of the Committee on Banking and Currency of the U.S. Senate relative to Senate Resolution 125, 76th Cong., 1st Sess.*, April, 1941, pp. 54–56; also Robinson, *op. cit.*, pp. 44–47.

[13] Applicants for admission to insurance, particularly newly organized banks, are expected to provide adequate capital in relation to prospective asset volume and, in any case, not less than $25,000 capital stock and $5,000 surplus. See *Annual Report of the Federal Deposit Insurance Corporation* (1939), p. 13.

[14] Net sound capital is defined as total capital less book value of loss or doubtful assets plus determinable sound banking value of assets not shown on the books of the banks. It represents the excess of the appraised value of the assets over liabilities.

[15] *Annual Report of the Federal Deposit Insurance Corporation* (1937), p. 15.

[16] *Ibid.* (1939), p. 12.

Thus it is clear that the Corporation fully subscribes to the theory that the primary function of bank capital requirements in a going system is to absorb losses and in that way enable the system to maintain continuous operation and uninterrupted service to the public. This position relegates to a position of secondary importance the older view that the function of bank capital requirements is to regulate the number of banks being formed, a matter which can be handled more simply and directly by merely refusing charters in cases where there is no clearly demonstrable need for new banks.

The emphasis which the Federal Deposit Insurance Corporation has given the 10 percent rule has aroused a certain amount of controversy regarding the theory of such a restriction as well as its practicability. Apparently, the corporation adheres to the belief that the best results are to be obtained by a flexible administration of capital ratio requirements in the light of the qualifying factors cited above, and is not prepared to assert that a statutory rule be laid down.[17] However, legislation which seeks this result has been introduced on occasion in Congress and, as has already been mentioned, a number of additional states have within recent years adopted such statutory rules.[18] The principle objection to a statutory rule is that the conditions affecting the adequacy of capital are so varied that the imposition of statutory ratio requirements would be unwise, at least until a formula is evolved which will test capital sufficiency on the basis of risk attendant to each class of assets. Any such capital ratio rule, whether statutory or administrative in nature, it is argued, ought to take account, not only of that portion of assets tied up in bank premises and hence not readily available, but, on the other hand, of those assets which, like cash, are nondepreciating in character. With this there seems to be general agreement. It has been explained by various persons that if a fixed rule were made mandatory by legislative action, or if the banks voluntarily adhered to such a ratio, they would at the upper limit either have to refuse deposits (the banks as a whole would cease granting loans and buying bonds) or increase capital funds.[19] Either alternative presents obvious difficulties. Consideration of

[17] Cf. address of Hon. Leo T. Crowley, Chairman of the Federal Deposit Insurance Corporation, "Bank Capital Ratios Today" before Wisconsin Bankers Conference, April 7, 1942.

The Federal Deposit Insurance Corporation in outlining suggestions for state legislation has never recommended legislation specifying capital ratios but merely "revision of legislation specifying minimum capital" (see p. 30, *Annual Report* for 1938).

[18] Some states appear inclined to leave the matter to the policy of the Federal Deposit Insurance Corporation. For example, South Carolina in 1939 stipulated that, in addition to all other requirements to be observed in obtaining a charter for a banking institution, the paid-in capital must be "sufficient to qualify such bank for membership in the Federal Deposit Insurance Fund." (See *Annual Report of the Federal Deposit Insurance Corporation* (1939), p. 32.)

[19] See Institute of International Finance of New York University, *op. cit.*, p. 25.

this aspect of the subject will be postponed until the conditions responsible for the present capital position have been reviewed.

THE PRESENT CAPITAL POSITION OF THE BANKS

It is well known that the laws governing the capital accounts of national banks remained substantially unaltered until 1900 when banks were permitted to organize with lower capitals, and that no substantial changes were made again until 1933 when the requirements were restored to the levels prevailing before 1900. In 1933 and 1935 several comparatively minor changes were made regarding double liability, surplus, etc., as mentioned earlier in this chapter. Thus, from the legislative standpoint, the situation today is much the same as it has always been, despite radical changes in the functions of the banks and their relation to the economic system.

The reduction in capital requirements effected by the 1900 law revealed a lack of wisdom because it was made during a period when deposit banking was undergoing a significant transformation from a basis on which a large fraction of the funds was supplied by capital accounts to one on which the large fraction is derived from demand liabilities issued to depositors. In other words, by 1900 banking already was being conducted on a thin margin of equity, a margin which during the succeeding years was to become much thinner.

Prior to the establishment of the Federal Reserve System many of our banking difficulties were attributable to inelasticity in the reserve organization and the currency mechanism, rather than to the actual solvency of the institutions themselves, but since then they have been caused in no small part by inadequate bank capital in relation to the kinds of assets held by the banks. Studies of bank failures covering the period of the twenties have had comparatively little or nothing to say regarding the capital position of the banking system. Hardy, in reviewing the proposed safeguards to enable the banking system to meet severe shocks and widespread insolvency, was one of few to stress the need for more ample capital and surplus in relation to deposits.[20] It was Hardy's observation that the rate of bank failures was only partially the result of the rate of shrinkage of assets and the adequacy of the organization for distributing the risks, but that "it is also a function *of the size of the margin provided for absorbing losses before they impair solvency.*" [21]

[20] Charles O. Hardy, *Credit Policies of the Federal Reserve System* (Washington, D.C., 1932), p. 344. The other factors discussed were enforcement of more rigid standards of asset policy, greater size of banks and diversification of investment, branch banking, and provision of more ample support of weak banks.

[21] *Ibid.*, p. 345. Italics mine.

It was not until after the establishment of the Federal Deposit Insurance Corporation that any comprehensive study was undertaken regarding the capital position of the banking system. The controversy during the preparation of that law and subsequently indicates that the subject of bank capital was regarded primarily as a scheme for insuring, or guaranteeing, the deposi-

TABLE 17

PERCENTAGE RATIO OF BANKS' OWN RESOURCES TO THEIR PUBLIC LIABILITIES EXCLUDING ACCEPTANCES AND SUNDRY ACCOUNTS, SELECTED COUNTRIES, SELECTED YEARS, 1913–37[a]

	1913	*1920*	*1929*[b]	*1933*	*1937*
Europe					
Austria	33.3	7.5	15.1	15.3	11.2(1936)
Belgium	24.3	15.1	25.6	29.5	14.5
Czechoslovakia	—	11.6	12.2	11.3	9.2
Denmark	30.8	14.7	17.5	19.0	18.7
Finland	22.0	24.9	19.4	18.4	13.4
France					
Deposit banks	19.8	8.9	8.3	8.9	9.4
Investment banks	55.3	32.9	19.2	29.3	23.2
Germany					
Commercial banks	30.3	4.0	7.5	7.7	8.8
Netherlands	52.8	29.4	28.0	36.0	26.3
Norway					
Commercial banks	18.3	24.2	18.7	19.0	16.9
Sweden	32.0	18.7	18.6	15.6	14.6
Switzerland	21.7	16.7	15.2	15.3	14.1
England and Wales	10.1	6.5	7.4	6.7	6.1
Scotland	12.7	5.7	10.1	10.2	9.2
Ireland	14.1	5.7	9.8	9.2	9.8
North America					
Canada	17.5	9.6	9.8	11.2	9.6
United States of America, all commercial	19.8	12.0	15.4	17.2	12.5
Latin America					
Argentine	39.0	—	17.8	18.6	11.7
Brazil	36.0	20.9	20.4	19.7	
South Africa and Oceania					
Union of South Africa	16.2	8.4	12.2	9.9	8.6
Australasia	22.2	13.5	20.2	21.2	19.5

[a] Sources: League of Nations, *Commercial Banks 1913–1929* (Geneva, 1931), p. 26, Table IV; and "Money and Banking," I, *Monetary Review 1938/39,* 170, Table XIII.

[b] Data for 1929 were corrected where differences existed between amounts shown in *Commercial Banks 1913–1929* and "Money and Banking 1938/39," Vol. I, *Monetary*

tor, rather than as a device for protecting the solvency of the banks themselves. Not until recently, under the leadership of the Federal Deposit Insurance Corporation, has it been recognized that supervision over the quality and amount of bank assets is a basic function of, and prerequisite to, the success of deposit insurance.

A number of students have remarked upon the fact that the ratio of capital accounts of the banks to total assets was decreasing before the First World War and that the change was accelerated by the tremendous expansion of bank assets during and since that war. This development was not peculiar to American banking; indeed, it appears to have been a worldwide phenomenon, as is clearly revealed by Table 17.

Special circumstances might be cited to explain the trend indicated by these data in the case of particular countries.[22] However, the most signal fact is that the trend was universal and that it is one which persists unto the present day. The basic explanation lies in the great expansion in bank assets accompanied by the growth of bank liabilities. In this connection it is to be noted that the greatest expansions occurred in periods of war finance or of inflation; generally speaking, whenever the banking system was called upon to cover the gap between demand for funds and the supply forthcoming as a result of voluntary savings. Throughout this period there were only brief intervals when the ratio of capital to deposits exhibited any inclination to revert to higher levels formerly prevailing. In the United States the most severe declines in capital ratio occurred in periods of rapid asset growth, notably 1896–1900 and 1915–19, and again, 1933–40, when banks failed to expand their capital to a degree commensurate with the expansion in assets.

In the United States, it appears to have been true that the relative rise in deposits is partly to be explained by the fact that the national banks were permitted by the Federal Reserve Act to receive time deposits and to the extent that these pertained to the nature of savings, they did not spell an expansion of purchasing power by the banking system of the sort produced by the issuance of demand deposits. In other words, the expansion of bank deposits in relation to bank capital is partly mitigated by the assumption of savings bank functions by the commercial banks since 1914. Thus, the ratio of capital to assets (or to deposits) of the banking system has been undergoing a steady decline for many years. This tendency has not yet been

[22] In Germany, Austria, Hungary, and France, for example, the drop in the capital ratio was due partially to actual loss of capital as a result of currency inflation, while the capital revaluation and new issues since stabilization failed to restore the gold value of the banks' own funds to their prewar level.

arrested, and today the system is operating on a smaller relative margin of capital than at any time in its history.[23]

The Federal Deposit Insurance Corporation, realizing that its ability to perform the guarantee of deposits depends in the final analysis upon adequate bank capital, has conducted careful studies of the position of the banks regarding capital. It found that the ratio of net sound capital of the insured commercial banks to the appraised value of their assets at the time of their 1940 examinations was 9.7 percent. If the capital supplied by the Reconstruction Finance Corporation is left out of account, and only privately owned capital considered, the ratio was 9.1 percent. It is estimated that subsequent to the examination dates in that year there was a further deterioration in the ratio so that by the year's end it was closer to 9.0 percent.[24] For all operating commercial banks in the United States and its possessions, the ratio of book value of capital to total assets was 9.5 percent at the end of 1940 and was lower than at any time on record. This compares with 11.7 percent on June 30, 1920; 14.1 percent, June 29, 1929; 11.8 percent June 30, 1937; and a range of fluctuation between 1919 and 1939 of between 11 and 16 percent.[25]

In Table 18 net sound capital is expressed as a percentage of the appraised value of assets, the deposits, and the total capital accounts of all insured commercial banks which were examined by the Corporation for the years 1933–40. The banks covered in this table are mainly insured banks not members of the Federal Reserve System. Comparable data for banks examined by other Federal agencies have not been compiled for years prior to 1938.

On the basis of examinations of insured commercial banks, including those examined by other Federal agencies, the Corporation found that in the year 1939 there were ten insured banks with no sound capital and an additional seventy-five with sound capital ratio to appraised value of assets of less than 5 percent, these two groups together having deposits of $385,000,000. Insured banks with sound capital of less than 10 percent numbered 2,884 having deposits of $30,000,000,000. About $600,000,000 additional capital was needed to bring these banks up to the minimum standard. It was estimated that approximately one half of the 996 noninsured banks in

[23] The Brookings Institution in 1940 concluded that the banking system was greatly undercapitalized and gave its opinion that a ratio at least as high as that of 1929 is necessary in the interests of banking stability, while pointing out that the success of the deposit insurance system depends in the last analysis upon the adequacy of banking capital. See H. G. Moulton, *et al., Capital Expansion, Employment and Economic Stability* (Washington, D.C., 1940), p. 125.

[24] See *Annual Report of the Federal Deposit Insurance Corporation* (1940), p. 47 n.

[25] *Annual Report of the Federal Deposit Insurance Corporation* (1939), p. 12.

TABLE 18

NET SOUND CAPITAL, INSURED COMMERCIAL BANKS EXAMINED BY THE FEDERAL DEPOSIT INSURANCE CORPORATION, 1933–40 [a]

Expressed as a Percentage of Various Items

	Appraised Value of Assets	*Deposits*	*Total Capital Accounts*
1933 [b]	9.62	11.15	45.12
1934	13.38	15.80	67.17
1935	13.98	16.58	76.51
1936	14.38	17.09	90.92
1937	13.12	15.33	92.25
1938 original [c]	12.64	14.64	87.78
1938 uniform [c]	12.77	14.81	88.83
1939	12.40	14.30	90.69
1940	12.09	13.90	93.62

[a] Source: *Annual Report of the Federal Deposit Insurance Corporation* (1940), Table 135, p. 186.

[b] Based on examination for admission to insurance in late 1933 and early 1934.

[c] Results of all examinations made in 1938 were tabulated both on the basis of original procedure and of uniform procedure.

operation December 31, 1939, were known to have capital accounts below the minimum standards of the Corporation, namely 10 percent.[26]

Furthermore, the Corporation found that in the light of other tests of adequacy, such as the quality of assets, 3,000 more banks (other than the 2,884 deficient above) had a capital below the reasonable minimum considered satisfactory in the light of the nature and quality of assets and other qualifying factors. From an absolute standpoint, it was found that at the end of 1939 approximately fifteen hundred small insured banks had sound capital and surplus of less than $30,000.

On the basis of examinations of 13,437 banks for the year 1940, the comparable findings were as follows:

TABLE 19

DISTRIBUTION OF BANKS ACCORDING TO NET SOUND CAPITAL RATIO, 1940

	Number	*Deposits*
Banks with no sound capital	7	$39,000,000
Banks with sound capital less than 5 percent of appraised value of assets	49	210,000,000
Banks with sound capital less than 10 percent of appraised value of assets	2,872	36,740,000,000

[26] *Ibid.*, p. 23.

The examinations revealed that there were seventy-two banks with deposits of $378,000,000 which possessed no sound capital except that represented by the investment of the Reconstruction Finance Corporation.

Nearly one fifth of the banks, holding almost two thirds of the deposits in all insured commercial banks, had net sound capital of less than 10 percent of the appraised value of assets. A comprehensive comparison for the years 1939 and 1940 is set forth in Table 20:

TABLE 20

PERCENTAGE DISTRIBUTION OF BANKS ACCORDING TO RATIO OF NET SOUND CAPITAL TO APPRAISED VALUE OF ASSETS, 1940 AND 1939 [a]

Insured Commercial Banks

	Number of Banks		*Deposits*	
	1940	*1939*	*1940*	*1939*
Banks with ratios of:				
$0.00 or less	0.1	0.1	0.1	
$0.01 to $4.99	0.4	0.6	0.4	0.7
$5.00 to $9.99	21.3	20.7	63.5	57.6
$10.00 to $14.99	45.4	44.1	29.0	32.1
$15.00 to $19.99	21.1	21.5	4.5	6.6
$20.00 to $24.99	7.7	8.3	1.5	1.7
$25.00 or more	4.0	4.7	1.0	1.3
All banks	100	100	100	100

[a] Source: *Annual Report of the Federal Deposit Insurance Corporation* (1940), Table 20, p. 46.

In recent years the proportion of banks with net sound capital ratios of less than 5 percent of deposits continues to be smaller than in the early years of deposit insurance. However, the proportion with net sound capital ratios of less than 10 percent, while higher than at the time of admission to insurance, was lower than in any of the early years of deposit insurance as demonstrated in Table 20 for insured banks not members of the Federal Reserve System. Data for members of the Federal Reserve System are not available for these years but would show a somewhat similar trend.[27]

The Corporation observed that the decline in capital ratios from 1939 to 1940 represents a continuation of the trend which has been in evidence since 1936 due to the growth in deposits and assets at a more rapid rate than the growth in capital accounts. During this period two conflicting developments were in evidence. On the one hand, the number of hazardous and very weak banks was reduced, but on the other, more banks fell into the group with capital accounts less than 10 percent of assets.[28]

[27] *Ibid.*, p. 51.

[28] *Annual Report of the Federal Deposit Insurance Corporation* (1940), p. 45.

TABLE 21

PERCENTAGE DISTRIBUTION OF BANKS ACCORDING TO RATIO OF NET SOUND CAPITAL TO DEPOSITS, 1933–39 [a]

Insured Commercial Banks Not Members of the Federal Reserve System

	1939	*1938 Uniform*	*1938 Original*	*1937*	*1936*	*1935*	*1934*	*1933* [b]
Banks with ratios [c] of:								
$0.00 or less	0.1	0.1	0.5	0.2	0.3	0.5	0.6	10.0
$0.01 to $4.99	0.6	0.5	1.8	0.9	1.9	1.6	1.9	9.6
$5.00 to $9.99	12.4	12.1	14.0	13.8	10.0	10.9	10.5	14.9
$10.00 or more	86.9	87.3	83.7	85.1	88.8	87.0	87.0	65.5
All banks	100	100	100	100	100	100	100	100

[a] Source: *Annual Report of the Federal Deposit Insurance Corporation* (1939), p. 51.
[b] Examinations for admission to insurance in 1933 and early 1934.
[c] Ratio of net sound capital to deposits is used for historical purposes because distribution according to net sound capital ratio to appraised value of assets was not available for earlier years.

In general, the small banks were found to have higher ratios of net sound capital than did the large banks, as shown in Tables 22 and 23. This would seem to reflect several influences, the fact that small banks tend to be located outside the financial centers and are engaged in a distinctly different type of business, holding assets which require a larger capital protection, as well as the fact that statutory capital requirements often only provide for an absolute minimum amount on organization which has only the remotest relation to the actual or eventual size of the banks. (See later discussion of relation of capital to kind of assets.)

CRITICISM OF CAPITAL RATIO TESTS

Some writers have found grounds for disagreement with particular capital ratio tests employed, while others disagree with the findings of the Corporation and have taken the position that the decline in capital ratios is by no means as ominous as it might appear. Prather argued that if the ratio is calculated in terms of capital to invested funds (loans, investments, and real estate owned) it will permit recognition of the increasing proportion of univested funds for which no protection against shrinkage in value is necessary; that is, it will afford a true measure of capital to risk assets.[29]

The Federal Reserve Bank of New York, in a study of twenty-seven New York City banks, 1934–39, found that whereas the ratio of total capital to

[29] Charles L. Prather, *Money and Banking* (Chicago, 1940), p. 354.

Table 22

DISTRIBUTION OF NUMBER OF INSURED COMMERCIAL BANKS BY SIZE AND BY NET SOUND CAPITAL RATIOS PER $100 APPRAISED VALUE OF ASSETS, 1940[a]

	All Banks	Dollar Deposits								
		100,000 or Less	*100,000 to 250,000*	*250,000 to 500,000*	*500,000 to 1,000,000*	*1,000,000 to 2,000,000*	*2,000,000 to 5,000,000*	*5,000,000 to 10,000,000*	*10,000,000 to 50,000,000*	*Over 50,000,000*
Banks with ratios of:										
$0.00 or less	7	—	2	—	—	2	2	—	1	
$0.01 to $4.99	49	1	3	5	4	13	11	5	7	
$5.00 to $9.99	2,872	8	76	366	728	622	503	230	250	89
$10.00 to $14.99	6,112	31	650	1,681	1,549	1,103	720	215	128	35
$15.00 to $19.99	2,829	86	863	745	539	330	195	45	25	1
$20.00 to $24.99	1,032	102	446	206	145	74	36	17	4	2
$25.00 to $29.99	325	73	128	50	43	19	10	1	—	1
$30.00 to $34.99	131	47	41	19	9	6	3	3	3	
$35.00 or more	80	37	21	14	5	—	3			
All banks	13,437	385	2,230	3,086	3,022	2,169	1,483	516	418	128

[a] Source: ***Annual Report of the Federal Deposit Insurance Corporation*** (1940), Table 133, p. 184.

TABLE 23

DISTRIBUTION OF DEPOSITS IN MILLIONS OF DOLLARS OF INSURED COMMERCIAL BANKS BY SIZE AND BY NET SOUND CAPITAL RATIOS PER $100 APPRAISED VALUE OF ASSETS, 1940[a]

	All Banks	*Dollar Deposits*								
		100,000 or Less	*100,000 to 250,000*	*250,000 to 500,000*	*500,000 to 1,000,000*	*1,000,000 to 2,000,000*	*2,000,000 to 5,000,000*	*5,000,000 to 10,000,000*	*10,000,000 to 50,000,000*	*Over 50,000,000*
Banks with ratios of:										
$0.00 or less	39	—	—	—	—	2	6	—	31	
$0.01 to $4.99	210	—	1	2	3	19	31	32	122	
$5.00 to $9.99	36,740	—	22	144	539	897	1,594	1,586	5,504	26,454
$10.00 to $14.99	16,816	3	125	612	1,102	1,543	2,134	1,476	2,234	7,587
$15.00 to $19.99	2,627	7	155	266	383	460	609	302	389	57
$20.00 to $24.99	889	8	73	70	102	104	110	118	102	201
$25.00 to $29.99	444	6	20	18	32	27	31	5	—	305
$30.00 to $34.99	135	3	6	6	6	9	9	19	77	
$35.00 or more	20	2	3	5	3	—	7			
All banks	57,920	29	405	1,124	2,169	3,060	4,531	3,539	8,459	34,604

[a] Source: *Annual Report of the Federal Deposit Insurance Corporation* (1940), Table 133, p. 184.

total deposits declined from 17.2 percent to 12.2 percent, the ratio of total capital to total deposits less cash assets only declined from 26.3 percent to 21.5 percent, and the ratio of capital to total invested funds from 19.9 percent to 17.3 percent.[30] It concluded that, "there is no single ratio of bank capital to the volume of invested funds which can be considered satisfactory under all conditions" and that the importance of the decline in the ratio of capital to deposits had been exaggerated.

The Superintendent of Banks in the State of New York, in an analysis of the capital position of the banks in that state for the years 1914–40, concluded that, "since the decrease in capital ratio has been occasioned by large increases in deposits, the greater part of which has been retained in cash, it seems reasonable that this factor should be considered in the determination of adequacy of capital." [31] After making such an adjustment in the calculation of capital ratios he contended that the capital position of banks and trust companies in that state continued to be fully adequate, that this was true "even without taking into consideration the fact that increases in security investments during recent years have consisted almost entirely of additional investments in government obligations . . . "

He further observed that "it should be noted that the present ratio of 19.32 percent is higher than that for any of the first fourteen years" and "less than one percentage point lower than the average for the twenty-six year period: when measured on this basis the capital position of banks and trust companies in this State continues to be fully adequate."

This conclusion hardly seems warranted by the statistics. The data still show that the ratio for 1940 is the lowest for the twelve years despite the improved cash position. More significant than this, however, is the fact that the same data showed that the ratio was improving all during the 1920s, especially from 1924 to 1931 when the rate of bank failures was steadily increasing, revealing that not enough capital was present to absorb the losses which were being incurred, and suggesting that the expansion in speculative bank assets might have been restrained had more capital been required. The periods in which the ratio worsened were 1915–19 and 1931 to date, both periods of heavy credit expansion, especially against the bank asset government bonds.

The evidence seems abundant that in the past the banking system has suffered from serious inadequacy of capital, and that at the present time

[30] Federal Reserve Bank of New York, *Monthly Review of Credit and Business Conditions,* April, 1940, p. 27.

[31] *Annual Report of the Superintendent of Banks,* State of New York (1940), pp. 14–17.

the capital position of the system is rapidly deteriorating even after allowance is made for the great absolute and relative growth in reserve credit. Earlier in this chapter it was argued that the creation of bank reserves is not a true substitute for bank capital, certainly not where reserves are used as a basis for an inflationary expansion of bank assets whose values, in the long run, must be validated if losses are to be avoided. The fact that the expansion in assets (and deposits) in the last ten years has been characterized principally by an expansion in cash and in the government bond holdings of the banks, which no one denies are relatively the highest grade asset available to the individual bank, does not mean that evil consequences are absent. It is, indeed, fortunate from the standpoint of individual banks that the quality of their assets has been relatively improved. Nevertheless, it remains true that their capital position has been weakened, and that the banking system, as a system, has become more and more vulnerable to fluctuations in the values of assets which could not be liquidated in very great volume without involving losses and destruction of bank capital.

The Problem of Improving the Capital Position

This raises the question: How can the capital position of the system be improved? The ideal answer is fundamentally simple. Either the banks must acquire larger capital, or else their assets must be prevented from further expansion relative to given capital. The difficulty is in putting either or both solutions into effect, through workable means. The range of optimum capital is limited, on the one hand, by the desire and need of the banks for earnings and, on the other, by the risk that is involved in expanding assets to an amount which is excessive in relation to the size of capital account.

Statistical studies show rather clearly that the profitability of bank capital as measured by net current operating earnings is correlated inversely with the ratio of capital to total assets.

Thus Thompson says: [32]

> We have ascertained that in the smaller banks generally the capital accounts are a larger proportion of total assets. The data shown in Table IV (for insured commercial banks not members of the Federal Reserve System) would appear to indicate that the relationship of total capital account to total assets was much more important in determining profitability of capital as measured by net current operating earnings than was the size of bank.

[32] Donald Thompson, "Trends in Bank Earnings and Expenses," *Journal of the American Statistical Association,* XXXIII No. 202 (June, 1938), 327-32.

TABLE IV

(*reproduced from Thompson, ibid.*)

NET CURRENT OPERATING EARNINGS PER $100 OF TOTAL CAPITAL

Accounts of Insured Commercial Banks not Members of the Federal Reserve System, Calendar Year 1936

		Banks with Ratios of Total Capital Accounts to Total Assets				
	All Banks	*10% or less*	*10% to 20%*	*20% to 30%*	*30% to 40%*	*40% to 90%*
Banks with deposits of: #						
$100,000 or less	6.05	12.28	8.19	5.57	4.23	3.78
$100,000 to $250,000	8.31	12.36	9.04	6.19	4.85	5.77
$250,000 to $500,000	9.81	12.93	9.60	6.25	5.40	5.48
$500,000 to $1,000,000	9.97	14.32	9.36	5.48	4.90	2.50
$1,000,000 to $2,000,000	9.31	13.90	8.65	4.75	4.17	0.50
$2,000,000 to $5,000,000	8.61	12.21	8.19	5.54	4.58	2.50
$5,000,000 to $10,000,000	9.36	12.75	9.52	5.10	5.63	
$10,000,000 to $50,000,000	9.76	15.19	7.92	4.38	4.58	
More than $50,000,000 @	—	—	—	—	—	—
All banks	8.89	13.35	9.15	5.88	4.53	4.00

Deposits are averages of end-of-month figures.
@ Figures for this group are not representative.
Note: Data are for banks operating throughout the year.

If this be the case, then it would follow that the imposition of higher capital requirements in the form of a capital ratio would tend to limit bank earnings and perhaps render difficult the attraction of capital to the banking business. This may be subject to some qualification.

It has been pointed out by Jones that the inverse correlation found to exist between the rate of earnings on capital and the capital ratio is to be explained in part by the fact that for banks with a low capital ratio, risk to the stockholders is greater and, if correction is made for assumed losses on total assets, no correlation is found to exist.[33] This correction assumes that the quality of assets in all cases was the same (that is, that rate of loss was independent of capital ratio). Granting the reasonableness of such a correction, it remains true that a capital ratio requirement, uniform for all banks, would discourage venturesome capital which otherwise might be attracted by the lure of a high profit rate resulting from the fact that the bank was operated on a thin margin of equity capital.

The fact is that there are two kinds of risks to be considered: One is the risk attendant upon the quality of assets; the other is the risk associated with a large volume of assets in relation to capital. Theoretically, the re-

[33] Homer Jones, "Some Problems of Bank Supervision," *Journal of the American Statistical Association,* XXXIII, No. 202 (June, 1938), 339.

quired capital ought to be governed by the risk attached to each class of assets as well as to the total assets in relation to the amount financed by capital.

Thompson found that the data are inadequate and do not reveal the extent to which banks suffer losses on different types of assets.[34] In the absence of such information, it is not surprising that supervisory authorities have concluded that each case must be considered on its merits with primary regard to the character and condition of loans and investments until a formula is evolved which will test capital sufficiency on the basis of risk attendant to each class of asset.[35] However, this merely means control of quality of bank assets, but there remains the need, as Jones pointed out, of exercising an influence over the respective proportions of a bank's funds which represent equity and which represent debt.[36] This the supervisory authorities and the lawmakers have failed to do.

The condition of the banking system today, when viewed from the standpoint of the capital position, is a serious one even when no account is taken of the particular risk characteristics of particular asset categories. This is a direct outcome of the era of low money rates which, by reducing the per unit return on bank assets, has necessitated a larger volume of assets in relation to capital in order to yield the same rate of return.

A study of the earnings of national banks since 1890 seems to indicate that the banks have been able to make a fair return on invested capital whether the capital ratio has been high or low, but it happens that in the earlier years the prevailing level of interest yields on banks' assets was high, whereas in later years, and especially of late, it has been low.[37] The maintenance of the return on invested capital has therefore been due largely to a rising ratio of earning assets to invested capital and partly to a contraction in expenses especially interest paid on deposits.

During the twenties the combination of fairly high yields on assets permitted the accumulation of surplus, and, in the years 1927–29 an actual improvement in the capital ratio, but even that was of but small aid toward meeting the tremendous losses of 1932–34. In the long run an expansion in earning assets is not going to provide the earnings needed to absorb inevitable losses.

Today the banking system is being impaled on the horns of a dilemma. The great growth in its earning assets since 1932 has consisted largely of government bonds, but a continued rise or maintenance in their valuations is dependent upon the continuance of easy money conditions which mean a

[34] Thompson, *op. cit.*

[35] *Annual Report of the Superintendent of Banks*, State of New York (1940), p. 17.

[36] Jones, *op. cit.*, p. 335.

[37] J. M. Peterson, D. R. Cawthorne, and P. H. Lohman, *Money and Banking* (New York, 1941), p. 192.

low rate of return on earning assets. Thus, the attraction of a new capital based on profit possibilities is dependent upon the enlargement of earning assets or the restoration of higher yields on earning assets. Either eventuality constitutes a threat to the capital structure of the banks. In the first case, it means a lower capital ratio and smaller relative capacity to absorb loss. In the second case, it means actual depreciation in the value of assets now held and consequent impairment of capital accounts.

The inherent consequences to the capital position of the banking system resulting from attempts to perpetuate easy money conditions do not seem to have been fully appreciated by students of these questions. Low yields on high-grade securities, particularly government bonds, have been produced by their continued purchase by banks by means of deposit issue. The creation of bank credit is the mechanism by which the rate of interest (yields on securities) was forced below that which would have been determined by the voluntary savings of the community.[38] In essential respects, this is a process in which government debt is monetized with resulting depreciation in the money yield on these debts.

In its unfolding the process has fed on itself since the banks became more and more desirous of enlarging their assets as the per unit return on securities declined. Expenses and overhead were reduced through effecting economies in operation and through cessation of interest payments on deposits, but they could not be cut below a certain minimum. When that point was reached, banks became more and more desirous of enlarging their assets as the unit yield disappeared. Even with the expansion of securities holdings, they were unable to augment their investment income with sufficient rapidity to offset the decline in income from other sources.[39] Thus, in one respect, the banking system is the unwitting cause of its own predicament, for, as its securities investments grew, its deposits grew, and its capital ratio deteriorated.

A cessation or reversal in the rate of expansion in bank assets in a period when the total supply of securities is expanding would impose upon the market a powerful influence tending to reduce the valuations of securities. A policy of perpetual easy money induced within the framework of existing banking institutions by the enlargement of bank reserves inevitably confronts the problem of the solvency of the banking system. There seem to be valid reasons for presuming that the catena of enlarged bank reserves, increased bank purchases of securities, lower unit yields on banks' earning

[38] Cf. Robert B. Warren, *The Search for Financial Security* (New York, 1940), p. 46.

[39] Cf. Murray Shields, *Interest Rates: an Analysis of Supply and Demand Factors* (lithographed MS, copyright 1941), pp. 45–46. See also *Annual Report of the Federal Deposit Insurance Corporation* (1940), pp. 48–50.

assets, followed by further enlargement in earning assets to compensate for lower yields, eventually endangers the capital position. Thus, while an easy money policy designed to facilitate financing of the Government's deficit may prove workable within the span of a business cycle, such a policy cannot be pursued indefinitely, or as part of a secular program, without the adoption of additional controls intended to revoke the right of individual banks to decide their asset policy independently, or without the need of additional machinery by which to facilitate the absorption of losses in asset values should the situation be allowed to develop extemporaneously.

The Capital Ratio Device

The preceding discussion should serve to emphasize the inevitable consequences of an inflationary policy of credit expansion which goes beyond the bounds of the potential loss absorption powers of the capital of the banking system. This raises the question whether the capital ratio device can serve any useful purpose in the control of credit. The use of the capital ratio requirements as a credit control device has received virtually no consideration in banking theory.

Credit control by the central bank from its beginning has rested upon the manipulation of the reserves of the banking system with a view to inducing desired action by the banks. Traditionally, the instrument used was the discount rate, which was intended to make it more or less expensive for banks to acquire reserves. This was later supplemented by open-market operations which were used to vary the size of member bank reserves upon the initiative of the central bank. In 1935 the Board of Governors of the Federal Reserve System was empowered to vary the amount of required reserves. In each case the theory of controlling bank credit has rested upon control of the reserves of member banks, and this, more often than not, has involved creation or destruction of reserve credit, at times more or less arbitrarily, and nearly always without any way of predetermining the full consequences of such action. There is no doubt that such devices have their place especially in offsetting, or compensating, changes in reserves brought about by other factors, such as currency hoarding, gold movements, etc., or even in stimulating an expansion of credit. However, if the expansion in commercial bank credit is induced by the creation of reserves by the central bank, it is not possible to limit the expansion by destruction of these reserves once they become employed in supporting the superstructure of credit erected upon them without adversely disturbing the government bond market. Therefore, it would seem that if the aim of the authorities is to limit the further growth in bank assets (and thereby deposits) a simple and direct approach would be to impose a limit upon the growth of bank assets by laying down a specified relation between them and the capital of banks. An outside limitation such as this would mean that beyond the specified limit no bank could acquire net additional earning assets unless it were able to increase its capital, though it would be free to change its holdings within the limit established, and it could continue to receive deposits which in practice would be offset by corresponding increases in cash in the case of the individual bank.

If the aim is to limit the expansion of bank credit, a capital ratio requirement would accomplish this result just as effectively and more directly than a limitation upon deposits in relation to reserves or of assets in relation to reserves. At the same time it would leave the individual bank free to carry such reserves as it deemed necessary in the light of existing conditions and of its position with respect to the other banks. There is a definite advantage in that the reserve position, as such, of the affected banks is not upset, as is the case where the central bank either destroys reserves through open-market sales or renders them unavailable through increases in reserve requirements. The incidence would fall on banks which are overexpanded relative to capital, rather than on those which are overexpanded relative to reserves. In a functional sense, an individual bank does not become overexpanded with relation to its reserves so long as its relation *vis à vis* other banks is in equilibrium, but it may become overexpanded in relation to capital even though its reserve position may be ample. The same is true for the system.

A capital ratio requirement would not impugn the theory of deposits based on bank assets, nor divorce the money-creating function from the lending function as would a 100 percent cash reserve requirement, but would limit expansion power to controllable limits set by the estimated ability of banks to absorb loss. It would be supplemented by the machinery for loss redistribution of the Federal Deposit Insurance Corporation.

The imposition of a relative limit upon the expansion of earning assets in relation to capital account of individual banks seems preferable to limitations such as those embodied in the 100 percent Reserve Plan because it would provide a limiting point toward which the banking system in time could become oriented. This limit would be designed to prevent the danger inherent in reducing the capital margin to such an extent that comparatively small fluctuations in asset values could succeed in wiping out bank capital, and to prevent inflation of bank assets, even where based on government bonds, from proceeding to the point where, in order to protect the solvency of banks, it would become necessary to freeze the holdings in the banking system either by a reserve requirement in which government bonds would be eligible to count toward the satisfaction of the requirement, or an increased reserve requirement based on reserve credit issued against acquisition by the central bank of government bonds formerly held by banks. In either case the control of the money supply would be subject to criteria not necessarily evolved upon principles as such but determined by expediency like war finance.

OBJECTIONS TO THE IMPOSITION OF STATUTORY CAPITAL RATIOS

Most objections to the capital ratio device have not been based upon its theoretical properties as a credit control mechanism, but rather upon the feasibility of its introduction into a banking system comprised of many thousands of heterogeneous units. It is recognized that an inflexible statutory rule would not take into account the risk variation among different classes of bank assets, and a simple ratio would not, therefore, be appropriate to all banks. Moreover, it is argued that it would fix a limit upon the earnings of some banks unless they were to acquire more speculative assets. The chief objection, however, is that "adequate capital, like sound management, can not be legislated into existence." [40]

Deposit banks in various countries show marked differences in function and structure. Likewise, within the United States, deposit banks are by no means a homogeneous class of institutions, either with respect to the kinds of assets held, i. e., the kinds of transactions financed, or the kinds of deposit liabilities assumed.

In Table 17, it was evident that capital ratios in various countries show significant differences. These differences have been attributed by some students to differences in functions. For example, in the Netherlands, the check and deposit system has not been developed to the same extent as in countries like the United States or England. This has been due to the competition of a postal check and transfer system and the practice of some municipalities of establishing transfer and deposit systems of their own. The inclination of the Dutch people to place savings directly in securities, rather than in bank deposits, is said to explain the relatively small volume of deposits in the Dutch banking system.[41] However, this does not necessarily explain why the ratio of capital to deposits is so high. In any case, because of this high ratio, it would appear that the Dutch banks have been correspondingly free to devote their resources to foreign investments and other purposes which in some banking systems

[40] Institute of International Finance of New York University, *op. cit.*, p. 26.

[41] *Money and Banking*, eds. Major B. Foster and Raymond Rogers (New York, 1940), p. 675. See also Institute of International Finance, *op. cit.*, pp. 23–24.

would have been incompatible with the maintenance of a deposit currency system supported by only a small margin of capital. It seems logical to suppose that the appropriate amount of capital used by a banking system is dependent primarily upon the kind and quality of banks assets, and secondarily upon the character of the deposit liabilities.

German banking for many years was noted for its accomplishments in the financing of industrial development. A characteristic feature of the great German D banks was the large proportion of fixed assets representing extensions of credit to underwrite the fixed capital equipment of industry. While the exact extent of the direct financial involvement of the German banks in this type of asset is difficult to ascertain, comparatively it has always been greater than in other countries, even though it has not been on as great a scale as sometimes supposed. Whale, in his excellent study of *Joint Stock Banking in Germany,* found that the policy of the German banks and their active participation in industrial finance did not involve them in losses on such a scale as to threaten their safety because of the practice of diversifying their interests and of maintaining secret reserves (surplus) in addition to observing a large proportion of capital to liabilities.[42]

Foxwell, in comparing English and German banking before the First World War, pointed out that the English banks carried enormous call liabilities on minimum reserve and worked mainly on their customers' capital, not their own, whereas the German banks traded on their own resources and held larger reserves.[43] In the light of this, he observed that the German banks could extend industrial capital and trading ventures without risk to depositors, especially as their shareholders were content with modest dividends. On the other hand, the chief economic function in which the resources of English banking were engaged was the circulation of two currencies, the deposit and check system in which most domestic payments were made, and the London bill which served as the clearing instrument of the financial world. The heavy responsibility imposed in the flotation of these currencies, he explained, limited the power of the English banking system to finance industry and to assume the risks inherent therein. Continental banks, on the other hand, were comparatively free of currency responsibilities and therefore able to attend to other banking duties.

In the United States, the differences in function and structure of city banking and country banking are well known. One such difference is found in the concentration of country bank assets as contrasted with the diversi-

[42] P. Barrett Whale, *Joint Stock Banking in Germany: a Study of the German Credit Banks before and after the War* (London, 1930), p. 329.

[43] H. S. Foxwell, *Papers on Current Finance* (London, 1919), p. 104.

fication which city banking enjoys. The dependence of country banks upon the welfare of the particular agricultural specialty of the local community and the limited number of commercial and manufacturing enterprises, in turn closely associated with the local type of agriculture, prevents adequate diversification. In the past, country banks customarily extended more long-term fixed, or "capital," credit to borrowers than did city banks, and therefore became less liquid. Finally, country banks have been morally unable "to shirk the responsibility of lending the greater part of their resources locally." In these respects the determinants of the kind and quality of country banks' assets "are radically different from those of a city bank." [44]

Accordingly, it is to be expected that the capital ratios of country banks would be higher than those of city banks. This is found to be the case and is illustrated in Table 24 showing the ratio of book value of total capital accounts to loans and investments of various classes of banks for which statistics are available currently in the Call Reports.

TABLE 24

RATIO OF CAPITAL ACCOUNTS TO EARNING ASSETS, VARIOUS CLASSES OF BANKS, DECEMBER 31, 1940 [a]

	Total Capital Accounts	*Loans Plus Investments*	*Ratio*
	In thousands of dollars		*Percent*
All insured banks	$6,673,453	$42,561,103	15.7
Member banks Federal Reserve System	5,697,516	37,126,067	15.3
All national banks	3,528,246	23,647,914	14.9
All state member banks	2,169,270	13,478,153	16.1
Country members	1,908,681	10,825,906	17.6
Banks not members, but insured	975,937	5,453,036	17.9
New York City members	1,615,077	10,910,333	14.8
Chicago members	269,746	2,377,314	11.4
Reserve city members	1,094,012	13,012,514	8.4

[a] Source: Board of Governors of the Federal Reserve System; Member Bank Call Report, No. 85, *Condition of Member Banks December 31, 1940,* and Federal Deposit Insurance Corporation, *Assets and Liabilities of Operating Insured Banks,* Report No. 14.

Population of the places in which banks are located appears to be an important factor in determining both the size of banks as well as their functional characteristics which, in turn, seem to exercise an influence on the capital ratios. Table 25 shows that small banks are more often located in places of small population. It has already been noted that small banks tend to have higher capital ratios than large banks. Table 26 for

[44] United States Congress Banking and Currency Committee, 71st Cong., 3d Sess., Hearings pursuant Sen. Res. 71, "Memorandum on Country Banking" by Robert B. Warren, pp. 655–60.

TABLE 25

NUMBER OF OPERATING UNIT COMMERCIAL BANKS, GROUPED ACCORDING TO AMOUNT OF DEPOSITS AND POPULATION OF CENTER IN WHICH LOCATED, JUNE 29, 1940[a]

		Population								
	All Banks	*Less than 250*	*250 to 500*	*500 to 1,000*	*1,000 to 2,500*	*2,500 to 5,000*	*5,000 to 10,000*	*10,000 to 25,000*	*25,000 to 50,000*	*50,000 or More*
Banks with deposits of:										
$100,000 or less	707	222	262	147	43	8	5	6	2	12
$100,000 to $250,000	2,582	409	883	809	386	44	17	11	2	21
$250,000 to $500,000	3,084	138	495	997	1,075	256	70	18	9	26
$500,000 to $1,000,000	2,910	27	113	441	1,103	692	318	113	26	77
$1,000,000 to $2,000,000	2,044	4	11	62	322	545	567	305	72	156
$2,000,000 to $5,000,000	1,403	—	2	1	36	130	295	509	191	239
$5,000,000 to $10,000,000	418	—	—	—	—	4	21	96	115	182
$10,000,000 to $50,000,000	263	—	—	—	2	—	2	14	31	214
More than $50,000,000	40	—	—	—	—	—	—	—	—	40
None or not available	41	4	7	6	8	2	—	—	—	14
All banks	13,492	804	1,773	2,463	2,975	1,681	1,295	1,072	448	981

[a] Source: *Annual Report of the Federal Deposit Insurance Corporation* (1940), p. 116.

Table 26

PERCENTAGE RATIO OF TOTAL CAPITAL ACCOUNTS TO TOTAL ASSETS, ALL COMMERCIAL BANKS SUBMITTING REPORTS TO THE FEDERAL DEPOSIT INSURANCE CORPORATION, GROUPED ACCORDING TO POPULATION OF CENTER IN WHICH LOCATED, 1940 [a]

	All Banks	Population								
		Less than 250	*250 to 500*	*500 to 1,000*	*1,000 to 2,500*	*2,500 to 5,000*	*5,000 to 10,000*	*10,000 to 25,000*	*25,000 to 50,000*	*50,000 or More*
Number of banks	*6,871*	*574*	*1,246*	*1,550*	*1,466*	*682*	*462*	*337*	*143*	*411*
December 30, 1939	12.57	14.14	14.40	13.41	12.68	12.27	12.72	12.16	12.88	12.15
December 31, 1940	12.70	14.58	14.72	13.69	12.98	12.58	12.82	12.30	13.15	12.06

[a] Source: *Annual Report of the Federal Deposit Insurance Corporation* (1940), p. 215. These banks comprise mainly nonmembers of the Federal Reserve System, but insured. As such they are mostly small banks located in places of small population. Assets are averages of figures for December 30, 1939, June 29, 1940, and December 31, 1940.

a special group of small banks (those submitting reports to the Federal Deposit Insurance Corporation in 1940, numbering 6,871 and comprising mostly non-member insured banks) reveals that even among small banks capital ratios bear a noticeable degree of correlation to population of the centers of location.

The theory that the amount of required capital ought to be related to the kind and quality of assets finds no uniform degree of adherence in the policies of banks. Tables 27 and 28 show the distribution of insured commercial banks examined in 1940 according to net sound capital ratios when grouped by ratios of fixed and substandard assets to the appraised value of total assets.[45] Inspection indicates that banks are distributed according to capital ratio in much the same way whether the proportion of fixed and substandard assets is high or low. Evidently, the maintenance of large capital in relation to risk assets does not appear to be a general practice.[46]

SOME ALTERNATIVE METHODS OF REINFORCING BANK CAPITAL

It remains now to consider several alternative devices by which the capital accounts of banks have been reinforced with a view to increasing the potential capacity of banks to absorb losses.

Double Liability

For many years the holders of stock issues of national banks, and most state banks, were subject to double liability in that they not only assumed the risk of losing their original investment, but, in addition, were liable to assessment up to the par value of the stock in order to cover losses if assets were insufficient to satisfy the claims of creditors. This liability was removed from the shares of national banks in 1937 by prior amendment of the National Bank Act, and since that time has been eliminated from the shares of banks chartered under state laws. Its re-

[45] Fixed and substantial assets include fixed assets not criticized, as well as all substandard assets. Fixed assets consist of banking house, furniture and fixtures, and other real estate. Substandard, applied to total assets, loans, securities, fixed assets, and miscellaneous assets, represents the appraised value of all assets believed by the examiner to involve a substantial or unreasonable degree of risk, and hence to be undesirable or hazardous for bank investment. See pp. 86–87, *Annual Report of the Federal Deposit Insurance Corporation* (1940).

[46] However, on a composite group basis, there is a tendency for the proportion of substandard assets to increase as capital ratios increase, and also as the size of bank, as measured by deposits, decreases. See *Annual Report of the Federal Deposit Insurance Corporation* (1940), Table 130, p. 172. The logical inference is that the higher capital ratio among small banks is offset qualitatively by inferior assets.

TABLE 27

DISTRIBUTION OF INSURED COMMERCIAL BANKS EXAMINED IN 1940, ACCORDING TO NET SOUND CAPITAL RATIO AND FIXED AND SUBSTANDARD ASSETS RATIO[a]

	All Banks	*Net Sound Capital per $100 of Appraised Value of Assets*								
		$0.00 or Less	*$0.01 to $4.99*	*$5.00 to $9.99*	*$10.00 to $14.99*	*$15.00 to $19.99*	*$20.00 to $24.99*	*$25.00 to $29.99*	*$30.00 to $34.99*	*$35.00 or More*
Banks with fixed and substandard assets per $100 of appraised value of assets of:										
$0.00	46	—	2	13	17	11	1	—	2	
$0.01 to $4.99	5,022	—	14	1,518	2,291	799	271	82	28	19
$5.00 to $9.99	4,481	—	4	829	2,188	978	318	113	38	13
$10.00 to $14.99	2,116	2	4	294	970	523	220	63	20	20
$15.00 to $19.99	1,005	—	5	114	408	288	126	30	23	11
$20.00 to $24.99	418	—	5	59	141	130	49	16	12	6
$25.00 to $29.99	200	2	6	19	69	60	24	12	5	3
$30.00 to $34.99	75	1	3	11	19	21	14	4	2	
$35.00 or more	74	2	6	15	9	19	9	5	1	8
All banks	13,437	7	49	2,872	6,112	2,829	1,032	325	131	80

[a] Source: ***Annual Report of the Federal Deposit Insurance Corporation*** (1940), p. 184.

TABLE 28

DISTRIBUTION OF DEPOSITS IN THOUSANDS OF DOLLARS OF INSURED COMMERCIAL BANKS EXAMINED IN 1940, ACCORDING TO NET SOUND CAPITAL RATIO AND FIXED AND SUBSTANDARD ASSETS RATIO [a]

	All Banks	*Net Sound Capital per $100 of Appraised Value of Assets*								
		$0.00 or Less	*$0.01 to $4.49*	*$5.00 to $9.99*	*$10.00 to $14.99*	*$15.00 to $19.99*	*$20.00 to $24.99*	*$25.00 to $29.99*	*$30.00 to $34.99*	*$35.00 or More*
Banks with fixed and substandard assets per $100 appraised value of assets:										
$0.00	133,782	—	6,966	93,263	19,292	6,482	767	—	7,012	
$0.01 to $4.99	34,534,419	—	144,299	26,014,976	7,423,060	638,908	267,305	25,123	17,478	3,270
$5.00 to $9.99	15,802,267	—	11,501	8,563,389	5,826,105	806,267	233,819	348,855	7,835	4,496
$10.00 to $14.99	4,309,567	1,430	9,025	1,256,510	2,319,615	507,743	156,084	21,951	33,334	3,875
$15.00 to $19.99	1,878,535	—	6,490	573,165	838,198	319,587	106,406	18,368	14,461	1,860
$20.00 to $24.99	655,888	—	7,762	116,624	224,048	203,057	44,777	11,404	47,521	695
$25.00 to $29.99	304,333	3,415	12,941	33,212	113,398	70,963	49,114	11,871	7,011	2,408
$30.00 to $34.99	166,752	30,751	2,861	41,278	38,973	37,349	11,771	3,666	103	
$35.00 or more	134,004	3,752	7,864	47,183	13,216	36,951	18,500	2,746	56	3,736
All banks	57,919,547	39,348	209,709	36,739,600	16,815,905	2,627,307	888,543	443,984	134.811	20,340

[a] Source: *Annual Report of the Federal Deposit Insurance Corporation* (1940), p. 185.

moval had been advocated on the ground that it never proved entirely satisfactory as a device for protecting the depositor owing to inability to collect assessments, that it was an obstacle to the raising of new capital,[47] and that the necessity for it ended with the adoption of deposit insurance. Actually, roughly 45 to 50 percent of the assessments against national bank shares were made good,[48] although some students believe that more might have been collected had certain administrative reforms been inaugurated.[49] In any case, this device was only of advantage to the depositor once the bank had failed and assets proved to be insufficient. It did not serve to prevent failure nor to provide the margin of excess of assets over liabilities in which contraction in values might be absorbed in order to avoid failure and liquidation. However, double liability did impose the burden of loss upon the owners of banks and was a kind of supplementary form of bank capital.

Deposit Insurance

Federal deposit insurance as now operated in the United States is a mechanism for redistributing losses incurred in banking operations. The individual bank is relieved of its loss assets and of a corresponding volume of deposits through their assumption by a special agency, the Federal Deposit Insurance Corporation, which then either liquidates the assets or, after writing them down, disposes of them to other banks in the system. Deposit insurance is essentially a mechanism of redistributing losses and to this extent it strengthens and extends the effectiveness of the capital structure of the banks in the system.

The Federal Deposit Insurance Corporation was capitalized by the sale of its stock in the amount of $150,000,000 to the United States Treasury and $139,000,000 to the Federal Reserve banks. During its operation, 1933–34 to 1940, the Corporation accumulated a surplus of $207,000,000 resulting from excess of income over expenses. Income is derived principally from assessments upon insured banks in the amount of one-twelfth of one percent per annum of total deposits, but an additional income is derived from earnings on the Corporation's assets, chiefly government bonds, and some loans to weak or failed banks. Expenses consist chiefly of losses on loans involved in merging weak banks and losses in failed banks.

[47] United States Congress, Senate, Committee on Banking and Currency, Hearings, 74th Cong., 1st Sess., on S. 1715, *To Provide for the Sound, Effective and Uninterrupted Operation of the Banking System* (Washington, D.C.,), Part I, pp. 149–51.

[48] *Annual Report of the Comptroller of the Currency* (1936), p. 29.

[49] Jones, *op. cit.*, p. 337.

Nominally, the Corporation guarantees deposits of individual depositors up to $5,000, but this limitation only operates if the Corporation confines its disbursements to paying insured deposits in failed banks. Since 1939, the Corporation to an increasing extent has anticipated failures and taken steps to facilitate the merger of weak and hazardous banks with strong institutions, taking any losses involved by virtue of bad assets unacceptable to the absorbing bank. In these cases the depositors in the weak institutions have been covered 100 percent.

As matters now stand, the Corporation derives the bulk of its income from assessments and from interest on government bonds in which its original capital was invested, so that, while a part of the cost of bank losses in weak or failed banks falls upon the general public (to the extent that income to pay interest is raised through general taxation as it would be under a balanced budget), the major portion of the burden falls on the banking system collectively, and may to some extent be shifted to the public through service charges. Injustices seem to result from the method of levying the assessment in the form of a flat premium and on the basis of total deposits regardless of whether or not the deposits are fully insured, rather than in accordance with risk being covered. The plan, therefore, is not purely mutual in character. However, if these injustices be disregarded, there can be no question that the capacity of the system to absorb losses is greatly strengthened and that the public accordingly is benefited.

Deposit insurance of this kind suffers from two inherent weaknesses which probably could never be fully compensated or corrected so that the cost would be levied in accordance with the specific risk covered. The reason for this is that the risk of loss on bank assets, that is, the risk of failure, is not always an independent event in the statistical sense and hence not subject to calculation in accordance with the law of probability based on the normal curve of error, as is the case, for example, with life insurance. On the contrary, depreciation in bank assets and bank failures frequently result from a common cause. Moreover, the conditions and forces which give rise to failures in one period are not the same as those operating in another, so that past experience does not always afford a satisfactory guide for statistical calculation of the probability of failures in the future. Thus, the method of levying the assessments to cover losses must be worked out on an arbitrary basis. As already stated, under the plan as it now operates, this cost is levied upon all insured banks at a flat rate based on total deposits regardless of whether or not they are insured. The device whereby loss in weak and failed banks is divided among the strong banks, however, should not be allowed to permit laxity in bank management, and in all cases of excessive loss the deficient management should be removed, otherwise the scheme will, as its opponents for many years have argued, place a premium on bad bank management.

In the final analysis, no scheme can succeed unless, in the first place, the banks possess adequate capital for the absorption of loss, or enjoy current income sufficient to cover the current rate of loss in the system. The only real ultimate protection to the Federal Deposit Insurance Corporation lies in there being available capital already in the banking system out of which the losses first can be absorbed so that the Corporation may be able to recover amounts paid in subrogation to the claims of the insured depositors, or in loans against bad assets. When the capital of the individual banks is exhausted, the resources of the Federal Deposit Insurance Corporation automatically assume the burden of loss. The requirement of adequate individual bank capital is the bulwark by which the system is protected and even this will not suffice unless the Corporation through its supervisory powers insists upon high standards and restraint when loans and investments are first made.

Loan Insurance

Another device by which a given quantity of bank capital can be made more effective in so far as loss absorption is concerned is the insured loan. The practice of insuring loans has had only limited application almost entirely within the field of mortgage banking. It is best illustrated by the insurance of mortgages now effected through a special agency of government, the Federal Housing Administration. This agency insures banks and other lending institutions against losses they may sustain in financing alterations and improvements on real property, in the construction of residential homes, and in the construction of large-scale housing projects. The insurance of Title 1, or modernization and repair loans, covers losses up to 10 percent of the face value of loans whose individual amounts are limited to $2,500, and whose maturities are limited to three years and thirty-two days. In 1939 the Administration was authorized to levy a premium for insurance thereafter granted under this Title not to exceed three-fourths of one percent. In the case of home mortgages under Section 203, however, the insurance covers the entire loan which, in the general case, must be limited to $16,000, not to exceed 80 percent of the appraised value of the property with a maturity of not over twenty years and with amortization of principal throughout the life of the loan. The interest rate charged by the lender must not exceed 4½ percent, to which is added a premium of one-half of one percent by the Federal Housing Administration charged to the borrower. All applications for insurance of small-home mortgages are received by the Federal Housing Administration insuring offices from lending institutions so that the original selection of risks is made by the lender, but if such risks meet with the standards established by the Federal Housing Administration, a commitment to insure will be issued to the mortgagee when the loan is executed in accordance with the terms of the application.

For the purpose of covering its insurance commitments, the Federal Housing Administration has set up three funds which are deposited with the Treasurer of the United States. Title 1 liability outstanding is not allowed to exceed $100,000,000, a sum originally set aside by Congress for this purpose.

Insurance premiums collected from contracts on small home mortgages executed under Section 203, along with fees from rental housing projects insured under Section 207 prior to amendments to the National Housing Act of February 3, 1938, are deposited in a mutual mortgage insurance fund. Since February 3, 1938, receipts from all new housing projects insured under Sections 207 and 20 are being credited to a separate housing insurance fund.

As cash accumulates in excess of the needs of the Federal Housing Administration, the Secretary of the Treasury, upon request of the Federal Housing Administrator, invests such cash in obligations of the United States or in obligations guaranteed by the United States. Payments on account of losses to mortgagees is accomplished by issuing debentures and certificates of claim in exchange for property deeded to the Administrator. The policy of the Administration has been to keep the amount of debentures outstanding at approximately the value of the property on hand acquired through default, so that the investments of the insurance fund, except for minor items, correspond with the excess of the resources over the liabilities of the fund.

The organic act provided that mortgages accepted for insurance should be classified into groups such that mortgages in any group should involve substantially similar risk characteristics and have similar maturity dates. A separate insurance fund was to be set up for each group. Originally, the initial premium receipts on account of mortgage insurance were classified by premium and maturity dates only, but it was intended after study of risk characteristics so to classify the mortgages in order that various borrowers be given the benefit of the premium accruals on a scientific and equitable basis.[50]

In principle, the insurance of mortgage loans on homes is a device for pooling risks and spreading losses by levying upon borrowers a flat premium. In default, reserves are used to cover losses which otherwise

[50] *First Annual Report of the Federal Housing Administration, for the Period June 27, 1934, to December 31, 1934,* p. 19.

would have been assumed by the lender, had he been willing to make the loan. Like all forms of insurance, this device is intended not only to protect individuals against loss, but to equalize losses by spreading risks.

Unlike deposit insurance, which was intended to relieve the depositor of the risk of loss, loan insurance is intended to relieve the lending institution of loss. In deposit insurance, losses on loans are first absorbed out of bank capital and only when that is exhausted are they absorbed by the Federal Deposit Insurance Corporation out of funds accumulated from charges levied against banks. In Federal Housing Administration loan insurance, losses are first absorbed by the Federal Housing Administration from its reserves accumulated from premiums levied on borrowers. Thus, bank capital is relieved from any loss absorption function.

Abstractly, such insurance could be extended to cover all the earning assets of a bank with the result that individual banks would be relieved of all loss absorption arising from the inability of borrowers to repay. That cost would be imposed upon the borrowing public, as described above, in the form of a specific surcharge, while presumably the ordinary costs of maintaining banking facilities, overhead, and current operating expense would be borne by the banks as usual out of current income realized from interest charges on loans or service charges to depositors. However, there are reasonable objections to the inclusion in this plan of other types of earning assets such as investments acquired in the open market. If the device of insurance were applied to all bank assets, it would mean that individual banks would no longer be forced to assume the risks of granting credit. Consequently, it is hardly to be expected that they would be permitted discretion in analyzing and selecting risks, with the result that one of the basic banking functions, that of measuring and underwriting risks, would be transferred to some other institution, in this case a Federal agency.

At the present time there certainly appear to be no advantages in completely divorcing this function from banks, merely to have it assumed by another set of institutions or even by a Federal agency. Therefore, it would seem wisest to leave this underwriting function in the charge of the banks; but since this requires that the banks also be made to bear the losses, they should be forced to pay the risk premiums if the plan is extended to cover additional assets. This cost in the end would be passed on to the borrowing public in the form of a higher interest charge, or else to the depositing public in the form of service charges.[51]

[51] Some authors regard interest in this connection as a type of risk premium. See H. Parker Willis and George W. Edwards, *Banking and Business* (rev. ed.; New York, 1925), p. 19.

The principle of insuring loans should occupy an important place in banking, especially in a system composed of thousands of rather small unit banks such as exist in the United States, because it affords a means of averaging and combining losses. Its feasibility, however, will be limited by the availability of a sufficiently large body of loans whose characteristics from the standpoint of risk are sufficiently homogeneous to permit actuarial treatment and whose form can be technically standardized, in respect to interest, maturity, amortization, collateral, and other terms of the loan contract. A start has been made in the case of mortgages on residential property under the aegis of the Federal Government, but the potentialities of this device as yet have hardly been tested.

Chapter IX

COMMERCIAL BANKING IN THE FUTURE

THE FOREGOING CHAPTERS have dealt with a variety of topics whose claim to relevancy lies in their bearing upon the functioning of the banking system. In this the final albeit inconclusive chapter an effort will be made to indicate the kind of remedial action which must be taken if the functional mechanism of banking is to be kept in working order.

The dual nature of banking functions was first examined, and it was shown that the functions of issuing the means of payment and of providing credit and money capital, although separable for analytical purposes, are simultaneously performed by deposit banks in the process of monetizing debts. The essence of the modern banking process was found to lie in the functional dependence of the supply of money upon variations in bank assets. The mechanical ability of the banking system to expand and contract its own credit against cash, loans, and securities was shown to be very extensive; but it was explained that any theory of money and banking, if it is to be realistic, should take into account the nature of the debts which are monetized and the institutional framework within which the money-issuing function is performed. It was argued that the chief weakness of contemporary monetary theory is that it often takes for granted the elastic creation or contraction in the supply of money and loses sight of the importance of the basis of bank credit. Thus, it is apparent that a large part of contemporary monetary theory does not concern itself with the banking process but is exclusively preoccupied with the effects of injections of fiat money upon the economy. Monetary theory abstracts from the banking framework and, for that reason, is rendered much less useful as a guide to administrative policy than would otherwise be the case. On the other hand, banking theory has been slow to adjust itself to the reality of changed financial technique; furthermore, credit theory continues to be predicated largely upon the point of view of individual banks.

Attention was turned to a description and analysis of the changes which took place in the composition of bank assets. It was found that the decline in commercial loans and the rise of non-self-liquidating assets were not due to alteration in physical capital requirements but rather to changes in financial technique and to growth in the total supply of money. These changes involved a shift from direct to indirect injection of bank credit into the economic system, and the conversion of the business community from a net debtor to a net creditor of the banking system. It was thus that the banks unintentionally relinquished their traditional function of serving as umpires in the direction and use of funds for economic purposes and assumed the primary task of financing the government and other intermediary lenders and spenders.

The growth in corporate securities in the 1920s and government securities in the 1930s meant that the banks absorbed an increasing fraction of total debt and came to rely to an increasing extent upon assets whose liquidity depended upon shiftability in markets in which the banks themselves were the chief participants. Obviously, this is the case today with government bonds of which the banks hold 43 percent of the outstanding marketable supply. Abandonment of the principle of self-liquidation in bank assets also meant the banks must rely for repayment of the debts held upon sources of income or savings which are unrelated to the specific use of their credit by borrowers. In addition, the means of repeatedly testing the productive quality of credit by its continuous cancellation and renewal has been impaired by the lengthening of the average maturity of bank assets.

Bank credit was found to have been written up at a rate exceeding the rate at which monetary savings of individuals and non-banking institutions assumed the form of "time" deposits and capital funds. It had earlier been noted that the monetization of debts in this way was tantamount to the substitution of bank credit for savings. Employment of bank credit in competition with savings was, of course, an indispensable device for the prosecution of cheap money policies.

Attention was then turned to the implications of the erection and multiplication of bank credit upon a narrow capitalization. The conclusion was reached that the overexpansion of bank credit upon any type of assets, except cash, relative to capital account, was incompatible with the solvency of the banking system.

A system whose peculiar technique is the writing up of demand liabilities, which in the long run can only be canceled by liquidation of the debt-assets which were monetized in their creation, runs the danger of experiencing a repetition of its insolvency in 1933. It runs this risk despite the steps which have since been taken to suspend the convertibility of bank liabilities into standard money, despite the introduction of deposit insurance, and despite the indefinite augmentation of reserves by gold imports and central bank credit creation. These merely removed checks which formerly operated, albeit unsatisfactorily, to inhibit the expansion of bank credit. Now that redemption of money in gold for domestic purposes has been abolished, and central bank credit made of indefinite elasticity, the question of the appropriate volume and kind of bank assets has become all the more important. What measures are likely to be taken to preserve unimpaired the structure of credit which is now being created?

With the outbreak of the Second World War, two things seemed clear. One was that the only way to avoid involvement of the banking system in the same mistakes that were made in financing the First World War was to place the debt arising from the deficit in the hands of non-banking institutions and individuals, and to supplement this policy with the most drastic kind of taxation in order to keep the deficit as small as possible. The other was that the successful mobilization of the country's resources could not be accomplished by monetary means; rather it could be achieved only by the strongest kind of nonmonetary devices including taxation, price fixing, priorities, and rationing, if misdirection of production and consumption and inflation of commodity prices were to be avoided.

On the contrary, the banking machinery is still the principal device for underwriting and holding issues of government debt. Current policies seem to conceive of it as the residual dumping place for all debt which is difficult to place elsewhere at given interest rates. This has meant further expansion of the deposits of the banking system. As long as the fetish of financing the war at an arbitrarily predetermined interest cost is reverenced, the United States Treasury is compelled to rely upon the continued monetization of government debt by the banking system as the indespensable mechanizing of cheap financing. Such a policy requires also the creation of additional reserves by the Federal Reserve banks by purchases of bonds, in the open market and directly from the Treasury, to the extent that the member bank system shows unwillingness to buy more bonds as its capital ratio diminishes.

Various reforms have been advocated in recent years designed to bring under control the overissue of bank credit. Whereas earlier kinds of banking regulation were designed to prevent overissue, the regulatory history of American banking in the last fifty years has been concerned more predominantly with the provision of liquidity through central bank assistance. However, in recent years it has been recognized that measures are now needed to limit the supply of money. Such proposals have ranged from the 100 percent reserve plan, which would prohibit the creation of deposits except in accordance with reserves placed at the disposal of member banks by the central bank,[1] to the proposals of the qualitative school to limit, by policy or by law, the proportion of "investment" assets so as to avoid their excessive monetization.[2] Occasionally, a modest suggestion has been voiced that banking be functionally specialized by the separation of banking which employs the technique of deposit creation from banking which involves the collection of savings and financing of fixed capital formation.[3]

The major conclusion of this book is that the future of the commercial banking system of the United States turns upon a fundamental choice regarding the purposes to which the banking system is to be devoted. Essentially this is a choice between a banking system whose primary purpose is to provide an exchange or payments mechanism based upon careful judgment of the type of debts which are monetized, and a banking system whose chief purpose is the attainment of nonmonetary objects, such as the financing of government deficits, the promotion of investment, or the development of public works. The importance of this choice lies in the necessity of designing the banking machinery and adapting its framework to the purposes to which it is to be devoted.

A banking system whose chief task is to provide circulating media, and to serve as a clearing mechanism, requires a different kind of organization and structure from one whose main object is to finance capital formation, easy money policies, etc. In the former case, it was shown that such a system operates with highly liquid assets and can exist on a small capital investment, whereas a banking system which is devoted to the latter purpose must be designed so as to be able to take the risks of investment as well as those which result from fickle changes in the disposition of the public to hoard, save, or consume. Such a system cannot survive without

[1] A penetrating analysis of the 100 percent reserve plan is to be found in Leonard L. Watkins, *Commercial Banking Reform in the United States*, "Michigan Business Studies," Vol. VIII, No. 15 (Ann Arbor, Mich., 1938).

[2] See William E. Dunkman, *Qualitative Credit Control* (New York, 1933); Ralph W. Robey, two articles in *The Annalist*, February 27 and March 6, 1942; and Fred L. Garlock and B. M. Gile, *Bank Failures in Arkansas*, Bulletin No. 315 (Agricultural Experiment Station, University of Arkansas, College of Agriculture), pp. 66–68. Dunkman advocated restriction of fixed capital assets to the amount of bank capital plus savings deposits; Robey proposed the establishment of maximum ratios of investment assets to bank capital; Garlock advised requiring a minimum proportion of liquid assets to deposits.

[3] See, e. g., Fred L. Garlock, *Country Banking in Wisconsin during the Depression*, Technical Bulletin No. 777 (United States Department of Agriculture, July 1941), p. 107. R. S. Sayers, in *Modern Banking* (London, 1938), p. 229, cited the fact that the mixed banks of Europe did much to increase the risk of severe banking crises in many countries and that, as a result, the legislatures compelled the separation of their work as deposit banks from their work as investment trusts. A similar effort was made in the United States in the Banking Act of 1933 which required the separation of the securities affiliates, but no real functional separation has ever been achieved.

substantial protection in its capital account and without assuming a much greater voice in the type of activity it finances than has traditionally been expressed by it in the past. Even so there is as yet no agreement as to what extent such a system can be allowed to manufacture credit by monetizing debts, if unrestricted markets in those debts are to be allowed to prevail.

Ideally speaking, there is much to be said for a return to a banking system whose assets would be narrowly restricted to the highest quality representing the financing of short-term self-liquidating transactions. Such a system, however, would need to take account of the changed organization of the business world and the techniques employed in its financing. Such a system would be expected to provide a much smaller quantity of money than that to which the economy has become accustomed in the past, and it would have to be functionally and physically separated from the conduct of other types of lending.

A realistic appraisal of the conditions of the present day hardly can avoid the conclusion that there is no possibility in the immediate future of rationalizing the banking business through reduction in its holdings of fixed assets and government securities and its restoration to a credit basis consonant with a smaller supply of money. This is because the decision has already been made to employ the banking system for the purpose of financing the deficit to whatever extent is needed in order to gain the nearsighted advantage of cheap financing cost.

The probability is that the preoccupation with the exigencies of war finance will mean that nothing further will be done to cope with the inflation of the banking system until conditions which call for action are actually faced. If the past is any guide, this means that rectification will take the form of improvisation. What sort of devices, then, are likely to be improvised in order to strengthen the system as it reveals signs of strain?

Since the major problem which the system will face is that of solvency, it would be well to examine the general way in which this problem might be attacked. The preceding chapter discussed the subject of bank capital in detail and reviewed several possible lines of action, such as the further development of deposit insurance, bank asset insurance, the imposition of capital ratio requirement, etc., but it is doubtful whether these measures alone would be adequate to the task of fortifying the system against probable strains. Additional possible lines of action will now be considered.

The solvency problem might be approached in one or all of three ways. The first possibility concerns measures for the replenishment of bank capital; the second, measures designed to maintain by direct action the asset values of the banks; and the third, measures for preventing, or discouraging, the conversion of deposits into hand-to-hand currency.

The replenishment of bank capital has already been considered in Chapter VIII where it was argued that a perpetual easy money policy is incompatible with the growth of bank earnings, the accumulation of surplus, or the sale of capital stock to the public. The only alternative, therefore, would be the sale of stock to the Government. Precedent for such action is to be found in the purchases of preferred stock in banks since 1932 by the Reconstruction Finance Corporation. When the solvency of the system is again threatened, the machinery for the re-employment of this device lies conveniently at hand.

The second possible approach is to prevent the liquidation of bank assets. Under free competitive market conditions the maintenance of the money value of government bonds would depend upon the willingness of banks, who are the chief holders of such bonds, not to sell them except at times when other buyers are willing to purchase them at prevailing prices. Here the traditional device of open-market operations has already been used for the purpose, not only of creating additional reserves, but of maintaining the price level and structure of the market. However, it does not appear likely that this device can be rendered effective in times when banks are unwilling to add to their holdings, or when all banks are inclined to sell simultaneously in volume. In a crisis, the device of suspending trading below fixed price minima, or the adoption of conventional values by the examining authorities, may for a while artificially preserve intact the solvency of the banking system, but such action could avoid *sub rosa* trading only if individual banks were permitted to protect their reserve position by having unlimited access to the Federal Reserve banks.

In the final analysis, it would appear that measures may become necessary to prevent the liquidation of bank assets by more direct action, as for example, by a requirement that banks hold special reserves in the form of government bonds as collateral against their deposits. Such a requirement might be expressed in various ways. The chief consideration, however, would be to freeze in the banking system the great volume of government debt which it had acquired and to prevent its liquidation except under controlled conditions.[4]

There remains for consideration a type of action designed to discourage

[4] A requirement relating government bond holdings to deposits would not be workable, since it would interfere with flexible financing of additional demands for bank credit. Therefore, some other index would have to be chosen, either an absolute figure, or perhaps a multiple of capital. Cf. Lawrence H. Seltzer, "The Problem of Our Excessive Bank Reserves," *Journal of the American Statistical Association*, XXXV, No. 209 (March, 1940), 24.

depositors from converting deposits into hand-to-hand currency, and thus causing contraction of bank reserves and inducing liquidation of bank assets. Here several possibilities suggest themselves. First, it is conceivable that deposits in insured banks might be given the quality of legal tender, that is, made acceptable legally for the payment of all debts as is now the case with the note issues of the United States Treasury and Federal Reserve banks. The purpose of this device would be merely to give to deposits a legal property which they now lack as compared to higher forms of lawful money. The success of such action would depend upon the extent to which the public could be convinced that the quality of bank deposits was of equality with other available forms of money.

A second device for offsetting the deflationary effects of a currency drain would be to extend the circulation privilege to outstanding government bonds so that the banks could issue their own notes, a privilege which was taken away from them in 1935. This would permit demands for hand-to-hand currency to be met by conversion of deposits liabilities into note liabilities and would avoid reduction in bank reserves as is the case where the principal note issue available is that of the Federal Reserve banks. The issue of Treasury currency would accomplish a similar result.

These proposals are not advanced as recommendations, but merely to illustrate the possible lines of action which would follow the further perversion of the banking mechanism into an instrument for the unlimited monetization of debt. If this occurs, then it will be impossible for the system to operate within the kind of framework to which it has been accustomed. The function of banking as a supplier of productive credit, limited by some criterion to income-producing activities, can only be restored by ridding the system of its inflated assets. This is capable of achievement only by first balancing the Federal budget. The alternative is to consider the assets of the system as the given independent quantity, and to adapt the framework to fit the requirements of the kind and amount of assets the system holds. If the foregoing analysis has done nothing else it is to be hoped that, at least, it indicates that banking is an institution whose organization and structure must be adapted to the purposes to which it is to be devoted. "The Banking Business is an ancillary business—it is the servant, not the master of political economy." [5]

Obviously, alterations in the framework of the kind described would involve the further surrender by the bankers of the exercise of independent judgment, which they once enjoyed, to the extent that they are to be protected by the Government or the central bank. Clearly, the assumption by the State of the managerial and directive functions formerly performed

[5] Robert B. Warren, *The Search for Financial Security* (New York, 1940), p. 30.

by the banking system would carry with it the obligation to subsidize and support that system when earnings are low as well as when losses occur.

While it is true that banking, as it has been practiced in the past, may have no place of predominant importance in a system where the State assumes ever increasing control over the direction of productive effort, nevertheless, the functions of the banking and credit organization of modern society are essential to the division of labor and specialization of effort. They cannot be dispensed with until such time as some overruling authority is able to force industry into channels which are necessary to produce commodities in the relative proportions appropriate to the satisfaction of consumers' tastes and preferences.[6]

[6] H. Parker Willis and George W. Edwards, *Banking and Business* (rev. ed.; 1925), p. 500.

APPENDICES

APPENDIX A

Data for Table 7

Ratio of Notes Payable to Total Assets

MERWIN'S SMALL CORPORATIONS SAMPLE

	Total Notes Payables for Five Groups [a]	*Total Assets for Same Five Groups* [b]	*Ratio of Notes Payables to Total Assets*
	(In Thousands of Dollars)		*(In Percent)*
1925	2,983	29,504	10.1
1926	3,195	30,878	10.3
1927	3,259	32,272	10.1
1928	3,355	34,406	9.8
1929	2,940	37,125	7.9
1930	2,669	34,451	7.8
1931	2,674	31,473	8.5
1932	2,497	27,864	9.0
1933	2,512	27,457	9.1
1934	2,277	26,620	8.6
1935	2,251	27,053	8.3
1936	2,309	28,261	8.2

[a] Compiled from data presented in Charles L. Merwin, Jr., *The Financial Characteristics of American Manufacturing Corporations*, T.N.E.C. Monograph No. 15, Appendix F, Tables 1-A to 1-E. The five groups included: banking; men's clothing; furniture; stone and clay products; and machine tool.

[b] Compiled from data presented in *ibid.*, Appendix A, Tables 1-A to 1-E.

APPENDIX B

Data for Chart 1

DOLLAR VOLUME OF NOTES PAYABLE OF SELECTED SAMPLES OF MANUFACTURING AND TRADE CORPORATIONS

(*In Thousands of Dollars*)

Year	Manufacturing		Trade
	Large Corporations [a]	*Small Corporations* [b]	*Large Corporations* [c]
1920	785,687	....	63,359
1921	431,608	....	33,001
1922	272,446	....	4,340
1923	323,733	....	12,153
1924	223,405	....	4,081
1925	162,387	....	5,157
1926	166,499	3,237	6,193
1927	152,256	3,259	6,719
1928	171,622	3,355	19,941
1929	161,826	2,940	38,910
1930	72,322	2,669	25,614
1931	44,562	2,674	18,654
1932	34,752	2,496	28,056
1933	64,957	2,512	35,183
1934	129,510	2,277	20,590
1935	193,566	2,251	19,515
1936	189,574	2,309	3,045
1937	285,068	....	4,337
1938	142,639	....	3,502
1939	88,165	....	12,186

[a] From National Bureau of Economic Research, *The Financing of Large Corporations, 1920–39* by Albert R. Koch (MS June, 1942). The sample includes eighty-four

LOANS AND DISCOUNTS "COMMERCIAL IN FORM"[a]
(HUNT'S SERIES, NATIONAL BANKS, 1920–39)
YEAR ENDING JUNE 30, OR NEAREST DATE

Year	*Millions of Dollars*
1920	10,264
1921	9,025
1922	7,969
1923	8,372
1924	8,338
1925	8,376
1926	8,656
1927	8,455
1928	8,745
1929	7,909
1930	7,590
1931	6,788
1932	5,150
1933	3,826
1934	3,666
1935	3,735
1936	4,073
1937	4,928
1938	4,776
1939	4,096

---

corporations whose names are listed in Appendix A with the following companies excluded for the years indicated:

Automobiles and trucks: Dodge, 1920–22; Hudson, 1920; Maxwell, 1920; Yellow Truck, 1920, 1921

Food other than meat packing: Hershey, 1920

Iron and steel: Jones & Laughlin, 1920, 1921; Youngstown, 1920

Machinery: Elliott-Fisher, 1920–25; Midvale, 1920–22

Petroleum: Pacific, 1920; Shell, 1920, 1921

[a] Pearson Hunt, *Portfolio Policies of Commercial Banks, 1920–1939,* Appendix, Exhibit C.

[b] Data furnished by Albert R. Koch from National Bureau of Economic Research, *The Financing of Small Corporations in Five Manufacturing Industries, 1926–36* by Charles L. Merwin, Jr. (MS 1942). The sample includes 381 corporations with assets of $250,000 or under in five industries: baking; men's clothing; machine tools; stone and clay; and furniture.

[c] Koch, *op. cit.* The sample includes twenty-seven corporations whose names are listed in Appendix A with Ginter (a predecessor of First National Stores) excluded in 1920, 1921.

APPENDIX C

Analysis of Change in Deposits

june 30, 1920–october 10, 1924 [a]

(In Millions of Dollars)

Increase in Deposits		6,200
Factors of Increase:		
Return of money from circulation	500	
Increase in monetary gold stock	1,900	
Increase in Treasury currency	300	
Increase in bank loans and investments	4,800	
Increased acquisitions of securities and bills discounted by Federal Reserve banks	000	
Increase in real estate owned by banks	700	
		8,200
Factors of Decrease:		
Increase in capital Funds	1,000	
Net indebtedness to foreign banks	100	
Commercial bank float	200	
Errors and omissions	700	
	2,000	2,000

[a] Source: Based upon the analysis of the credit superstructure presented in William Adams Brown, Jr., *The International Gold Standard Re-interpreted, 1914–1934* (New York, 1940), I, 575.

Analysis of Change in Deposits

october 10, 1924–june 30, 1928 [a]

(In Millions of Dollars)

Increase in Deposits	9,300
Factors of Increase:	
Increase in loans and investments	10,800
Increase in real estate owned by banks	400
Rise in commercial bank float	500
Errors and omissions	300
	12,000

[a] Source: Based upon analysis of the credit superstructure presented in Brown, *loc. cit.*

Factors of Decrease:	
Decline in monetary gold stock	400
Increase in money in circulation	000
Decline in Treasury currency	000
Decline in net indebtedness to foreign banks	200
Reduction in government securities and bills held by Federal Reserve banks	300
Increase in capital funds of banks	1,800
	2,700

Analysis of Change in Deposits

AT ALL BANKS AND IN THE POSTAL SAVINGS SYSTEM DECEMBER 31, 1929–JUNE 30, 1933 [a]

(In Millions of Dollars)

Decline in adjusted demand deposits	8,500	
Decline in adjusted time deposits	6,600	
Increase in United States Government deposits	–700	
		14,400
Factors of Increase:		
Increase in bank holdings of United States Government securities	3,100	
Decline in bank capital	2,900	
Purchase of securities by Federal Reserve banks	1,500	
Decline in deposits of foreign banks	500	
Other factors, net influence	200	
		8,200
Factors of Decrease:		
Decline in bank loans	19,700	
Decline in bank holdings of securities other than United States Government securities	1,900	
Increase in money in circulation	1,000	
		22,600

[a] Source: Martin Krost, "The Significance of American Deposit Movements since 1929," paper delivered before the American Economic Association, Fifty-second Annual Meeting, December 28, 1939. Krost's data are based upon all banks including mutual savings banks and the postal savings system.

Analysis of Change in Deposits

at all banks and in the postal savings system june 30, 1933–december 30, 1936 [a]

(In Millions of Dollars)

Increase in adjusted demand deposits	11,100	
Increase in adjusted time deposits	3,600	
Increase in United States Government deposits	400	
		15,100
Factors of Increase:		
Increase in bank holdings of United States Government securities	9,500	
Increase in bank holdings of other securities	700	
Increase in Postal Savings System holdings of United States Government securities	900	
Increase in monetary gold stock	5,400	
Increase in silver certificates issued	800	
Purchase of securities by Reserve banks	400	
		17,700
Factors of Decrease:		
Increase in currency in circulation	500	
Decline in bank loans	800	
Increase in bank capital	800	
Increase in deposits of foreign banks	400	
Other factors, net influence	100	
		2,600

[a] Source: Krost, *op. cit.*

Analysis of Change in Deposits

at all banks december 30, 1936–december 30, 1940 [a]

(In Millions of Dollars)

Increase in deposits exclusive of interbank deposits		11,300
Factors of Increase:		
Increase in investments	1,400	
Increase in loans	2,300	
Increase in monetary gold stocks	10,700	
Increase in monetary silver stocks (as measured by increase in silver certificates issued)	600	
Other factors, net influence	100	15,100

[a] This analysis is based on change in deposits, exclusive of interbank deposits, and is not strictly comparable with Krost's analysis for previous years. For explanation of method and sources of data see *Federal Reserve Bulletin,* March, 1941, pp. 210–11.

Factors of Decrease:		
Sale of securities by Federal Reserve banks	200	
Increase in bank capital	400	
Increase in currency in circulation	2,200	
Increase in deposits of foreign banks at Federal Reserve banks	1,000	3,800

APPENDIX D

Data for Chart 4

NATIONAL BANKS, YEARS ENDING JUNE 30 OR NEAREST DATE THERETO

(In Millions of Dollars)

	Capital Funds [a]	*Savings and Time Deposits* [b]	*Total*	*"Investment" Assets* [c]	*Real Estate Loans Plus Investments Plus "Loans, Non-Commercial in Form"* [d]
1915	2,106	1,321	3,427	3,954	....
1916	2,103	1,716	3,819	4,722	....
1917	2,199	2,173	4,372	5,427	....
1918	2,250	2,336	4,586	6,819	....
1919	2,364	2,776	5,140	8,553	....
1920	2,622	3,463	6,085	7,482	7,534
1921	2,796	3,677	6,473	6,948	7,005
1922	2,848	4,074	6,922	7,824	7,843
1923	2,876	4,686	7,562	8,076	8,515
1924	2,916	5,158	8,074	8,707	8,783
1925	2,970	5,810	8,780	10,021	10,029
1926	3,089	6,178	9,267	10,617	10,604
1927	3,239	7,088	10,327	11,889	11,894
1928	3,571	8,050	11,621	13,560	13,547
1929	3,674	7,889	11,563	13,203	13,184
1930	3,976	8,097	12,073	13,986	13,846
1931	3,756	8,045	11,801	13,934	13,798
1932	3,280	6,958	10,238	12,203	11,997

[a] See *Annual Report of the Comptroller of the Currency* (1940), p. 322; *ibid.* (1938), p. 723.

[b] Statistical Abstract (1938), p. 257, or American Bankers Association pamphlet *Savings Deposits and Depositors* (1940).

[c] Calculated by multiplying the percentages of total earning assets in the form of "investment assets" (loans secured by stocks and bonds, loans on real estate, and bonds) as given in Willis and Chapman, *The Banking Situation* (New York, 1934), by total earning assets, as obtained from the *Annual Reports of the Comptroller of the Currency.*

[d] Hunt, *op. cit.*, Exhibit C.

DATA FOR CHART 4 (*continued*)

	Capital Funds	*Savings and Time Deposits*	*Total*	*"Investment" Assets*	*Real Estate Loans Plus Investments Plus "Loans, Non-Commercial in Form"*
1933	2,875	5,912	8,769	.....	11,459
1934	3,001	6,498	10,499	.....	13,273
1935	3,087	6,869	9,956	.....	14,264
1936	3,165	7,188	10,353	.....	16,119
1937	3,212	7,534	10,746	.....	15,928
1938	3,274	7,599	10,873	.....	15,142
1939	3,390	7,693	11,083	.....	17,004
1940	3,477	7,894	11,371	.....	.....

APPENDIX E

Required Relationship of Total Capital Accounts to Deposits in State Banks [a]

State	*Kind of Bank*	*Minimum Rate*	*Law*	*Enforcement*	*Remarks*
Arizona	All	10 percent	Rev. code 1928, Sec. 221	None	
California	Commercial	10 percent of unsecured deposits up to $1,000,000; 5 percent in excess of $1,000,000	Gen. Laws, Sec. 652–19	Enforced	Deposits not to be increased if ratio is not met
	Savings	10 percent to $1,000,000; 5 percent, $1,000,000 to $3,000,000; 3 percent, $3,000,000 to $25,000,000; 1 percent, over $25,000,000	*Ibid.*		
	Trust company	Same as commercial and savings	*Ibid.*		
Colorado	All	10 percent of unsecured deposits	Col. Statutes Annotated, 1935, Title 2, Ch. 18, Sec. 28	Lax	If surplus equals capital, undivided profits may be included at discretion of commissioner. Combined capital and surplus must equal 10 percent of deposits
Indiana	All	10 percent of unsecured deposits	Burns Annotated Statutes, 18–603	At discretion of commissioner	Banking department may require bank to increase capital or decrease deposits. Banks are exempt if cash plus government bonds equals 50 percent of deposits

Iowa	Savings	Capital and/or surplus must equal 5 percent of liabilities	Iowa Code 1935, Sec. 9176		Authorities regard condition of bank and capability of management rather than fixed ratio
Michigan	Commercial and savings	10 percent of unsecured deposits up to $1,000,000; 7.5 percent to $2,000,000; 6.7 percent to $3,000,000; 7.5 percent to $4,000,000; 8 percent to $5,000,000	Statutes Annotated Section 11897–41 Supp. Effective Aug. 1, 1940		Commission may change requirements for individual banks
Minnesota	All	4 percent of unsecured deposits	Mason's Statutes Sec. 7899–12		Commissioner attempts to get 10 percent
Mississippi	Commercial, stock savings, and trust companies	8 percent of deposits; 6⅔ percent with permission of State Comptroller	General Laws, 1934, c. 146, No. 41	Discretionary	The 1934 amendment decreased the general requirement from 10 percent to 8 percent and extended the provisions to cover savings banks which formerly were exempt. In 1940 the law was amended to permit the state supervisory authority to waive the requirement every six months for an indefinite period
Nebraska	Commercial	10 percent of unsecured deposits	Cumulative Supp. of compiled Laws 8–122	Lax	Applies to banks organized after May 15, 1935, with capital stock of less than $25,000. If deposits are more than ten times capital stock and surplus, capital stock must be increased. (Banks whose average deposits for the twelve-month period next preceding the month in which a dividend was declared are in excess of ten times the combined capital and surplus must carry 20 percent of accumulated net profits to surplus.) (Not enforced.)

APPENDIX E (*continued*)

Required Relationship of Total Capital Accounts to Deposits in State Banks

State	*Kind of Bank*	*Minimum Rate*	*Law*	*Enforcement*	*Remarks*
Nevada	All	8 percent of unsecured deposits	Compiled Laws (Hillyer's), 747–19	Enforced	Deposits not to be increased if ratio is not maintained
New York	All	Capital stock, surplus and undivided profits, 10 percent of net deposits	Sec. III, Subsec. 2	At discretion of Banking Board	May require bank to credit surplus with portion of net profits. Banking department considers 14 percent adequate, 10 percent minimum. In theory is as urgent as Federal Deposit Insurance Corporation, but not in practice
North Carolina	Commercial, stock savings, and trust companies, with branches or tellers' windows	10 percent of deposits	Code Ann. (Michie, 1939), 220 (r)		
North Dakota	Commercial	10 percent of unsecured deposits	Compiled Laws, Ch. 93, Sec. 17, 1935 Session laws		For banks organized after 1935
	Savings	5 percent of deposits	Ch. 96, Sec. 49, Session laws of 1931		
Rhode Island	Commercial and trust companies	10 percent of deposits exclusive of savings deposits	General Laws of Rhode Island, 1938, c. 133, No. 2		

South Dakota	Commercial, stock savings, and trust companies	$6\frac{2}{3}$ percent of deposits	Code (1939), Sec. 6.0303		Banks with capital of less than $15,000 must increase it to $15,000 if deposits exceed capital and surplus by more than ten times
Texas	All	10 percent down; varies with size of bank	Vernon's Statutes 1936, Sec. 506	At discretion of Banking Commission. Each case is enforced on its own merits	
Washington	Commercial incorporated in cities having population of 25,000 or over but located outside central business district thereof	10 percent of deposits	Rev. Stat. Anno. (Remington, 1932)		
Wisconsin	Commercial and trust companies	Deposits limited to fifteen times unimpaired paid-in capital plus ten times undistributed surplus	Statutes 1931, Sec. 220.075	Enforced	Bank must increase capital or surplus to meet ratio. Failure to do so may result in forfeit of charter. Correction usually made by transfer to surplus or by increase in common capital by payment of common stock dividend, rather than injection of additional capital.

[a] Information regarding Mississippi, North Carolina, South Dakota, Rhode Island, and Washington is based on American Bankers Association, *Compilation of State Statutes Requiring . . . . Ratio between Capital and Surplus and Deposits,"* and reference to state codes in order to ascertain currency of the laws. Information regarding the rest of the states is based on information furnished by the Federal Deposit Corporation.

BIBLIOGRAPHY

AUTHORS AND THEIR WORKS

Andarkar, Bhalchandra, The Theory of Monetary Policy. London, P. S. King and Son, 1935.

Anderson, B. M., Jr., "Bank Expansion vs. Savings," *Chase Economic Bulletin,* June 25, 1928.

—— "Bank Money and the Capital Supply," *Chase Economic Bulletin,* November 8, 1926.

—— The Value of Money. New York, Macmillan, 1917.

Angell, J. W., Investment and Business Cycles. New York, McGraw-Hill, 1941.

Bangs, Robert B., "Public and Private Debt in the United States, 1929–1940," *Survey of Current Business,* United States Department of Commerce, November, 1941.

Barnett, George E., State Banks and Trust Companies, National Monetary Commission, S. Doc. 659, 61st Congress, 3d Session. Washington, D.C., United States Government Printing Office, 1911.

Beckhart, B. H., "Monetary Policy and Commercial Bank Portfolios," *American Economic Review,* Supplement, Vol. XXX, No. 1, March, 1940.

—— Qualitative Credit Control, prepared for the Commission on Banking Law and Practice, Association of Reserve City Bankers, Bulletin No. 10, June, 1936.

Bradford, Frederick A., Money and Banking, rev. ed. New York, Longmans, Green, 1941.

Brown, William Adams, Jr., The International Gold Standard Re-interpreted, 1914–1934, 2 vols. New York, National Bureau of Economic Research, 1940.

Cassel, Gustav, The Theory of Social Economy, tr. by S. L. Barron. New rev. ed., New York, Harcourt, Brace, 1932.

Chapman, John M., Commercial Banks and Consumer Installment Credit. New York, National Bureau of Economic Research, 1940.

Clark, Evans, ed., The Internal Debts of the United States. New York, Macmillan, 1933.

Cole, G. D. H., ed., What Everybody Wants to Know about Money. London, Victor Gollancz, 1933.

Copeland, Melvin T., "Marketing," in Recent Economic Changes, Vol. I. New York, National Bureau of Economic Research, 1929.

Crowley, Hon. Leo T., Bank Capital Ratios Today. Address before Wisconsin Bankers Conference, April 7, 1942.

Currie, Lauchlin, "The Decline of the Commercial Loan," *Quarterly Journal of Economics*, Vol. XLV, No. 4, August, 1931.

—— The Supply and Control of Money in the United States. Cambridge, Mass., Harvard University Press, 1935.

Curry, O. J., Utilization of Corporate Profits in Prosperity and Depression. University of Michigan, Bureau of Business Research, "Michigan Business Studies," Vol. IX, No. 4. Ann Arbor, Mich., 1941.

De Marco, A. De Viti, Die Funktion der Bank, tr. from Italian by H. Fried. Vienna, Julius Springer, 1935.

Dewing, Arthur S., The Financial Policy of Corporations. 3d rev. ed. New York, Ronald Press, 1934.

Dunkman, William E., Qualitative Credit Control. New York, Columbia University Press, 1933.

Durbin, E. F. M., The Problem of Credit Policy. London, Chapman and Hall, 1935.

Edwards, George W., The Evolution of Finance Capitalism. New York, Longmans, Green, 1938.

Edwards, Gurden, Changes in Bank Earning Assets. New York, Economic Policy Commission, American Bankers Association, 1936.

Ellis, Howard S., German Monetary Theory. Cambridge, Mass., Harvard University Press, 1934.

Foster, Major B., and Raymond Rodgers, Money and Banking. New York, Prentice-Hall, 1940.

Foxwell, H. S., Papers on Current Finance. London, Macmillan, 1919.

Garlock, Fred L., Country Banking in Wisconsin during the Depression, United States Department of Agriculture Technical Bulletin No. 777, July, 1941.

—— and B. M. Gile, Bank Failures in Arkansas, Agricultural Experiment Station, University of Arkansas, College of Agriculture, Bulletin No. 315, March, 1935.

Gibson, J. Douglas, "The Changing Character of Bank Assets," *Canadian Banker,* Vol. XLV, No. 1, October, 1937.

Greef, A. O., The Commercial Paper House in the United States. Cambridge, Mass., Harvard University Press, 1938.

Gregory, T. E., "Money," in The Encyclopaedia of the Social Sciences, Vol. X. New York, Macmillan, 1933.

Hansen, Alvin, Fiscal Policy and Business Cycles. New York, Norton, 1941.

Hardy, Charles O., Credit Policies of the Federal Reserve System. Washington, D.C., The Brookings Institution, 1932.

Hargreaves, E. L., "Debt," in What Everybody Wants to Know about Money, ed. G. D. H. Cole. London, Victor Gollancz, 1933.

Harrod, R. F., "Currency and Central Banking," in What Everybody Wants to Know about Money, ed. G. D. H. Cole. London, Victor Gollancz, 1933.

Hart, A. G., Debts and Recovery. New York, Twentieth Century Fund, 1938.

Hawtrey, R. G., Capital and Employment. London, Longmans, Green, 1937.

—— Currency and Credit. 2d ed., London, Longmans, Green, 1923.

Hayek, F. A., Prices and Production. 2d rev. ed., London, George Routledge and Sons, 1934.

Heckscher, Eli F., "The Bank of Sweden in Its Connection with the Bank of Amsterdam," in The History of the Principal Public Banks . . . , ed. by J. G. Van Dillen. The Hague, Martinus Nijhoff, 1934.

Hersey, Arthur B., "Sources and Uses of Corporation Funds," *Journal of the American Statistical Association,* Vol. XXXVI, No. 214, June, 1941.

Hicks, J. R., Value and Capital. Oxford, Clarendon Press, 1939.

Hunt, Pearson, Portfolio Policies of Commercial Banks in the United States 1920–1939. Harvard University Graduate School of Business Administration, "Business Research Studies," No. 24.

Jacoby, Neil H., Government Loan Agencies and Commercial Banking, address before the American Statistical Association, December 28, 1941.

James, F. Cyril, The Economics of Money, Credit, and Banking. 2d ed., New York, The Ronald Press Company, 1935; 3d ed., rev., 1940.

Johns, C. H. W., Assyrian Deeds and Documents, 4 vols. Cambridge, England, Deighton, 1898–1923.

Jones, Bassett, Debt and Production. New York, John Day, 1933.

Jones, Homer, "Some Problems of Bank Supervision," *Journal of the American Statistical Association,* Vol. XXXIII, No. 202, June, 1938.

Keynes, John Maynard, The General Theory of Employment, Interest and Money. New York, Harcourt, Brace, 1935.

—— A Treatise on Money, 2 vols. New York, Harcourt, Brace, 1930.

Koch, Albert R., The Financing of Large Corporations, 1920–39. Preliminary and confidential MS; New York, National Bureau of Economic Research, 1941.

Krost, Martin, The Significance of American Deposit Movements since 1929, paper delivered before the American Economic Association, Fifty-second Annual Meeting, Philadelphia, December 28, 1939.

Kuznets, Simon, National Income and Its Composition 1918–1938. New York, National Bureau of Economic Research, 1941.

—— National Income and Its Composition 1919–1935. New York, National Bureau of Economic Research, 1937.

Landmann, Julius, "Banking, Commercial History to the Close of the Eighteenth Century," The Encyclopaedia of the Social Sciences, Vol. II. New York, Macmillan, 1933.

Lavington, F., The English Capital Market. London, Methuen and Co., 1921.

Lindahl, Erik, Studies in the Theory of Money and Capital, English tr. New York, Farrar and Rinehart, 1939.

Lutz, F. A., "The Structure of Interest Rates," *Quarterly Journal of Economics,* Vol. LV, No. 1, November, 1940.

Machlup, Fritz, "The Liquidity of Short Term Capital," *Economica,* Vol. XII, No. 37, August, 1932.

—— The Stock Market, Credit, and Capital Formation. New York, Macmillan, 1940.

Mack, Ruth P., The Flow of Business Funds and Consumer Purchasing Power. New York, Columbia University Press, 1941.

Macleod, Henry Dunning, The Theory and Practice of Banking with the Elementary Principles of Currency, Prices, Credit, and Exchanges, 2 vols. London, Longman, Brown, Green and Longmans, 1885.

—— The Theory of Credit, 2 vols. London, Longmans, Green, 1890.

Means, Gardner, "Bank Debts," in The Internal Debts of the United States, ed. Evans Clark. New York, Twentieth Century Fund, 1933.

Merwin, Charles L., Jr., Financing Small Corporations in Five Manufacturing Industries, 1926–36. New York, National Bureau of Economic Research, 1942.

—— The Financial Characteristics of American Manufacturing Corporations, Temporary National Economic Committee, 76th Congress, 3d Session, Monograph No. 15. Washington, D.C., United States Government Printing Office, 1940.

Mitchell, Waldo F., The Uses of Bank Funds. Chicago, The University of Chicago Press, 1925.

Morton, Walter A., "Liquidity and Solvency," *American Economic Review,* Vol. XXIX, No. 2, June, 1939.

Moulton, H. G., "Commercial Banking and Capital Formation," *Journal of Political Economy,* Vol. XXVI, 1918.

—— Financial Organization and the Economic System. New York, McGraw-Hill, 1938.

—— The Formation of Capital. Washington, The Brookings Institution, 1935.

—— G. W. Edwards, J. D. Magee, and Cleona Lewis, Capital Expansion, Employment and Economic Stability. Washington, The Brookings Institution, 1940.

Peterson, J. M., D. R. Cawthorne, and P. H. Lohman, Money and Banking. New York, Macmillan, 1941.

Prather, Charles L., Money and Banking. Chicago, Richard D. Irwin, 1940.

Richards, R. D., The Early History of Banking in England. London, P. S. King and Son, 1929.

Rist, Charles, History of Monetary and Credit Theory from John Law to the Present Day, tr. by Jane Degras. New York, Macmillan, 1940.

Robertson, D. H., Banking Policy and the Price Level, rev. ed. London, P. S. King and Son, 1932.

—— Essays in Monetary Theory. London, P. S. King and Son, 1940.
Robey, Ralph W., "Amended Reserve Act Could Check Banking Laxity," *Annalist*, Vol. XXXVII, No. 946, March 6, 1931.
—— "The Progress of Inflation," *Annalist*, Vol. XXXVII, No. 945, February 27, 1931.
—— Purchasing Power. New York, Prentice-Hall, Inc., 1938.
Robinson, Roland I., "The Capital Deposit Ratio in Bank Supervision," *Journal of Political Economy*, Vol. XLIX, No. 1, February, 1941.
Sayers, R. S., Modern Banking. London, Oxford University Press, 1938.
Schumpeter, Joseph A., Business Cycles, 2 vols. New York, McGraw-Hill, 1939.
—— The Theory of Economic Development, tr. Redvers Opie. English ed., Cambridge, Mass., Harvard University Press, 1936.
Schwenzer, Walter, Zum Altbabylonischen Wirtschaftsleben. Leipzig, J. C. Hinrichs, 1915.
Seltzer, Lawrence H., "The Problem of Our Excessive Bank Reserves," *Journal of the American Statistical Association*, Vol. XXXV, No. 209, March, 1940.
Shields, Murray, Interest Rates: an Analysis of Supply and Demand Factors. Lithographed MS, copyright 1941.
Sloan, Laurence H., Corporation Profits. New York, Harper and Brothers, 1929.
Smith, Frank P., and Ralph W. Marquis, "Capital and Surplus as Protection for Bank Deposits," *Bankers Magazine*, Vol. CXXXIV, No. 3, March, 1937.
Snyder, Carl, Capitalism the Creator. New York, Macmillan, 1940.
Sprague, O. M. W., and Randolph Burgess, "Money and Credit and Their Effect on Business," in Recent Economic Changes, Vol. II. New York, National Bureau of Economic Research, 1929.
Steiner, W. H., Money and Banking. New York, Henry Holt, 1933.
—— and Eli Shapiro, Money and Banking. New York, Henry Holt, 1941.
Suviranta, Br., "The Shiftability Theory of Bank Liquidity," in Economic Essays in Honour of Gustav Cassel. London, George Allen Unwin, 1933.
Terborgh, George, "Manufacturing Inventories during and after the World War," *Federal Reserve Bulletin*, July, 1941.
Thomas, Rollin G., Modern Banking. New York, Prentice-Hall, 1937.
Thomas, Woodlief, "The Banks and Idle Money," *Federal Reserve Bulletin*, March, 1940.
Thompson, Donald, "Trends in Bank Earnings and Expenses," *Journal of the American Statistical Association*, Vol. XXXIII, No. 202, June, 1938.
Tresckow, W. von, Merchants of Debt: a Study in the Changing Character of American Banking and Its Effect on Securities. New York, Young and Ottley, June, 1936.
Tucker, Rufus, "The Growth of Large Corporations and the Formation

of Capital," in Capital Formation and Its Elements. New York, National Industrial Conference Board, 1939.

Van Dillen, J. G., ed., History of the Principal Public Banks Accompanied by Extensive Bibliographies of the History of Banking and Credit in Eleven European Countries. The Hague, Martinus Nijhoff, 1934.

Von Beckerath, Herbert, Modern Industrial Organization. New York, McGraw-Hill, 1933.

Wall, Norman J., Agricultural Loans of Commercial Banks, United States Department of Agriculture, Technical Bulletin No. 521, July, 1936.

Warren, Robert B., The Search for Financial Security. New York, Columbia University Press, 1940.

Watkins, Leonard L., Commercial Banking Reform in the United States, Vol. VIII, University of Michigan, Bureau of Business Research, "Michigan Business Studies," No. 5. Ann Arbor, Mich., 1941.

Westermann, W. L., "Warehousing and Trapezite Banking in Antiquity," *Journal of Economic and Business History,* Vol. III, No. 1, November, 1930.

Whale, P. Barrett, Joint Stock Banking in Germany: a Study of the German Credit Banks before and after the War. London, Macmillan, 1930.

Wicksell, Knut, Lectures on Political Economy, 2 vols. New York, Macmillan, 1935.

Williams, John H., The Implications of Fiscal Policy for Monetary Policy and the Banking System. Address before a joint session of the American Economic Association and the American Statistical Association, New York, December 28, 1941.

Willis, H. Parker, Monetary Control. Address before United States Department of Agriculture Graduate School, Washington, D.C., April 4, 1936.

—— Money—Its History and Purposes. Unpublished address, New York University Forum (Nassau College), Hempstead, N.Y., February 18, 1936.

—— and Jules I. Bogen, Investment Banking, rev. ed. New York, Harper and Brothers, 1936.

—— and John M. Chapman, The Banking Situation. New York, Columbia University Press, 1934.

—— John M. Chapman, and Ralph W. Robey, Contemporary Banking. New York, Harper and Brothers. 1933.

—— and George W. Edwards, Banking and Business, rev. ed. New York, Harper and Brothers, 1925.

Willis, J. Brooke, "Commercial Bank Lending and Its Relation to Capital Financing," *Financial Reporter,* Vol. III, No. 253, November 4, 1937.

Winakor, Arthur, Capacity to Pay Current Debts, University of Illinois, Bureau of Business Research, Bulletin No. 53, October 6, 1936.

—— Maintenance of Working Capital of Industrial Corporations, University of Illinois, Bureau of Business Research, Bulletin No. 49, January 23, 1934.

Woodward, Donald B., "Changes in Capital Financing," *Journal of the American Statistical Association,* Vol. XXXIII, No. 201, March, 1938.

Young, Allyn Abbott, An Analysis of Bank Statistics. Cambridge, Mass., Harvard University Press, 1928.

OTHER WORKS, PAMPHLETS, DOCUMENTS, AND OFFICIAL PUBLICATIONS

American Bankers Association, The Answers of the American Bankers Association in Reply to Part 9 of the Questionnaire of the Committee on Banking and Currency of the U.S. Senate relative to Senate Resolution 125, 76th Cong., 1st Sess., April, 1941.

—— Changes in Bank Earning Assets. New York, Economic Policy Commission, American Bankers Association, 1936.

—— Compilation of State Statutes Requiring Surplus at Time of Organization of Banking Institutions, Accumulation of Surplus by Banking Institutions, Ratio between Capital and Surplus and Deposits, prepared by the Legal Department, 1936. Mimeographed MS.

—— The Earning Power of Banks. New York, Research Council of the American Bankers Association, 1939.

—— Savings Deposits and Depositors. New York, Research Council of the American Bankers Association, 1930, 1935, 1940.

Association of Reserve City Bankers, Term Loans of Commercial Banks. Privately printed, 1938.

Banking Act of 1933, The, Public No. 66, 73d Congress, June 16, 1933.

Banking Act of 1935, The, Public No. 305, 74th Congress, August 23, 1935.

Board of Governors of the Federal Reserve System, Banking Studies 1941.

—— "Deposits by Classes of Depositors," *Federal Reserve Bulletin,* May, 1940.

—— "Distribution of Demand Deposits by Economic Classes," *Federal Reserve Bulletin,* October, 1939.

—— Federal Reserve Charts on Bank Credit, Money Rates, and Business and in Banking Studies, 1941.

—— Member Bank Call Report, No. 85, Condition of Member Banks, December 31, 1940.

—— Regulation A, October 1, 1937.

—— "Term Loans by Banks to Commercial and Industrial Concerns," *Federal Reserve Bulletin,* July, 1939.

Bureau of Foreign and Domestic Commerce, United States Department of Commerce, Survey of Current Business, September, 1941.

Comptroller of the Currency, Annual Reports for Year ended October 31, 1936; year ended October 31, 1914, Vol. I; and year ended October 31, 1940.

Federal Deposit Insurance Corporation, Annual Reports for years ended December 31, 1934–40.

Federal Deposit Insurance Corporation, Assets and Liabilities of Operating Insured Banks, December 31, 1940, Report No. 14.

Federal Housing Administration, First Annual Report for the Period June 27, 1934, to December 31, 1934.

Federal Reserve Bank of New York, Annual Report for Year Ended December 31, 1941.

—— *Monthly Review of Credit and Business Conditions,* April, 1940.

Institute of International Finance of New York University, Ratio of Capital Funds to Deposits of Commercial Banks in the U. S., Bulletin No. 112, October 14, 1940.

—— Some Aspects of the Mounting Public Debt, Bulletin No. 119, February, 1942.

League of Nations, Commercial Banks 1913–1929. Geneva, 1931.

—— Commercial Banks 1929–1934. Geneva, 1935.

—— "Money and Banking, 1938 / 39," Vol. I, Monetary Review. Geneva, 1939.

—— Statistics Relating to Capital Formation, Studies and Reports on Statistical Methods, No. 4. Geneva, 1938.

National Bureau of Economic Research, Recent Economic Changes, 2 vols. New York, McGraw-Hill, 1929.

—— The Volume of Consumer Installment Credit, 1929–1938, Bulletin No. 79, September 1, 1940.

National Resources Committee, The Structure of the American Economy, Part I. Washington, D.C., United States Government Printing Office, June, 1939.

Secretary of the Treasury, Annual Report for the Year Ended June 30, 1940.

Standard Statistics Co., The, New York, N.Y., "Standard Trade and Securities," Standard Earnings Bulletin Supplements, Composite Financial Statements. Published annually to 1939.

Superintendent of Banks, State of New York, Annual Report for the Year Ended December 31, 1940, Part I. Legislative Doc. No. 24, 1941.

United States Census Bureau, "Sales Finance Companies and Bank Holdings of Installment Paper," Census of Business, 1939. Sixteenth Census of the United States, 1940.

—— Statistical Abstract of the United States, 1938. Washington, D.C., Government Printing Office, 1939.

United States Congress, 71st, 3d Session, Congress Banking and Currency Committee. Hearings pursuant Sen. Res. 71, To Make a Complete Survey of the National and Federal Reserve Banking Systems, Part V. "Memorandum on Country Banking" by Robert B. Warren.

United States Congress, 74th, 1st Session, Committee on Banking and Currency, Senate, Hearings on S1715, To Provide for the Sound, Effective, and Uninterrupted Operation of the Banking System, Part I.

United States Congress, 75th, 3d Session, Temporary National Economic

Committee, Hearings, Investigation of Concentration of Economic Power, Part I, "Economic Prologue." Washington, D.C., United States Government Printing Office, 1939.

United States Congress, 76th, 1st Session, Temporary National Economic Committee, Hearings, Investigation of Concentration of Economic Power, Part IX, "Savings and Investment." Washington, D.C., United States Government Printing Office, 1940.

United States Congress, 76th, 3rd Session, Temporary National Economic Committee, Monograph No. 15, *see* Merwin, Charles L., Jr.

—— Temporary National Economic Committee, Monograph No. 27, The Structure of Industry.

—— Temporary National Economic Committee, Monograph No. 37, Savings, Investment, and National Income. Washington, D.C., United States Government Printing Office, 1941.

United States Congress, 77th, 1st Session, Committee on Interstate and Foreign Commerce, House, Hearings, Proposed Amendments to the Securities Act of 1933 and to the Securities and Exchange Act of 1934, Part II, committee print, November 7–19, 1941.

United States Treasury Department, Bureau of Internal Revenue, Statistics of Income. Various years.

INDEX

VITA

Willis, J(ohn) Brooke, born July 17, 1909, Washington, D.C. Education: Dartmouth College, A.B., 1930; School of Engineering, Columbia University, B.S., 1932; School of Business, Columbia University, M.S., 1933; George Washington University, Sanders Fellow in Economics, 1935–36 (academic year); School of Business, Columbia University, candidate Ph.D., 1936– —. Employment: Jewel Tea Company, economic research and reports, 1933–35; Agence Economique et Financière (Paris, France), New York correspondent, 1937–39; London *Financial News,* New York correspondent, jointly with others, 1937–38; same for *De Telegraaf* (Amsterdam, Holland). Lecturer in Banking, Columbia University, 1938– —. Published articles: "Commercial Bank Lending and Its Relation to Capital Financing," *Financial Reporter,* November 4, 1937.

Bei Fragen zur Produktsicherheit wenden Sie sich bitte an:
If you have any questions regarding product safety,
please contact:

Walter de Gruyter GmbH
Genthiner Straße 13
10785 Berlin
productsafety@degruyterbrill.com